CO
KIL

COSTA KILLER

JON CLARKE

ROBINSON
London

Constable & Robinson Ltd
3 The Lanchesters
162 Fulham Palace Road
London W6 9ER
www.constablerobinson.com

First published by Robinson,
an imprint of Constable & Robinson Ltd, 2005

Copyright © Jon Clarke, 2005

The right of Jon Clarke to be identified as the author
of this work has been identified by him in accordance with the
Copyright, Designs and Patents Act, 1988.

All rights reserved. This book is sold subject to the condition
that it shall not, by way of trade or otherwise, be lent, re-sold,
hired out or otherwise circulated in any form of binding or cover
other than that in which it is published and without a similar condition
including this condition being imposed on the subsequent purchaser.

A copy of the British Library Cataloguing in
Publication Data is available from the British Library.

ISBN 1-84529-064-X

Printed and bound in the EU

1 3 5 7 9 10 8 6 4 2

Contents

Contents

Acknowledgements

Thanks for this book must first and foremost go to all the characters who have given time and helped to make it work. From Tony King's family, to the countless other people he came into contact with – it could not have been written without you. They include Louise Deravairere, Celia and Ingrid Pantoja, Simon Bowers and hack extraordinaire the late Nigel Bowden (a.k.a. Slippery of the Costas).

Thanks must also go to my wife Gabriella for being so long-suffering and supportive, my mother for her get-up-and-go and my father for inspiration. I should also like to thank my agent Robert Smith, my editor Pete and everyone else at Constable & Robinson. Cheers Claire for the help with some of those tricky documents, John Leech for a tour of all the grisly sights and Steve Kinchington at Scotland Yard for the background and thoughts.

Introduction

It is, of course, a cliché, but in the case of the 'Costa Killer', as it has come to be known, the truth is undoubtedly stranger than fiction. The best crime writers would certainly be hard-pressed to come up with a plot so far-fetched and complicated: with its twists and turns, its intrigue, its intricacy and the range of characters involved. A case beset with incompetence and greed, a loophole in the law and, most importantly, the tragic deaths of two young teenagers. A case that took over five years to solve and awash with aggression and violence: the only code that most of its characters know. No one comes out well. No one! The police, the courts and particularly the accused: a trio of dubious characters from the murky world of timeshare on Spain's Costa del Crime.

Naturally, the plot hinges around murder; in this case two young Spanish teenagers. The first was the homicide of Rocío Wanninkhof, a pretty 19-year-old, stabbed to death in 1999, her body dumped half-naked, and bizarrely covered in stones, just a few hundred yards inland from the upmarket tourist Mecca of Marbella.

Said to be Spain's most complicated murder case, with over 500 suspects, the supposed killer was arrested after a year, tried, found guilty and sentenced to 15 years in prison. And then four years later on came the bombshell when, looming large and in the frame; enter Tony King – a.k.a. the Holloway Strangler – accused of the murder of Rocío and of another teenager, Sonia Carabantes, in 2003. His DNA is found at the scene of both crimes.

An occasional bouncer or 'clumper' (to use the Costa term for hired hand or heavy), he must, of course, be guilty. Soon becoming the second most famous Englishman in Spain after David Beckham, he's quickly banged up and beaten up, with a convenient first-night confession for the cops. It all looks cut and dried and after the usual trial-by-media – something of an art form in Spain – all that's left to do is throw away the key!

But yet there was more . . . with the much suspected involvement of King's former boss and best friend Robbie Graham, the classic psycho, smooth and charming, with a love of knives and a nasty habit for using them against women. Some 15 years in timeshare – working with the likes of the infamous John Palmer and Dennis New – this man is good, oh so good. A compulsive liar and cheat, with debts around the globe, he's got a colourful charge sheet back home in England, and a love of sex, the more violent the better.

Pulled in by the police just days after King's arrest, few on the Costa del Sol who knew him were surprised. With a reputation for sexual deviance and a vicious way with women, it seemed only a matter of time before he was hauled up in front of the courts and banged up for something nasty. Indeed most former acquaintances of the pair – and there were many – were convinced that Robbie must have been guilty of the crimes for which King had initially been charged. With evidence to back up his love of sexual violence and depravity, the biggest surprise of all was when the courts let Graham go on a vague technicality.

And finally there is Dolores Vázquez, and joy of joys for the media, a *lesbian*, and the former lover of the dead girl's mother. A crafty, cold-faced manager of a timeshare resort, she became the main suspect for the 1999 Wanninkhof murder, despite any forensic evidence, and was pulled in and eventually taken to trial. While there is no hard proof, or indeed any clear motive, there are over two dozen unsubstantiated pieces of evidence to put to the court. It is certainly convincing and, of course, the jury bites!

There have already been a thousand column inches on the 'vicious, ruthless woman' and she goes down – until on appeal another judge orders a retrial. Nearly two years in prison awaiting trial, with the prospect of more, it certainly comes as something of a major twist, to say the least, when another man's DNA turns up at the scene.

But such is the intrigue in the case of the 'Costa Killer' that either way – whether Tony King was there or not, whether he is found guilty or not – the truth is much to the Spanish public, not to mention the family, will remain convinced for years to come that Dolores or Robbie Graham – and possibly both – were culprits in the murder of Rocío Wanninkhof. Confused? You need to read on!

Chapter One

The Drama Unravels

The only traces of Sonia Carabantes Guzman were a series of bloodstains and a few personal belongings. On the way back home from a night out with friends, the 17-year-old had been just a few steps from her house when she was attacked by an unknown assailant and bundled into a car. There were various signs of a struggle with a bloody handprint found on the hood of a neighbour's van and a pool of blood measuring 20 centimetres in diameter alongside it. Ominously nearby, a trail of her blood tapered away until it finally faded in the middle of the road. It wasn't long before a bloodstained shoe, her bag and mobile phone, smashed to pieces, turned up just two dozen metres from her front door.

Popular and pretty, the auburn-haired Spanish girl had only been living in the mountain village of Coin for two years, since persuading her parents to move back from Switzerland, where she was born and her parents had lived for 30 years. She had always enjoyed her summer holidays in this part of southern Spain, hanging out with her extended family and practising her second language. The typical whitewashed Andalusian *pueblo*, which clings to an escarpment on the edge of the breathtaking Sierra de las Nieves National Park, she would spend her summers playing in the windy, narrow streets and exploring the surrounding countryside.

Sonia had been in her last year at school on the night she had disappeared while walking back from the village's annual Virgen de la Fuensanta carnival, which was in its penultimate night. It was around 5a.m. on Thursday, 14 August 2003, and she had been escorted all but the last 200 metres home by two friends who left her at a zebra crossing on the infamously treacherous mountain road that eventually leads to Ronda. From there she was already well in sight of her road, Calle del Pino, in the Felix Rodriguez de la Fuente urbanization. Nobody would have considered her to be in any danger.

Her killer had almost certainly also been at the carnival and attacked her as she reached a mini-roundabout just before the junction with her road. It was a violent assault and she had then been dragged to a vehicle that was parked in Calle del Pino. The signs of the struggle that had taken place did not bode well and family and friends straightaway feared for her life. It certainly had all the hallmarks of a sex attack and the police were quick to appeal for witnesses and for anyone with any information to step forward. The news was soon across the front pages of both the local Spanish press and the numerous English free-sheets that span the coast, and by the following night hundreds of locals had gathered to help search the area for the teenager. Within days an estimated 5,000 Spaniards, with a mixture of expatriate British, Dutch and Germans, had joined the search party, which was organized by the Guardia Civil and the local Protección Civil. Sonia's two elder brothers arrived from Switzerland, while one couple even turned up with a remote-controlled miniature helicopter armed with a video camera, to fly over nearby forest and waste ground sending back images.

For days teams kept up the search – many with dogs and covering ground as far afield as Marbella and Cartama – and Coin town hall showed its support by cancelling the remainder of the carnival celebrations. It was, of course, all everyone was talking about and the world stood still in Coin until five days later on 19 August, the young girl's body was found on a building site some five kilometres from her home.

Her body was found by a group of builders close to a series of industrial warehouses in the hamlet of El Pinar, near Monda. It hadn't been hard to locate due to the strong, almost over-powering smell of her decomposing remains. It was not a pretty sight. Half-naked and wearing just a T-shirt and bra, which was torn, the upper part her body had been covered with a pile of large rocks and stones.

But it was the injuries to her face – she had a broken nose and jaw and various teeth had been fractured – that really shocked investigators. She had clearly been attacked by a very violent man – something the autopsy results confirmed. Apart from the injuries to her face she had a fractured collarbone and, according to the coroners, the cause of death was by strangulation. Sources from the investigation added that they believed Sonia's attacker was not a professional, as it had been a rushed and sloppy job, with little attempt to cover any tracks. They added that there was a strong trail of clues and forensic evidence, which apparently included human hair, blood samples and even a discarded cigarette butt.

In a country where the instances of sex crimes and the dis-appearance of children are considerably lower than many other places in Europe, pandemonium quickly broke out, particularly as dozens of journalists had soon descended on the normally sleepy mountain town of Coin, which numbers some 17,000 inhabitants. The outcry to catch the killer was enormous and naturally, under pressure, local police forces swamped the area with detectives quickly announcing that they had identified some suspects, in particular two young men from the town, both around the age of 20.

They believed the local youths may have known Sonia and even participated in the ensuing searches and, unsurprisingly perhaps, the announcement was met by something of a witch-hunt in the small Andalusian town, which was once a strong-hold for the Moors and is situated in the middle of a fertile area known for its citrus groves. In a climate of fear not known since the days of the Inquisition, a whispering campaign began amid the quiet, traffic-free streets and clutch of fifteenth- and sixteenth-century churches, and a number of locals found themselves shunned, even spat at and totally harassed.

It led to one unfortunate young man filing an official complaint with the local Guardia Civil. The town's mayor Gabriel Clavijo and other town hall officials were forced to publicly appeal for calm and patience.

Police also appealed for a group of revellers who – between 5a.m. and 6a.m. on the morning in question – were, appar-ently, nearly hit by a white car on the road between Coin and the town's nearby fairground. The small white car was also seen by two witnesses in Coin around the time of Sonia's disappear-ance, driving fast and later that morning another witness saw someone washing a white car along the Pereila river, not far from where the body was found. Investigators also announced that they had found the dead girl's bloodstained knickers close to the scene.

Intriguingly, it soon became apparent that there were a number of disturbing similarities between Sonia's death and the violent murder of another teenager Rocío Wanninkhof, aged 19, some four years earlier. And to the untrained eye the similarities certainly looked remarkable. The two teenage girls had both been of a similar height and build and had connec-tions abroad. They had both lived in villages just five miles apart and both disappeared on the night of their local fiestas.

But most unusual of all, it quickly emerged, their bodies had both turned up half-naked, WITHOUT any evidence of sexual assault.

Detectives were, however, far less convinced, stating it was merely a coincidence, until, of course, the bombshell news dropped that there was in fact a DNA link between the two murders. At the beginning of September, reports showed that the DNA from samples of skin taken from underneath the fingernails of Sonia Carabantes, as well as saliva samples from a cigarette butt found near to her body, matched the DNA on a cigarette butt found at the scene of Rocío Wanninkhof's disappearance in 1999. Both cigarettes, it emerged, were from the brand Royal Crown and, according to a biologist at the Institute of Toxicology in Seville, it was '99.9996 per cent' likely that the samples came from the same person.

In a massive media scare across Andalusia, the two murders were straightaway being linked to the death of a third girl, Anna Lorente, in nearby Alora, in 2000, and the disappearance of María Teresa Fernández, aged 18, from nearby Motril, in August of the same year. Both had gone missing on the nights of their local carnivals while Fernández had, oddly enough, also grown up in Switzerland. There was an apparent serial killer on the loose and warnings were duly issued.

The Costa del Sol had never seen anything like it and, having recently relocated to Spain from London, I sent my first despatch of the case to the national newspapers in London, under the heading 'Costa Killer – Possible Serial Killer on the Loose in Spain!', warning British holidaymakers coming to Spain to be wary of a killer, 'who might be targeting foreigners'. I felt it would be of interest to the English press and even got a quote from a British embassy spokesman giving some loose advice on safety for young women, but while there was considerable interest, particularly from the red-top tabloids, nobody printed a word.

The next seven days, however, were as dramatic as any movie and the Spanish media went into overdrive. It started when police announced that they were looking for a man who may have had scratches on his body and in particular a bandage on his arm. DNA samples were voluntarily taken from various people close to the family or close to the investigation and police continued to appeal for potential witnesses to come forward that might have seen the white car, particularly after they found a car headlight cover that had bloodstains matching the DNA of the alleged attacker. Within days they also announced the reopening of the case of María Teresa Fernández, with investigators also looking into similarities with the murder of Anna Lorente, aged 20.

More pertinently came a massive outcry in the media from friends and family of the lesbian timeshare boss Dolores Vázquez, who had already been convicted of the murder of Rocío Wanninkhof (she was stabbed eleven times) in September 2001. Found guilty by a jury on numerous shreds of evidence (although none of it forensic, it should be pointed out), she had been sent to prison for 15 years, but soon released on appeal pending a retrial. Publicly declaring her innocence for the previous two years – but still under strict bail conditions – Vázquez – who had been the on/off girlfriend of Rocío's mother – had been due for a retrial on 14 October 2003. Unsurprisingly, under considerable pressure from her lawyers, the retrial was duly postponed until a later date, but with the prosecution cautiously insisting that she would remain a suspect.

Meanwhile, a few miles away in Alhaurín el Grande, certain questions were being raised about the activities of a local barman, Tony King, who had moved to Spain in the autumn of 1997. His girlfriend Mariluz Gallego – a cleaner, with whom he lived in a flat in the Emilia Olivares school – knew that he had gone to the fiesta of Coin alone on the night of Sonia's death and moreover hadn't returned until the early hours of the morning with cuts all over his body and a bandage on his arm.

His boss Simon Bowers also had cause for concern when King turned up at work the Saturday after the murder with a far-fetched story that he had cut his hand after a car crash on the way home from the fiesta. But it was at the house of his estranged wife Cecilia King, with whom he had a daughter Sabrina, that suspicions raised led to the crucial phone call that tipped off the police.

The decision had come after the London-born barman – who, it emerged had previously worked as a bouncer and as a timeshare salesman – arrived as usual to pick up his daughter for her weekly day out the following Saturday. Both Cecilia and new partner David Cooze, who lived in nearby Fuengirola, had been immediately suspicious about the injuries, which he admitted he sustained on the night of the Coin carnival. But when Tony contradicted himself about how he had sustained the injuries they became convinced of his guilt and after a couple of agonizing days of debate Cecilia took the brave decision to call the police.

Scandalously, perhaps, her initial tip-off to Scotland Yard on 11 September and another one the following day to Crime-stoppers fell on deaf ears – despite the British police having a long file on the criminal background of King. But finally, through sheer perseverance, Cecilia was taken seriously by Spanish detectives, who quickly arrived to speak to her. Indeed, they took her call on 13 September so seriously that they immediately decided to surreptitiously trail her errant husband for the next three days, until they had sufficient samples of saliva from a glass and a cigarette butt to get a DNA sample. When the two samples came back with a match – bingo! – they had their man.

Unsurprisingly, they didn't hang around and on Thursday, 18 September the sensational news dropped across European TV networks that a British man had been hauled in for

questioning over the two murders. It had first been seen as a newsflash on Spanish TV networks just before lunchtime that a British man with the initials 'T.A.K.' had been arrested in connection with the murders. It soon emerged that he was 38 years old and lived in Alhaurín el Grande.

Now the English press were interested and it sparked one of the biggest news stories of the summer, with literally dozens of journalists descending on the scruffy hillside town, which was just a couple of miles coast side from Coin. A dusty, fast-growing town – with a surfeit of cranes (said to be Spain's national bird) and piles of sand and cement – Alhaurín el Grande (not to be confused with Alhaurín de la Torre, its upmarket cousin and where, coincidentally, the British consul in Malaga resides) had a distinct frontier-like feel. Easily one of the hardest places in Spain to get to, with its complete lack of signs and appalling roads, it perhaps explained why King (and many of the other thousands of Brits) lived there.

It was straightaway apparent that the type of Briton living in the town – there are said to be over 3,000 now living among the official population of 18,000 – was hardly Home Counties or professional. Provincial accents and tattoos were very much in evidence, as were the clichéd signs for 'live Premiership footie' and 'steak and kidney pie'. There were also a fair amount of Union Jacks and very much a 'them and us' kind of feel. The divide between the building-fraternity Brits and the swamped locals was very obvious. 'Colonization' was the word used by many – and not surprisingly the vast majority of English neither spoke a dicky bird of Spanish nor frequented their host country's restaurants.

The growth had certainly been dramatic over recent years, a point hammered home during an interview with the consul Bruce McIntyre himself. 'While only a few British and other foreigners are officially registered – perhaps as little as ten per cent are on the *padrón*, as it is known – there are almost certainly a good many thousand there,' he said, during an interview in his central Malaga office. 'It certainly causes quite a few problems, not least because if they are not officially registered the district of Andalusia gets a lot less public money than it should get. In fact it is estimated that there would be as many as two new fully equipped hospitals, eight new medical centres and 400 more doctors if they were all officially registered. By not registering they are putting a huge burden on the existing infrastructure of the state. It doesn't make us popular.'

Alhaurín was certainly no exception, with, for example, about thirty British pupils attending the school where King's girlfriend was a cleaner, while three years earlier there had just been one. The two groups were 'not mixing', according to one parent, and teaching was becoming increasingly hard. Standards were falling and a few Spanish teenagers even admitted to me that it was frowned upon to be seen with *guiris*, the derogatory nickname for foreigners. With a Briton arrested for the murder of two young Spanish girls, the tension in the air was, understandably, palpable, to say the least.

The facts were straightforward. Anthony Alexander King had been arrested at 10.30a.m., along with his girlfriend Mariluz Gallego, a mother of three, when police had swooped on the grace-and-favour house they shared inside the walls of the Emilia Olivares school, where she cleaned part-time. After an exhaustive search of nearly four hours – in which police seized eight bags and a strongbox of evidence – King was led out of the home in which he'd lived for six months, and transferred to the National Police headquarters in Malaga. It had been a straightforward arrest, which was officially confirmed during the afternoon by Minister of the Interior Antonio Acebes, adding however that people should still 'be prudent, as the investigation is still going on.'

With passions at fever pitch, by the time King had been hauled out, a crowd of over a thousand angry Spaniards had

lined the road to shout abuse and chant the phrase: '*asesino,
asesino*' in unison. Their behaviour when he was handcuffed and
led away wearing yellow shorts, a black T-shirt and white
Adidas trainers, even surprised the police. Tempers flared to
such an extent that a number of residents actually attempted to
attack the British barman. With a denim jacket draped over his
head to stop the dozens of waiting photographers from getting
a picture he was an easy target and it certainly made for
dramatic photos, with people throwing bottles and aiming kicks
at the unmarked car, which carted him off. It was a well-orches-
trated operation with numerous papers duly tipped off, and
everything went to plan apart from the chief of police in
Malaga Florentino Villabona receiving a nasty cut on his head
from a stone that was thrown from the crowd in the mêlée.

With the overwhelming DNA evidence – not to mention the
seizure of his English-registered grey Mazda, which tellingly
had a headlight cover missing, as well as particles of blood from
the victim – some might say it was inevitable that he would
quickly confess to his involvement in the murders. Indeed,
according to police sources, he had confessed to the murders
within just a couple of hours of being detained and by the end
of the night he had also admitted to a string of other sex attacks
along the Costa del Sol.

King, it emerged, was certainly well known in the town, more
for what he didn't say than said. Immediately recognizable, he
was a well-built and taciturn man, who always wore shorts and
T-shirts to show off his muscles. Many people described him as
a quiet and solitary figure, who had a squeaky voice and
seemed wrapped as tightly as a coil. People queued up to talk.
'He seemed very cold and never said "hello" when he came in
my bar,' said waiter Antonio Jesús Lopez, who regularly sold
cigarettes to him. 'He always had a lot on his mind and seemed
to be an accident waiting to happen,' said bar owner Antonio
Gonzalez.

A few, who knew him better, described him as a decent, friendly bloke, who was a good masseur and reliable worker. Others, however, described him as 'creepy' and 'weird'. Indeed two teenage girls recalled how they had been chatted up by the barman late at night. One of them, Joanne Jackson, aged 18, from Ellesmere Port, near Liverpool, said: 'He came out with some really perverted lines, and really freaked me and my friend Amanda out. He was definitely angling towards trying to take us to bed. He was creepy and we were glad to get away from him.'

A keen smoker, who liked a drink, King had lived in the town for around three years and usually worked as a barman at the Bowers Arms, a typically down-at-heel and somewhat sleazy English pub that lined the main drag of Alhaurín el Grande. One of perhaps a dozen English pubs now plying their trade in the town, its welcome blackboard summed up the place. 'Janine and Simon welcome you to the Bowers Arms. Karaoke, Yorkshire Pud and Great Beers.'

The following day, its owner Simon Bowers decided to talk. He had spent the previous day cowering at home, like many of the British in town. Fearing a backlash against the *guiris* who in recent years had been swarming into the town from the coast, he gave a heartfelt speech at an impromptu press conference to the various representatives of the British tabloid press, who had hot-footed it over from England on the orders of their editors the previous evening. To put it in a nutshell, he said he felt betrayed by his former employee, whom he had never suspected of any such misdemeanour, but if he was guilty he deserved everything he got. He apologized to the parents of the two dead girls and said he hoped the English would be forgiven. It was a rousing speech and featured heavily on the evening's TV networks.

It transpired that Bowers had known Tony King for some three years since he had given him a job and a place to stay in his family home on the outskirts of the town. He claimed to be King's best friend and was the last person to socialize with him on the night before his arrest. While the press pack moved on rapidly to find the next big angle I decided to get to know Bowers, who proved to be a fascinating and useful source of information. Indeed, over a series of lengthy interviews, he and his wife Janine – who have since moved back to their family home town of Leeds after the police shut down their bar – gave a revealing insight into the mindset and behaviour of the British barman, who had lived with them on and off for nearly two years.

Most importantly, however, was their belief – the first people to come out and say it – that King was not guilty of at least one of the two murders; that of Rocío Wanninkhof. In fact, they never wavered from that belief in their final six months in Spain, and continually pointed the blame on King's other close friend and former colleague Robbie Graham, who, as it turned out, had been sensationally arrested three days after King.

The timeshare salesman had straightaway become a suspect on King's arrest and few people who knew him had any doubts that he had been in some way involved in at least the first murder. It later emerged through official police transcripts that his name had been mentioned many times during King's initial interrogations. King had treated Graham as a mentor and, according to many, had been under 'some sort of spell' while working for him. Police apparently made it a high priority to haul him in for questioning – along with his and King's former timeshare boss Jonathan Daniels, who was also dragged in for seven hours of questioning.

The problem the police had was in finding Graham, as the Mancunian – who was a well-known conman, with a reputation for violence – had recently moved out of an apartment in Calahonda, owing thousands in rent and saying he was going back to England.

However, in a clever police operation he was tracked down to a hotel in Nerja; a fashionable tourist resort 20 miles up the coast, the other side of Malaga. He was eventually hauled in by ten policemen, who grilled him for 48 hours, before being forced to charge him with the lesser charge of 'covering up for a murderer', with no better evidence to go on. They, like everyone else, had been highly suspicious that he may have had more involvement in the murders, particularly the murder of Rocío in 1999. They had come to this assumption after colleagues of the pair, who worked together at a timeshare company in Calahonda, insisted that they had both been out together on the night of Rocío's murder and – significantly – neither had come to work the following day.

They certainly acted like some sort of sinister double act, drinking in the same pubs, going to the same parties and often sleeping on each other's floors. Time and time again, over those early days I heard stories of Graham's violence, in particular to women, but he was not to be broken. With no hard evidence to go on, the wily salesman simply stuck to his loose story (it would later change many times) that all he knew of the murder was King's confession on the same night. And in an extraordinary judicial cock-up, to his good fortune, the authorities were forced to release him after three days when it emerged that the sentence for the crime of covering up a murder ran out after four years. It was a bizarre loophole, which unsurprisingly sent the Spanish press apoplectic with rage, particularly when a smirking Graham was seen being led out of Alhaurín prison, where King was also being kept, and was whisked off in a black Mercedes, hired by the *News of the World*.

But before his tabloid payday, the timeshare tout had a couple of aces up his sleeve and somehow talked the police into allowing him to undertake a voluntary hypnosis session in order to remember the night in question in 1999. It meant being taken up to Madrid, where during the highly controversial hypnosis he recalled a great deal more information about the time in question. While inadmissible as evidence in court, the transcripts were given far too much credence in the Spanish press and within days he was dumping a ton of shit on his former friend and colleague in the *News of the World*.

In the exclusive double page spread, Graham claimed that King had turned up at his flat on the night of the murder of Rocío and revealed that he had attacked the teenager on some waste ground. 'He said he'd hurt someone,' Graham spouted. 'He'd tried it on with her and she'd started screaming when he touched her up and he'd been a bit heavy with her. He said: "She's not moving – she's either unconscious or I've killed her." And he told me he'd thrown a knife in the sea.' A typically salacious red-top interview, it was also claimed in a bulleted list of points that King had:

- threatened to murder his estranged wife Cecilia and new partner David Cooze;
- had kept a stash of guns, knives and CS gas and;
- watched violent movies and porn for hours on end.

But soon came an even better angle for the British press. Splashed across the front page of the *Daily Mail* on Monday, 22 September 2003 was the sensational news that Tony King wasn't his real name after all. He was in fact Tony Bromwich, better known as 'the Holloway Strangler' for a string of terrifying sex attacks on women in 1986. Under the screaming five-deck headline: 'THE COSTA KILLER WAS SEX STRANGLER IN BRITAIN', the *Mail*'s experienced crime correspondent Stephen Wright wrote how King had received a ten-year prison sentence after a five-week reign of terror in which he used electrical flex to choke his victims before molesting them. The report went on to add that 'he attacked four women and a teenager and while none was raped, a sexual motive was involved'. Stirring stuff and suffice to say the following day every media organization in the country was camped outside Tony Bromwich's mum's house in north London. The story 'had legs', to use a Fleet Street phrase.

What seemed of particular interest were the similarities between his convicted crimes in England and the ones he was accused of in Spain. The fact that none of the English victims had been raped, like Sonia and Rocío, suggested a problem with impotence and sparked a deluge of new articles, both in the English and Spanish press, with the papers desperately attempting to track down any of King's family members, as well as his victims. His mother Lynda Bromwich sensibly refused to speak, simply taping a statement to the door of her house in north London. It was straight to the point and conclusive. It read: 'I wish to say the following: I love my son Tony unconditionally to the day I die. I do not believe everything that has been printed. I also know that a lot of lies have been said. I will never say another word to the media again.'

Next came a massive outcry, particularly in the Spanish media, about how this apparently prolific and dangerous sex offender was able to change his name so easily and then move abroad and immerse himself unchecked in Iberian society. The Spanish were simply appalled at the ease at which he had been able to change his name by deed poll and their anger intensified when it emerged a few days later that not only had King been an early suspect in the murder of Rocío Wanninkhof, but he had apparently 'fled' Britain, after being singled out as the main suspect in a violent sex attack on a teenage au pair at a train station in Surrey. It turned out there was CCTV footage of him on a nearby platform around the time of the attack and it had even been shown on *Crimewatch* the day after he had left the country (instigating dozens of phone calls naming him). Police knew where he had gone (they even had an address in Spain) but in a somewhat bizarre and warped loophole, they didn't attempt to extradite him to face charges. Instead they sent a warning to Spanish police to keep an eye on King, a warning that apparently fell on deaf ears.

There was also a mad scramble to find King's estranged wife Cecilia Pantoja, a former timeshare salesperson, who everyone knew would be the main prize for the Sunday buy-up merchants. News editors were screaming down the phone at their reporters to find her, but all anyone had to go on was that her partner David Cooze was an estate agent and they apparently lived in Fuengirola. One thing's for sure, the timeshare world was keeping incredibly tight-lipped and I had to really pull out the stops to find them.

The address had finally come through a Spanish TV contact who was working undercover on the story, and I arrived at David and Cecilia's house alongside the main N-340 highway outside Fuengirola, just as Cecilia had agreed to do a live TV broadcast about her husband the following day for national TV network Antenna 3 in Madrid. I managed to secure an interview for the *Sunday Mirror*, who had contracted me for the job and the deal was a simple, if painful, one. We would go to the capital that night – a five-hour drive away – and after her TV interview the following day, I could have my exclusive.

It was a long 24 hours, not arriving in Madrid until 5a.m., and then with a lot of high drama when – because of money wrangles – Cecilia walked out of the studio at the last minute, with the whole of Spain waiting on tenterhooks. I watched from my hotel room on national TV as she stormed out into the car park and got into her lawyer's car – tight-lipped – and drove off, goodness knew where. I naturally assumed the lawyer had negotiated a big pay deal with the *News of the World* or the *Mail on Sunday*, who had both sent teams down to secure an interview.

It certainly came as an amazing surprise when it turned out they had come back to my hotel and were sitting down in the dining room having a late breakfast. The rest of the day was spent frustratingly talking money and contracts and I didn't get to sit down to interview Cecilia until 10p.m. at night. It was Friday night and I had less than 12 hours to turn the whole article around for the Sunday. But the result was worth it, the story being splashed over the front page and on four pages inside. Under the headline: 'I Shopped My Costa Killer Husband', Cecilia told how she had met and married the 'sex monster' a year after he had got out of prison in England. She revealed how he spent all their money on drugs and that their sex life had rapidly dwindled as he got more and more into pornography and started to go out late at night while she was asleep. The trial-by-media (of which I had admittedly become a part) was in full swing.

In a deluge of articles that was to follow, one ex-boss told how King might have been a paedophile, as he leered at girls as young as nine. Gardening contractor John O'Connell, said: 'Some of the things he came out with were sick. He boasted he had sex with a girl of twelve, who he claimed was a prostitute. King said it took place in the back of our firm's pick up. He seemed to be proud of it. Whenever he saw a schoolgirl in uniform, even if she was only nine, he'd stop what he was doing for a good look and say: "She'd get it".'

O'Connell, who had employed King for nearly a year, added that the odd-job man carried a stockpile of dangerous weapons in his car. 'He had weapons on him all the time,' he said. 'There was a machete, samurai sword, sawn-off shotgun, knuckle-dusters and flick knives in the boot of his car.' He added that when he sacked him for making a crude remark at a woman, King told him he wasn't in the slightest bit upset as he had a job as a hit man lined up in Valencia for which he was due to get paid 30,000 euros.

Soon some of the victims had also come forward to talk about the attacks in England, while a series of alleged victims in Spain queued up to give their accounts about the attacks they had suffered at the hands of King. One woman, a mother of two in her forties, who gave her name only as María, claimed he almost beat her to death and tried to rape her in June 2001. Perhaps to satisfy the media's lust for blood he was very publicly being trawled to a series of identity parades up and down the Costa del Sol to see if any of the accusers could pick him out. Some did, but out of over half a dozen accusations, by the trial he had not been charged with a single one.

The story continued to dominate the headlines particularly when the following weekend the tabloids hit on a highly speculative story that King might even have been responsible for the murder of Milly Dowler, aged 13. It was the start of the silly season, and King was suddenly being blamed for dozens of unsolved murders, stretching back 16 years. Detectives from Norway even apparently got in on the act, according to the *Sun*, contacting the Spanish police through Interpol over the murder of Trudi Espas in Oslo in 1986. The killer had apparently used 'similar methodology' to King, who by this time, of course, had not even been convicted of *any* murders, let it not be forgotten.

While it all seemed highly implausible, police in the UK took it seriously enough to set up a special investigation unit and sent a trio of British police to Malaga in an attempt to talk to King about his movements in England. In the event they were unable to interview him (they were told by Spanish police that there was 'no chance' of interviewing their man).

And then was to come the most extraordinary and outrageous breach of legal protocol – not to mention prison security – imaginable. Somehow a Spanish lawyer, and sometimes journalist, David Rojo, managed to get into Alhaurín de la Torre prison under the guise that he was going to represent King. Incredibly he was able to talk the prison's most high-profile inmate into writing a couple of notes of apology to the families of the two dead girls. The result was explosive and, suspiciously, featured prominently as an exclusive in the *Sun* the following day. In the letters he admitted the two murders and said he was 'sorry'. In what appeared to be his real handwriting, he allegedly wrote to the mother of Rocío Wanninkhof saying: 'I am sick to the soul for what damage and pain I caused. I am sick and need help and beg for your forgiveness in this. And confessed everything in the hope that you would not have to go through another trial and suffer more.' He added, oddly: 'My deepest apologies for not owning up to the crime and causing a rift in your friendship with Dolores.'

Despite being charged with the murders, obviously any semblance of the idea of a free and fair trial had been thrown out of the window. Sub judice clearly did not exist in Spain and it seemed the media could write just about what it wanted. Indeed, soon the papers and magazines were claiming that King was some sort of necrophiliac and had kept some of Rocío Wanninkhof's bloody clothes as a trophy and that he had gone back time and again to the spot where he had dumped her body as police searched for it. They claimed that he got his kicks out of playing a sick sexual fantasy over the dead body while it lay prone and undiscovered for a month. Other leaks from police and judicial sources led to stories that he was addicted to films about sex and death and that he had watched a horror film about a serial killer called *Absence of Good*, hours before killing Sonia Carabantes.

To add salt to the wounds, the following month – even more incredibly – the police officially released statements in which King was said to have confessed to the murders. In the alleged confessions, taken in the days after his arrest, he was said to have admitted to stalking the victims and claimed he was a sexual pervert who could not get his kicks from normal sex. In the claimed confessions, made public by the courts, he said: 'I am mentally ill. I apologize to all women for being so ill. I know I am ill because I was touching her [Sonia], touching her breasts and the rest of her body. I believe she was dead by now. I am disgusting. When I approach them I feel like a hunter, a conqueror that has taken his prisoner or his target. I have no interest in sex with my partner and am not able to achieve orgasm. Stalking women, touching them and then, while I pleasure myself, remembering how my victims once walked, how I approached them, touched them and intimidated them – that motivates me more.'

In another alleged confession he admitted to dragging Rocío Wanninkhof by the hair across the waste ground near her home. He told how she put up a desperate struggle as he stabbed her ten times in the neck, abdomen and back. King, who had followed her in the car, said: 'I put the knife to her throat and told her to come with me. Rocío pushed me and tried to escape. She wouldn't stop struggling, fighting back, shouting. The last place I stabbed her was in the back. She fell to the ground and stopped screaming. I only wanted to touch her. She was young and I thought she would be afraid.' All in all Tony Alexander King was guilty as charged. Would a trial really be necessary?

Chapter Two

The Poor Little
'Please-and-Thank-You Boy'

Tony King's upbringing can best be described in two ways: traumatic and deprived. Perennially skint, with a violent father, a bullying older brother and a mother with emotional problems, some psychologists might say that his future in the crime world was clearly marked out from a young age. Add to that, considerable learning difficulties, stemming from his late-diagnosed dyslexia and you have a lad clearly disadvantaged in life.

Born Anthony Alexander Bromwich on 2 August 1965 at the Whittington Hospital, a scruffy concrete expanse at the foot of Highgate Hill, which, while so close to the leafy and affluent climes of Highgate and Hampstead always feels bogged down in the grimy suburbs of Archway and Holloway. Named after Dick Whittington who famously climbed Highgate Hill to seek his fortune, these days it is a typically run down and over-stretched London hospital at the sharp end of care.

Living almost all of his life within a mile or two of the hospital, there were, sadly, no streets paved with gold, or rags-to-riches stories for Tony, who like Dick Whittington was born into grinding poverty, but unlike the former Mayor of London, never managed to climb Highgate Hill to find his fortune.

The fact is his father Kenneth Frederick Bromwich was a violent, aggressive type, who seemed to take pleasure in beating up his wife and three children. A former pimp and spiv – who used his children to help sell his wares door to door – his longest steady job was working as a moulder in a factory, making plastic taps out of Bakelite. Psychologically unhinged, he would often disappear for months on end, leaving his wife Lynda with the unenviable task of trying to bring up their three children on the pittance he had left on top of anything she could cobble together from social security handouts and the odd part-time job.

Weighing in at 8lb 9oz – the heaviest of three siblings – Tony's only significant birthmark was a small turnover on his left ear (his daughter Sabrina was also born with one), which at his mother's insistence was later corrected. After the customary two weeks in hospital he was back with his older brother David at the tiny terraced house his parents shared with Lynda's grandmother in Highbury. Classic slum housing that had been earmarked for demolition, the long row of two-bedroom houses sat in a dead-end road called Ashburton Grove, which ironically is soon to become the glamorous £50m home of Arsenal FC. With a coal yard at one end and the municipal council dump at the other, it was considered to be one of the most polluted streets in the borough and was forever noisy with the constant movement of trucks and dustcarts.

Conditions indoors weren't much better, particularly when Tony's younger sister Angela joined the family the following year. All squeezing into one bedroom there was little room for their possessions, even less to swing a cat. With ancient flock wallpaper peeling off the walls and gas lamps still stuck to them, an outside loo at the end of the garden and holes in the stairs, the house had a distinct Dickensian feel. Add to that a moody, unpredictable father and a hyperactive older brother – who hardly ever slept – it certainly can't have been pleasant.

'It was smelly, damp and miserable. A run down house that hadn't been redecorated for decades,' recalls Tony's mother Lynda Bromwich, who still has terrible nightmares about the place. 'We hardly had enough change to feed the meter and it was always filthy with all the dustcarts and coal lorries going up and down all day. There was a dirty old junk room at the top, and the creaky stairs and shadows from the gas lamps used to give me terrible nightmares when I was growing up there. It makes me sick just thinking about it.'

While never actually starving (all the cooking was left to Lynda's grandmother, as Lynda was forced to go out looking for work), it was undoubtedly hard for the kids, who had no pocket money and little in the way of entertainment. Their father never bought them toys and they were the last family in the road to get a television, an ancient second-hand one at that.

Having been brought up by her grandparents, Lynda Cox – as she was born – had spent her whole life in that house. Her grandfather Albert, a former bus conductor, spent decades on sick leave after being poisoned by mustard gas in the First World War; her grandmother Mary was a Post Office worker. Her father was a squaddie from the Black Watch and her mother – who was only 16 when Lynda was born – had flown the nest to marry someone else when she was three years old, leaving her at the mercy of her grandparents.

It was a tough start in life and she must have been hoping that the person she ended up marrying would at least take her somewhere new. But sadly it was not to be. When she started dating Fred, as most people knew him, he not only insisted he didn't have two pennies to rub together, but refused to even tell her where he lived. She was only 17 when they met at a dance hall in Finsbury Park on one of her first – and rare – outings to a nightclub. Being a religious, God-fearing girl, who attended her local Methodist church two or three times a week, nightlife was usually spent hanging around the local park with her friends from Sunday school and she took an immediate dislike to the pushy cockney, who had greased-back hair and was clearly the worse for wear. He, however, refused to be outdone, and after three or four unsuccessful attempts to get the former May queen to dance, reluctantly slipped a note to her friend Sandra declaring his love. Two weeks later he had somehow found her address and hung around outside until she finally agreed to come out.

The warning signs were certainly there, and she soon discovered that he was already divorced from a Greek girl he'd met while serving with the British army in Greece (she later discovered they'd had a daughter he never saw and, tellingly, she says, was divorced on the grounds of 'cruelty'). But Fred – who was undeniably handsome, with a pair of searing blue eyes and an impeccable dress sense – eventually won her over and they began dating.

At first he was charming and sensitive, and while not one for flowers or expensive meals, he obviously made up for any shortcomings between the sheets. Aspiring to be a plumber, he would talk of buying a house and promised her holidays by the sea, which apart from one week in Clacton – where he disappeared after a few days leaving her to the mercy of the hotelier – failed to materialize. He would frequently come home very late with poor excuses and would disappear for weeks, sometimes even months on end to his own flat in nearby King's Cross.

He would always come back though, prompting his uncle to describe him to Lynda as 'like a dog who came back in the mating season'. She knows she shouldn't have put up with it but somehow Lynda stuck in there even when he started to turn violent following the birth of their first son David when Lynda was aged 19.

She remembers the beating well, the salivating, bug-eyed maniac kicking her over the sofa for not having prepared his supper when he got in from the pub one night at almost midnight. Sadly the attacks became depressingly regular (something which was backed up by Tony's grandmother, who witnessed many of them) and he would not only demand his supper be cooked when he got in, whether it was 7p.m. or 2a.m., but he would expect a roaring fire in the grate, even though he, more than anyone else, knew that the family could ill afford it.

And then on 8 September 1965 – their wedding day – came the bombshell. It was a month after Tony's birth and the small gathering of mainly family were trying to dry themselves out at the sausage-roll-and-beer-reception at Lynda's house after getting soaked on the walk back from Finsbury register office. It was a British classic like no other and it had poured down since dawn. There had even been a bucket on the altar to catch the drips. Things just didn't bode well for the future with Fred refusing to contribute a penny towards the wedding and Lynda and her mother paying for everything – including the £30 wedding ring.

A telephone call to a neighbour's house (they had no phone) had been received only an hour after arriving at the party. Lynda had dutifully stumbled around to the neighbour's in her new navy-blue Debenham's suit and frilly white blouse, her hair up in curls on top of her head. To call it a shock would be an understatement. On the other end of the line was a mad, hysterical woman, going by the name Lulu, who claimed she had been dating 'Kenneth', as she called him, for the previous nine months.

As Lynda vividly recalls: 'She was ranting and raving at me down the phone, saying: "How dare you marry my man?" and threatening to bash me up. It was so disrespectful I decided to have it out with her, first demanding her address and then storming off to find her. It turned out to be the flat near

Caledonian Road, where Fred had been living on and off for years and I literally shot up Holloway Road and got the first bus there. I was like a raging bull. I was so upset and seeing red and barged my way in and went straight for this girl. I remember my fist connecting with her right eye and dragging her to the floor. I won't say much except she had two black eyes and would have thought twice before making threats again.'

Eventually dragged off by Fred, who had followed hot on her heels, it didn't take her long to ascertain that Lulu was a 'call girl', as she puts it, and that she and another girl had been working for Fred from the flat for years. Half his clothes were in the bedroom and she had stormed out telling her rival that she was welcome to the 'good-for-nothing cheat', who she never wanted to see again.

And that, of course, should have spelt the end of the shortest marriage in history. But Lynda, who had gone back to cry on her mother's shoulder, was sadly for turning. Indeed after less than a week of tears and mourning, in which she had refused to talk to her new husband, she finally agreed to forgive him when he wrote a series of grovelling apologies in chalk in the road outside her house. He also promised to leave the pimping behind, which Lynda naively believed despite his new nickname in the road, Burlington Bertie, for his sharp dress sense and clever ways with ladies of the night.

Somehow lost on her, as she strolled around in practically rags ('he even quibbled about giving me ten shillings to buy a pair of plimsolls'), Fred in contrast would swan around in tailor-made suits from Savile Row and insisted that everything he wore was dry cleaned. Soon pregnant with Angela, she now admits she was naive not to raise an eyebrow as he would come and go (he would still often disappear for weeks on end) like a real Dapper Dan, togged up in a handmade mohair suit with crisp white Liberty shirts, a trilby hat and expensive Burberry-check umbrella.

Like a classic wartime spiv, he would often turn up with a job lot of this and that, be it tins of peaches, a pile of wigs, a box of tracksuits or, on one occasion, a thousand or more candles he had 'got off the back of a lorry', which he forced his children to help him flog to the neighbours one night when they had a power cut. Another time he set himself up as some sort of loan shark, having commandeered a £500 inheritance Lynda had received from her old Sunday school teacher. However despite sticking a series of adverts up in a few local newsagents' windows, he hardly had a call and had soon frittered away the money anyway.

It took a while, but Lynda finally discovered the truth about his second job as a part-time pimp, when she literally bumped into him walking out of her local launderette one day with these two girls on his arm, one straightaway recognizable, despite the coiffured blonde mop and bright red lipstick, as Lulu. 'In that moment I understood where he got his money from and why everyone called him Burlington Bertie. I was furious and ran across the road to confront these tarts, I'm afraid to say using some rather colourful language, until Fred finally stepped in and told me curtly: "Stop hassling my ladies!" and wandered off with them. We later had it out and he admitted he was still working as a pimp and after weeks of furious rows and one particularly bad night when he beat me up I decided to go to the police. The truth was he had been living off immoral earnings and these girls were keeping him in money. I remember the evening the police came round and I told them he was always beating me up, paid no money in maintenance for the kids and was also working as a pimp – and they, of course, did absolutely nothing about it.'

But Fred's behaviour doesn't appear to be out of line from his family, who according to Lynda, were all 'potty'. Apparently originating from the East End with vague Jewish roots, his family had relocated to Manchester and thrived as merchants. Fred had a sister, who – legend has it – stuck a meat fork in her husband, while Fred's father was a colourful story teller, who claimed at various times that he had been in the RAF, Army and Navy. Fred, according to Lynda, hated his parents, and while facts are sketchy, apparently spent a large part of his upbringing in care along with a brother. More certain is the fact that in the time he was married to Lynda he only once drove up to Manchester to see them. 'And when we arrived, the first thing this old git said to us was: "What do you want?" and wouldn't let us in.'

Like his father, Fred had an 'abnormal brain pattern', and was prone to lose his temper for the slightest reason. Perhaps frustrated by his footloose employment – Lynda insists that he did genuinely try to give up the pimping and was frequently on the dole and mooching around the house – his temper would flare up at the slightest thing.

The first bad attack had happened five months into her pregnancy with David. 'I can't remember what brought it on, but he just went nuts and it culminated in him kicking my pregnant stomach and me falling down the stairs,' recalls Lynda. 'The fact that I didn't miscarry was incredible, not that he'd have given a shit.'

And, of course, the violence didn't stop there. In fact it got worse and Lynda can still recall dozens of individual beatings, which became more regular, happening two or three times a week. 'I got beaten with shovels, pushed down stairs and hit with a chair and Fred always used to say that if I ever dared to leave him he would throw acid in my face. The slightest thing could set him off and he would go mental. It started with this look in his eye and a horrible grin on his face – a bit like Jack Nicholson in *The Shining*. When it happened you knew you were going to get hurt.'

One of the nastiest attacks happened when one Sunday morning at the age of four, a young Tony innocently dragged a large lump of wood covered in mud into the kitchen from the small garden at the back. His mother was busy preparing the Sunday roast and peeling the potatoes, while his father sat at the table poring over his favourite red-top newspaper, when suddenly he went berserk.

'You could see this look come across his face as he saw this filthy plank of wood come sliding across the floor,' recalls Lynda. 'I could see there was something brewing and shouted at Tony to take it out, but it was too late, his father had lost it and ran across the room, grabbed the piece of wood out of Tony's hand and started hitting me with it. Angela came running in and was screaming on my left arm, while Tony grabbed the other arm and David tried to pull me out into the garden, but there was nothing that could stop him. He had gone berserk and was belting me everywhere around the head, on the legs, and all I could think about was trying to protect the kids and not to go down under any circumstance as I knew if I'd fallen that could have been it. At one point I vividly remember just managing to pull Angela out of the way of a blow before we managed to run into the garden, where the neighbours could see what was happening. And I can tell you there was blood all over the place and my head and legs were black and blue by the next morning. I guess it was a miracle that nothing was broken.'

Hearing the attack from her bedroom their grandmother ran out to call the police, who were round in minutes and duly carted off a still snarling Fred to the cells. But, such is the way in so many cases of domestic violence, Lynda Bromwich refused to press charges against her husband, deciding to give him another chance, after he came grovelling back to her, having tried to commit suicide with a bottle of aspirins.

The pattern of violence followed by repentance was always the same and he would come back the next day begging for forgiveness. He also eventually agreed to have psychiatric analysis, which discovered through an ECG test that he suffered from hypertension and had 'an unnatural brain wave'.

Says Lynda: 'You couldn't find a softer, more stupid person than me. The truth was I fell in love with him and you always somehow hoped his behaviour would change, and somehow you figured it was good for the kids to have a dad around.'

And still the violence didn't stop. There was the time, for example, when Angela had sneaked out to join the local canal boating club against her father's wishes. 'Fred was furious,' Lynda remembers. 'And when she came in he grabbed hold of her and dragged her into the kitchen where I was washing up after supper. He told her she was going to learn a very valuable lesson today. "You disobeyed me! — now see your mum there . . . come on . . . look at her face . . . this is a lesson you are not going to forget," and he belted me full force in the mouth and went on beating me so badly that by the time he had finished I looked like Quasimodo. And do you know what he said to her at the end: "Now sweetheart, that'll be you next time." '

As Angela, now a mother of two in her late thirties, confirms: 'It went on for over twenty minutes until there was blood all over the floor. It was like a one-sided boxing match. It was sickening and we were all very shaken. But he was always attacking us and I remember him throwing Mum off the balcony, pushing her down the stairs and stuffing a pillow over her head. I also got my fair share of beatings and if anything went wrong he would make us line up in the hall until he found out who was guilty; if no one owned up we would all get a sound beating.

'I remember him frequently cracking his belt and coming towards us laughing with a manic grin on his face, before laying into us. I still have nightmares about that.'

But the worst of the beatings were reserved for Tony. Stubborn and often standing up to his father, rather than backing down like his brother and sister, he would find himself bashed around without mercy. One Christmas, for example, his father went mad because Tony wasn't able to work out how to put together a new Scalextric set he had been given by his mother. 'Fred couldn't understand the instructions either and got so frustrated he jumped all over the new set smashing it to pieces before punching me and Tony.'

Another memorable attack (surprisingly confirmed by his father) was when at the age of four or five Tony refused to put his pyjamas on in preparation for going to bed. While both parents remember it slightly differently, the long and short of it was his father 'beating the living daylights' out of Tony when he refused to get ready for bed. 'I went in and grabbed the little sod and smacked his bottom and forced him to put on his pyjamas,' recalls Fred, during an interview at his house in south east London. 'He needed to learn a lesson and I guess we came to blows.'

From then on the beatings came on an almost weekly basis for the youngster. While his elder brother David was more quick-witted and mostly able to steer clear of trouble and most of the time Fred couldn't bring himself to hit his daughter, Tony bore the brunt of his father's aggression. 'A combination of his learning difficulties and his stubbornness seemed only to inflame his father's ire,' remembers Lynda. 'Fred used him as a scapegoat and knocked any confidence he ever had out of him. He used to belittle him about his dyslexia, which just made things worse, as well as making him feel conscious about his voice, which was a little bit higher than other boys of his age. He even teased him by saying he sounded gay, which really upset him.'

By his own admission, Fred Bromwich was a disciplinarian. He got it from his own father, who brought his children up 'the hard way', as well as a particularly nasty experience in the army at the hands of his commanding officer, who picked on him for three years. As he recalls: 'This sergeant took an immediate dislike to me and haunted me every day. He would pick on me and hassle me for no apparent reason and constantly charged me with small petty offences. I think it was because I was too quiet for him. Like Tony, I was a shy, silent type and people didn't like it. I, like Tony, have learnt that to my cost.'

Ironically, now living as a born-again Christian (with iconic portraits tacked to the walls and a liking to wax lyrical about the Bible) during interviews he unwittingly makes frequent references to the attacks he meted out to his children. A clip round the ear here, a smack there, it is more than obvious that he was a physical man with a short temper.

Pacing up and down the homely kitchen of the house in Dulwich he shares with his second wife, a dancer, he at first appears restless, but soon intimidating, despite being well past retirement age. Short and stocky with piercing dark eyes and slicked-back hair, his physical side masks his obvious intelligence and, in truth, he is a fairly straightforward, even witty character, who is, without a doubt, as sharp as a pin. Looking out at the well-kept garden – one of his main hobbies these days – he does his best to come over as the caring, concerned parent, who did all he could for his children. Almost defensively listing all the opportunities he offered them (the boating holidays, the horseriding courses), he neglects to elaborate on the details or mention the context and circumstances surrounding them.

There were for example the ballroom dancing lessons he dragged the three children to at Morgan's Dance School in Holloway Road. Failing to see that dance classes were hardly something that pre-pubescent boys would be interested in (they hated them, according to Angela), Fred went on about how much fun they were and how he himself made it to 'silver and gold' in ballroom and Latin. The truth, however, is never far from his lips and it is not long before he reveals that David was 'too macho to be any good' and Tony was 'too introverted' and had 'legs like tree trunks'.

Their Sunday afternoon games perhaps sum the man up best. 'If it was rainy and we were cooped up inside we would play a game called "dead leg",' he recalls. 'It involved rolling up the carpet in the living room and removing anything else that could get broken and I would stand in the middle of the room while the three of them would come from all angles and try and give me a dead leg. The rules were that I was only allowed to stay in one position and parry them with my arms, but if I could grab them I got to give them a dead leg.'

Symbolically, perhaps, Tony failed to understand the game, and in a comment that speaks volumes, Fred adds: 'Tony just didn't get it and would always aim kicks at my body and get me in the kidneys and ribs. It really hurt and used to make me so mad.' It would usually end in another beating.

It was left, however, to his sister Angela to really test their father's mettle when at the age of 13 she reported him to the police for 'abuse'. It had happened not long after their parents had finally broken up and she had fallen out with her mother and gone to stay with an infamously troublesome Irish family, who lived up the road. Greatly upsetting her mother, the situation got worse when her brothers started to bunk off school and join her at the house full of grubby kids, who would hang around all day smoking and drinking. Eventually getting too much for their long-suffering mother, who tried everything to get them to go to school, she was forced into the one final option and called Fred to come round and discipline the children, in his own ever-subtle way.

'I went ballistic,' he recalls, adding in a delightfully under-stated way how he had gone round to Seamus's house and practically carried his sons home with 'a clip around the ear'.

The problem was that in the mêlée Angela had somehow slipped away and disappeared and her father reluctantly agreed to go to the local police station to report her missing only to discover that she had gone up to the very same place to fill out a complaint form about him having 'abused' her. It turned out she was still in the station – and while it has not been specified exactly what 'abuse' she meant – in a classic case of softly, softly police procedure they insisted father and daughter talk it through and took them home together in a panda car. Predictably, once home, recalls Angela, he literally punched her on the jaw and knocked her over. 'He sent me flying over the sofa and on to the floor and told me never to do anything like that again. I can't believe he didn't break my jaw.'

Perhaps betraying his new Christian values, not to mention ignoring almost certainly the real reason behind her problems, Fred claims: 'Angela was always a little madam, a real trouble-maker, and I am not at all surprised that she later became a drug addict. But it was always Angela and David who were the ringleaders. Tony was the quiet, introverted one, who would blithely go along for the ride.'

Surprisingly complimentary about his youngest son (who he has kept in touch with throughout his time in Spain) he recalled how he was an extremely popular boy at primary school and made a real effort in every subject. Attending Dalmeny school, by Holloway prison, he says his head teacher was encouraging about his efforts, and even put the three Bromwich children forward when the outside examiner came to analyse the school's performance. While David was always top of the class and one of the first boys in the school to get to grammar school, Tony excelled in practical subjects like woodwork and art.

Tony was also known for his politeness and garnered himself the nickname 'the please-and-thank-you boy', among the dinner ladies. He rarely caused any problems. 'He was the only child who never asked for anything, no money, nothing,' recalls his mother. 'While my other two, David and Angela, were self-centred and greedy and would always rush to the front door when I came in with shopping to see what they could grab. Tony would be the one to help me carry the bags to the kitchen and then make me a cup of tea. He did that with everyone. He had respect for people and a big heart unlike Angela and David.'

But the psychological problems he was suffering as a result of the violence he experienced at home started to become increasingly pronounced. For starters there were the skin problems, such as rashes and eczema that would creep over his body when he was upset. But soon he developed the more alarming affliction of asphyxia, a condition causing him to pass out from lack of breath when he was scared or anxious. As his mother recalls: 'It meant he would cry inwardly without a sound until he fainted through lack of breath and that would happen when Fred lost his temper.

'The poor fellow would go blue in the face and be shaking without making a sound. You could see the panic in his eyes, which would eventually roll back as he passed out. It was very scary and the doctor explained it as a natural phenomenon to allow him to start drawing breath again. It was his way of coping with the violence around him.'

The youngster also developed a severe problem with bedwetting. Tellingly, not stopping until his father moved out for a time when he was 12 years old, it was an almost nightly occurrence and made him frightened to go to bed in case it happened and his father found out. 'It caused terrible nightmares and a sleeping disorder, that lasts to this very day,' says his mother, who had to be extremely organized to prevent her husband finding out. 'Fred would go mad and clout Tony if he discovered he'd wet the bed and I always had to be up first to make sure I turned over the mattress or quickly changed the sheets. I always had to have a big pile of clean sheets ready to put on and there is no doubt that the effect on Tony was extreme. It is no coincidence that it ended almost the minute Fred had left and curiously stopped for six months when Fred ran off with this West Indian nurse when Tony was about nine.'

The problems would also have a profound effect on his schooling with his fellow classmates calling him names like 'smelly' and 'stinky' as a result of the distinct waft of urine clinging to his clothes. It was this, more than anything else that turned him into a loner. But while he rarely enjoyed school he refused, according to his mother, to bunk off. One former class-mate, who asked not to be named, said: 'Tony was a strange kid, who always sat near the back of the class and had few, if any, friends. He was quiet and introverted, I guess. But because he was tough and came from a hard family we didn't pick on him that much. Sure we called him smelly and teased him a bit, as he definitely ponged, but we didn't go overboard.

'He certainly wasn't stupid and made as much effort as anybody to learn, despite coming bottom in most subjects, and to be fair I think he was not a disruptive child like his older brother. I guess he had a lot of problems which the teachers never really got to the bottom of.'

This certainly seems to be the case, with the youngster only being diagnosed with dyslexia at the age of ten. The discovery was only made after his father talked to his head teacher at a school open day. A rare visit – in a period, when Fred Bromwich was apparently showing an interest in his son's development – he says he was told what beautiful handwriting his son had and led over to look at a couple of examples of his work on the wall. 'But when I looked at them closely I couldn't understand the words. While beautiful they were all mixed up and upside down,' he recalls. 'The headmistress said he always wrote like that, but phonetically he had no problems. I then asked her how he was doing in class academically and she said he was "not very good". I asked her where he stood in class and she replied "bottom in every subject". I was gutted and decided to get him some extra help.'

Working at the time at the world-renowned Ear, Nose and Throat hospital in Gray's Inn Road, in King's Cross, he says he met a doctor who recommended the Nuffield Foundation, where a child psychologist quickly diagnosed him with dyslexia. 'He would look at a tree upside down and think it was normal or not notice that a house had no front door. It was a classic case of dyslexia and on the psychologist's advice I opted to send him to a crammer prep. school where he could get the necessary tuition he needed.'

So at some point in his penultimate year at primary school the youngster was packed off to a private school in Kensington. While it is unclear who put up the money, he did attend the school, opting out of French and Spanish classes, in favour of extra maths and English. 'He was doing four times as much arithmetic as the others and at the end of the year he was bright enough to pass the entrance exam to get into Central Foundation Grammar school like his brother,' claims Fred proudly.

But while Tony's father might credit himself with helping his son overcome the problems caused by dyslexia, his sister recalls how his rather less orthodox methods at home must have scarred him for life. Having single-handedly decided to try and solve his son's learning disabilities, he took it upon himself to give him extra tuition in the evenings. This, says Angela, involved making him stand up and read in front of the family after supper and predictably ended in a thumping should he get his words mixed up. 'He would take his belt off and crack it as Tony began and you could see him get more and more frightened,' she recalls. 'Dad would literally hover over him and we would all wince waiting for the clout to come. It made him very nervous and he hated being humiliated. It was from about that point onwards that he would do anything to avoid being humiliated.'

Certainly, being at Central Foundation wasn't helping and within a year it became increasingly obvious that he was way out of his depth and, moreover, becoming a nuisance. Bullied by his fellow pupils and teased about his weight (according to a psychological report they called him 'fatty'), he started to bunk off with his older brother, who was also rapidly going off the rails. They would frequently fail to arrive at school at all or sneak out of classes to play on the slot machines up in Soho or King's Cross.

The truth, it later turned out, was that they, 'like their sister', were influenced by a new family of Irish tinkers, who had been moved into the estate from 'somewhere up north'. Their mother had long flown the nest and their father, a cabinetmaker by trade, was an alcoholic who rarely made it out of bed before midday. He was simply uninterested in his children's education and neither cared what they did all day, nor with whom they hung out with.

Angela, by now 13, was – in the words of her mother – 'like an animal let out of a cage' now that her father had gone (she would later have problems with drugs) and had pretty much moved into the neighbour's home full-time. And that is where Tony and David started disappearing each morning after being walked up to the bus stop at the end of their road by their mum. 'The buggers would wait till I'd gone out of sight and they would sneak back to their friends where they would spend the whole day messing around,' recalls Lynda. 'Understandably the school soon got fed up and asked them to leave and that was that.'

It should have meant the boys going to their local school Archway Boys, but fearing that they would continue to bunk off their mother petitioned their local education authority explaining the bad influence the local Irish family was having on them. It did the trick and the council agreed to send them, on a trial basis, to a boarding school in Louth, near Grimsby.

But problems soon emerged there as well, with both David and Angela being expelled within a couple of months for bunking off to return to London. Tony, in contrast, actually enjoyed being away from his overbearing family and lasted for a whole year until his parents apparently learnt of a nasty experience at the hands of one teacher. Recalls Lynda: 'Apparently this PE instructor who did not like Tony used to punch him in the jaw and make him say "thank you". It had

42

been happening almost every day for months and Tony was miserable. We phoned him to confirm it was true and stormed up there to confront the teacher, who surprisingly didn't deny it and gave some weak excuse that Tony needed discipline. Poor guy, after all the grief he got from his father, now he was getting it from a teacher. The damage is immeasurable.'

So back home he came to Holloway to live with his mother and for a time things were settled. He joined his brother at Archway Boys, where he started to make a few friends, particularly two West Indian boys, one now a solicitor's clerk, the other a driving instructor.

But the good times weren't to last for long when after a few months his father suddenly turned up out of the blue insisting that the whole family join him in a new life in the fast-growing new town of Telford, in Shropshire. He had landed a job as a plumber, and through a combination of coercion and charm he eventually got his way.

It is no surprise that they were all miserable, finding themselves in a smelly, unfurnished council flat on a busy road. A relatively humdrum, charmless town, recalls Lynda, they spent all their time mooching around the house missing their family and friends. While the beatings had stopped for a few weeks prior to the move they came back with a vengeance on arrival, and after a couple of months Lynda had had enough and early one morning gathered her things and the children and hitched back to London to stay with her long-suffering grandmother.

Fred, of course, was far from happy and got straight on the phone ordering them to come back and threatening to kill them if they didn't. 'We taped some of the threats and the police told us we could put him away for a few years,' says Lynda. Charges were duly made and while they were moved to a safe house in Goswell Road, Islington, Fred was ordered to sign on every day at the local police station in Telford to stop him from coming back to London. 'But of course, I dropped the charges when he came snivelling back from Telford all sweetness and light and promising to be good.'

They moved back into a new council house until a year or so later when the final straw came as the boys started hitting puberty and looked as if they might try hitting their father back when he got violent. On one occasion David, now 14, stepped in front of his mother one evening to prevent a thrashing and bore the full brunt of his father's ire. 'He took off his belt and whacked him around the face with the buckle end. He was lucky not to lose an eye and the next day had a terrible series of marks. I feared they would step in to help me and one of them would get killed. I had been able to somehow deal with it, internalize it, if you like, until then and I suddenly realized I had to be brave and draw the line.'

So two days later she took the three children to her grandmother's and called a solicitor to begin divorce proceedings. While Fred would regularly phone up with death threats and warnings of 'having to watch out on dark nights', the following year in 1978, not long before Tony's thirteenth birthday the decree absolute came through and she was finally rid of the man who had troubled her life for so long. Or so she thought. 'The truth is he would still come round and terrorize us whenever he wanted to.' But thankfully, after nearly a year of harassment he seemingly grew bored and moved on – much to the family's joy – to the other side of London.

Chapter Three

Girls and First Love

By the age of 14, Tony Bromwich was at last beginning to develop some self-confidence. Finally rid of the black cloud that was his father, he started to broaden his horizons and even take an interest in his appearance. He began wearing increasingly flattering clothes, including silk shirts and a Crombie jacket, and started to put gel in his hair. But most importantly, he began to take an interest in his physique. Still stung by the overweight tag he had inherited at Central Foundation, he made a point of watching what he ate and started to work out and do sit-ups and press-ups every night at home. He was soon the proud owner of a rippling set of biceps; something that didn't go unnoticed with the local girls.

'He grew more handsome by the day,' recalls his sister Angela. 'One minute he was this smelly little fat kid, quiet and put upon, the next I was getting charged in the playground by a dozen girls all asking me about my older brother. They would beg me for our address and ask me to put in a good word with him. They would also pass me notes, love letters really, to hand to him and he was fast becoming one of the local heart-throbs.'

Initially it all went over the young teenager's head and while his older brother took a keen interest in the opposite sex, Tony took up various sports as hobbies. He became surprisingly proficient in swimming (certificates and medals prove this) and he represented his local area in judo. He also began to attend a gym and got a BMX bike, which he would ride around the local skateboard parks. He started dreaming of being a professional bodybuilder and, in particular, hung out with a couple of West Indian friends he'd met at the gym, next to the infamously rough Archway Tavern pub on the polluted Archway round-about. One of them, it should be noted, had a prostitute as a mother and the group soon formed a cosmopolitan local gang, who were, if anything, more black than white.

He was also beginning to find his feet at school, where, according to his sister, he became something of 'a face'. In particular he hung around with a lad called Rocky, who now runs a cab business, and the class joker Joey Butler, a mixed-race boy, now working as a solicitor's clerk in London. They had first met at judo classes in the evening, but had become close mates, according to his sister, when Tony had stuck up for Joey, who was being picked on for being black. 'Tony abhorred racism and bullying and got into quite a few fights over it,' recalls Angela. 'Joey was really grateful for the support and they became a real double act. They would tear around the hallways running into classrooms in the middle of lessons and make faces at the teachers and run off. He had been so quiet and polite before, but now thanks to Joey, who was a real prankster, he was beginning to come out of himself. They were always having a laugh and began to hang around everywhere together and did judo in the evenings.'

Like most teens of that age, there were of course, a few scrapes with the law and Tony – who according to his family has always been the 'unlucky one' – would usually be the one to get caught. 'Nothing more than the odd punch-up or ding-dong' in the words of his mother, they would normally take place in local clubs and pubs, such as the Archway Tavern, a well-known salt-of-the-earth Irish pub, where there was always something going down.

But apart from the time he got a police caution for stealing from an allotment, there appears to be only one serious matter of note, when Tony and his brother had joined a gang to fight another group from a nearby pub. It was a friend's relative, who needed a bit of local support, and Tony and David agreed to go along as a bit of backup, or muscle, for lack of a better word. The problem was while they had both stuffed a handful of stones into socks and charged up the road to meet this gang, unfortunately for Tony, when the police turned up he was the only one with a weapon still in his hand. David had made sure he disposed of his weapon as soon as he'd heard the sirens. Tony, of course, hadn't and was pulled in for possession of a dangerous weapon, for which he got a £75 fine and a two-year conditional discharge, according to his mother.

'But neither Tony, nor David were criminally minded,' claims Lynda Bromwich. 'They never used to hang around on corners looking for people to mug. David was off with girls, while Tony was busy doing his sports. The truth is Tony was just unlucky and if anyone was going to get caught it was him.'

The odd scrapes apart, his mid-teens also coincided with the first period of relative stability for the family who, after moving around various council estates and housing associations in the north London triangle of Highbury, Holloway and Archway, finally landed the prize of a three-bedroom council house in Hornsey Rise, where his mother still lives today. While hardly the sort of des-res property associated with much of north London, the pleasant end-of-terrace cottage in Mulkern Road certainly had its charms. Despite being surrounded by ugly 1960s council houses, and with a distinct *frisson* of crime, the turn-of-the-century workman's cottage was roomy and had a decent garden.

It was here, in Mulkern Road, not long after his fifteenth birthday, that Tony lost his virginity to one of his sister's best friends, who had come to stay over for the night. Ann-Marie, or Pee Wee to her friends, was a precocious, attractive 14-year-old, who had developed a major crush on Tony, to the extent that she pestered his sister Angela for months for an introduction.

'She was bonkers about Tony and continually went on about him,' recalls Angela, who now lives around the corner from Mulkern Road. 'It was actually pretty tedious. I think it was the second night she stayed over and after flirting with Tony all evening in front of the TV she sneaked upstairs to his room in the middle of the night. I knew what she had planned and she didn't come down for at least an hour. When she came back she had this big grin on her face. She came over to stay as much as possible after that and would always sneak upstairs to have sex with Tony. He, of course, would act totally disinterested, but I knew he was enjoying the attention, not to mention the sex. He was still pretty shy with girls and didn't know how attractive he was. But the truth was he could lure any girl anywhere he wanted and Pee Wee certainly didn't have any complaints. In fact she told me the sex was great.'

Tony was soon dating a different girl every couple of months and would usually end up bringing them home for sex. His mother was a liberal woman and was happier to know that he was indoors enjoying himself rather than hanging around late in parks or nightclubs. 'There were certainly quite a few of them,' says Angela. 'He was always sowing his oats and would get through them like there was no tomorrow. First it had been David that liked the girls, but Tony was rapidly catching up.'

He would pull a lot of the girls while out with his mates at various nightclubs in London and before heading 'up west', as they would term the West End, they would spend hours in front of their mirrors preening themselves and making sure every hair was in place. Clothes-wise they were soon swept away by the casual craze that swept Britain in the early 1980s, insisting on wearing only the best designer labels such as Tachini and Fila, and between them they would often be wearing thousands of pounds worth of clothes.

More stability came for the lads (Angela had long parted the nest) when family friend Keith Rose, an East End printer, moved in with Lynda during Tony's final year at school. An affable, straightforward cockney he had been looking for somewhere to live after his wife died of cancer and he had lost their house. Dependable and calm, he was a great support to Lynda, and had soon landed Tony his first job as an apprentice printer at D&D Print Finishers, in Bow, East London.

Well connected in the printing trade he had pulled a few favours to land the post for Tony, who had no intention of taking his academic studies any further and indeed finished school at Archway Boys with no qualifications to speak of. So after a few months of messing around doing odd jobs in local pubs his apprenticeship agreement records that he was to begin the four-year post as a 'print trade finisher' on 4 January 1982 to finish on the same date in 1986.

He proved to be a model worker, running around doing all the grunt work and manning the series of imposing machines that printed everything from adverts for supermarkets to booklets on religion. His former boss Dave Hill recalls what a steady reliable worker he turned out to be. 'He was not the sharpest tool in the box, but he was strong as an ox and perfectly suited for the job. He ran the folding machine and did most of the packing for us. I had no complaints. Despite being a bit of a loner, he was a real gentle giant and didn't seem like he could hurt a fly. We all liked him.'

Getting in at 8a.m., he would get a lift to work from his step-father Keith, and would knock off at 4p.m., with a half-hour lunch break. While he would often be offered overtime up to 7p.m., he would normally be home before six having caught a bus up to East Aldgate tube station and from there home to Holloway. It was a steady routine that suited him. He certainly liked the money, and the new-found self-respect it gave him soon paid off.

Tony met Lynne Saunders, his first true love, on a night out in early 1983. A year into his apprenticeship, and growing more sensible by the day, it would prove to be one of the turning points in his life. It was practically love at first sight when he spotted the pretty secretary sitting at a table on the edge of the dance floor at the packed Lyceum nightclub on the Strand. It was a Friday night and the 17-year-old had been out to celebrate one of his workmates' birthdays in Covent Garden, and a few of them had ended up in the imposing white-pillared venue, a short walk up from Trafalgar Square.

Like two different worlds colliding, Lynne, an only child, was out with a group of friends from her workplace at prestigious merchant bank Morgan Grenfell in the city. Well dressed in a navy suit, she and a group of other secretaries from the bank perched around a table, while a handful of traders shuttled backwards and forwards to the bar to purchase the drinks. Giggling like schoolgirls after five or six Babychams, the girls had turned their attentions to a bit of 'talent spotting' as they liked to call it.

That was where Tony came in. With a bit of wedge in his pocket – Friday being payday – he had a newfound confidence and looked great in the jacket and slacks he had changed into from his work clothes. He took a shine to the petite brunette and the pair were soon on the dance floor rubbing up against each other, and although Tony could hardly be described as

John Travolta, he didn't disgrace himself. An hour or two later, after he had bought her a couple of drinks, they swapped numbers before he kissed her goodnight on the cheek and rushed off to get the last tube home.

His mother vividly remembers his mood when he got in around 1a.m. that night. 'I remember him coming in and telling me there and then that he had met someone nice. He was exhilarated and said, "Mum, she is a really nice, sweet girl, not like the wretched lot round here." I was really pleased for him. I knew he had had quite a few flings and was anything but a virgin, but I desperately wanted him to find himself a proper girlfriend.'

He had been decidedly distracted for the rest of the weekend and changed his mind every five minutes about when would be the best time to call her. He eventually settled on Sunday night about 8p.m. and they agreed to go on a date the following Wednesday near her home in Walthamstow. Tony's stepfather Keith remembers it well, having offered to give him a lift to Walthamstow station, close to the house she shared with her mother. 'Tony was so nervous,' recalls Keith. 'He rushed back from work and spent ages getting ready. He was a ball of nerves and the car absolutely reeked of aftershave and, of course, after all that she wasn't at the station when we got there. Tony was gutted and insisted we wait, so we ended up hanging around for nearly an hour when I finally told him it was time to go, and lo and behold just as we were driving off, he spotted her, walking up the high street. It turned out she had been waiting at a different entrance.'

But after the initial hiccup things went well and the relationship soon developed into a full-blown love affair to the point that they would see each other three or four times a week, normally on the nights that he wasn't working out at the gym, which were usually Mondays and Wednesdays. They more often than not went out near her home in Walthamstow, as

51

Lynne found it hard to get on with Tony's 'overbearing' mum. He would get a bus or tube over after work and they would go to the pub or to the cinema, before he would get the last tube back to Finsbury Park soon after midnight.

But while Tony was getting increasingly besotted with his new girlfriend, spending all his money on jewellery and other presents for her, his mother feared that the relationship was not doing him any good.

'She was a very quiet girl and very different from the girls Tony was used to meeting around our way,' says Lynda today. 'She was quite controlling and to be honest I found her cold and stand-offish and felt that she never made much of an effort to get on with us. She would come in and stand in the hall looking all nervous and never really muck in. It was quite clear that she vastly happier at her house in Walthamstow.'

To add to her dismay, within a year Tony had pretty much given up all his hobbies like judo and cycling, and stopped seeing his local friends. 'All he wanted to do was spend time with her and he was so incredibly fawning and attentive to her that he practically ignored everyone else. He sort of let go of all his friends. She wanted 100 per cent of his attention and what Lynne wanted Lynne normally got. He would spend all his weekly earnings on things like bracelets and earrings,' recalls his mother. 'After a time, I guess, we understood that he had completely fallen in love and were happy for him.'

But it was certainly anything but plain sailing for Tony. A somewhat demanding girlfriend, as his mother recalls, Lynne only saw things in black and white and didn't take kindly to Tony being late or arguing with her. Somewhat snobby about his poor, working-class background, she didn't like to mix with his family and most of the time insisted he spend time with her family and friends. Tony reluctantly went along with it, until a chance meeting with an Oriental girl, Irene Wong, who had literally stopped him in the street to ask for directions.

It was the spring of 1984 and the svelte Malaysian, who had been driving a soft-top Golf GTi, took a real shine to the handsome bodybuilder walking back home from the tube station. She had been looking for a local warehouse and Tony sent her in the right direction, but not before she could ask him for a drink and the pair swapped numbers.

When she phoned him at work the following day, Tony nearly had a heart attack, according to his mother, but agreed to go for a drink after work in the West End. It turned out to be a night he certainly hadn't bargained for, when she turned up in a skintight mauve catsuit, her nipples clearly showing, and insisted they only drank champagne. Fortunately for Tony, the Kuala Lumpur-born marketing boss – who was on a two-year placement in England – was not short of cash, through both her job and the backing of a wealthy family, and insisted on paying for all the drinks.

By 10.30p.m. the two were both roaring drunk and back at her stylish apartment just off Holborn High Street. Some 15 years his senior, the high-flying Malaysian, who had flawless porcelain skin and long flowing black hair, knew exactly what she wanted and gave Tony a sex lesson he would never forget. As his friend Simon Bowers says: 'Tony would often talk about this Oriental keep-fit and yoga fanatic, who taught him a lot about sex. He said she was incredibly demanding in bed and used to make him get into all sorts of weird and bizarre positions and hold them during sex. She dictated to him what to do and made him carry on for often hours on end. He said it really screwed him up.'

Either way, according to his mother, Tony really fell for this older woman and started on a torrid affair behind Lynne's back. Older and more confident about herself, Irene was soon a regular visitor to the King household in Holloway and became good friends with Tony's mother and sister, who would later visit her in Malaysia.

And for a few months Tony saw both Lynne and Irene, until one day the shit hit the fan and his girlfriend of nearly two years found out about his secret lover. She had suspected it for a while and went ballistic, but rather than finishing with him on the spot, she took it as the start of a battle and over the next few weeks the pair began a tug of war over Tony, which Lynne eventually won.

Somehow sensing a change in Lynne, who suddenly seemed to give him more respect after his infidelity, Tony threw himself even deeper into the relationship and it wasn't long before they began talking about marriage. At the end of 1984, Tony went down on bended knee at a pub in Walthamstow and three months later – on Valentine's Day 1985 – they held an engagement party at his mother's house in Holloway attended by family and a few friends. A wedding date was set for 7 July that year and the pair started looking for a house to move into together.

They had already saved up a fair amount of money and had according to his mother soon made an offer on a small two-bedroom house with a patio garden, in Chingford, a mile of so from Lynne's parents in Walthamstow. They had got a joint mortgage through the Abbey National (which had been no problem with her work at Morgan Grenfell and his steady work at the printers) and they had soon started buying all the furniture.

The register office was booked in Walthamstow and, according to Tony's mother, Lynne had already bought her wedding dress, which was in the process of being altered, when Tony was suddenly and dramatically arrested and charged with serious sexual assault.

Chapter Four

The Holloway Strangler

The timing certainly could not have been more dramatic. Just nine weeks before his wedding to Lynne on 7 May 1985, Tony King had been arrested in north London and charged with a string of sexual attacks for which he would later earn the sobriquet the 'Holloway Strangler'.

Taking place over a five-week period, between 27 March and 1 May 1985, the seven attacks around north and east London had been both unusual and vicious. In each case the victims had been garrotted and rendered unconscious, with the exception of two (for which he was found not guilty on a technicality) where a metal bar and a brick had been used to knock out the victims before they were assaulted.

Most of the attacks happened on Monday and Wednesday nights – on the days, it was claimed, that King went weightlifting rather than to see his fiancée. Between the ages of 15 and 33, all of the seven women were groped around the breast and vaginal area, normally from the outside of their clothing, and while King would occasionally 'kiss their naked breasts', he didn't attempt to rape or sexually abuse them and no semen was found at any of the crime scenes.

As all of this took place two decades ago, official records are hard to access but, according to a police source, one of the women, for example, was strangled unconscious only to come round to find her attacker 'on top of her on the pavement and sucking her naked breast'. Realizing that his victim had regained consciousness, King casually got up, dusted himself off and walked off at a brisk pace.

Another victim apparently came round to find King kneeling over her and 'fondling her breasts and rubbing her vagina through her jeans', while a third was pulled to the ground and rendered unconscious to come round ten minutes later on her own. The only evidence of the attack, apart from a sore neck, was that 'her jacket and jumper had been pulled up and the zip of her jeans undone'.

'He was a classic opportunist,' believes DS Steve Kinchington, the detective superintendent who was put in charge of liaising between Spanish and British police during the recent case. 'On the surface, he appeared to have a completely normal relationship and sex life, but in reality he had developed a severe personality disorder and reached the trigger point turning him into a deviant sex criminal.'

The DS, who holds the official file on King at Kingston police station in Surrey, believes the attacks revolved around masturbatory fantasies. Having worked on numerous complicated murder cases, such as the high-profile Stephen Lawrence case, he believes King is guilty of all seven earlier attacks and probably those in Spain. 'I studied the file in depth and spoke to a lot of the old victims and families and friends of King,' he says. 'They were all in a close proximity and his *modus operandi* was to knock them out, normally with a ligature, either on his way to work or on his way back home. I think the sexual step came later at home when he would play with himself fantasizing about the attack,' he says. 'It's the same as rapists who masturbate about their attacks until they get bored and have to go out and do it again to get a fresh memory. I think he was going out and doing his attacks in the same way.'

The DS adds that the type of attacks suggest someone with a sexual inadequacy, which might have stemmed from his fiancée mocking or ridiculing him during lovemaking. 'The fact that he had to render the women unconscious or comatose before molesting them hints that he didn't want them looking at him,' says the detective. 'It suggests he gets embarrassed in front of women and this might stem from problems of achieving erection in front of former or current girlfriends.'

Kinchington is also keen to stress the seriousness of the crimes and believes that King was extremely lucky that none of the girls died. 'Let's face it, when you strangle someone unconscious, there is a thin line between recovery and death. There are only seconds between unconsciousness and death and unless you are a real expert and know what you are doing you can easily kill someone. I believe that any one of those girls could easily have died. I have seen people killed by punches on CCTV and when you put a ligature around someone's neck and pull it tight it is pretty borderline whether you kill them or not. The fact is you are a real menace to society. What is also certain is that each and every one of those girls will all be mentally scarred for life.'

Of that there is no doubt and a couple of the victims have since come forward to recall their ordeals. One, Margaret Lotter, who was 16 at the time, bravely agreed to waive anonymity to recall the attack which took place on 1 May 1985, which has left her suffering from panic attacks and serious agoraphobia. She had been walking back to her best friend's house at about 5p.m. that afternoon when she had been jumped on by King in a subway.

'It happened very quickly,' she recalls. 'He jumped on my back, knocking me to the floor, then turned me round so I was facing upwards. I realized there was something round my neck – I looked and it was a long piece of blue twine or string, the sort of thing you'd use to tie up a parcel. He had his knees on my shoulders, pinning me down and his feet were on my legs. I couldn't move, scream, do anything. He had his face just inches from mine, his nose was nearly touching mine and as he pulled the string tighter he just stared into my eyes. I will never, ever forget those eyes – they were so piercing and just seemed to look right into me.'

Still suffering nightmares from the attack, the mother of a teenage boy, who lives in Bow, east London, was first struck by her attacker's baby face, despite the fact that he was 18 years old at the time. Convinced she was going to die and at King's mercy, it came as something of a miracle when a local bus driver walked into the subway scaring King into running off. Despite surviving the ordeal, which left her blue in the face with a nasty red mark around her neck, she had appalling psychological side effects for years.

'For months afterwards I wouldn't go anywhere on my own,' she says. 'My parents took me to work and picked me up, and I'd stay in at night and just watch TV. I had to sleep with my sister because I couldn't bear to be alone. Every time I closed my eyes I saw him – always those eyes – that face just inches from mine. I still have nightmares about that. He never says anything in the dream, I just see his face staring into mine.'

Margaret, who straightaway recognized the picture of King after he was arrested in Spain, adds, 'I'd always wondered what had happened to him after he was released and I'd often see men in the streets and think: "Is that him?" I count myself so lucky. I could easily have been raped, or murdered like those poor Spanish girls. He ruined my life and God knows how many other lives he's ruined. I just pray he's jailed for life this time.'

Another victim Christine Blewer, who also waived her right

to anonymity, had an even more sickening experience when she was hit on the head with a metal grinding tool King was alleged to have stolen from a machine shop next to the printer where he worked. One of the two attacks – for which King was found not guilty, due to the judge's direction on the basis that the *modus operandi* was different – Christine, then 25 years old, later miscarried her first child as a result of the attack.

On her way home from work on 15 April 1985, the contemporary dance teacher had come across King as she waited for a lift at her block of flats in east London. She remembers glancing at him as she stepped into the lift and was then hit over the head with such ferocity that she thought she had suffered an electric shock. As she lay dazed on the floor he tied her handwoven cashmere scarf tight around her neck and began undoing her clothes and in her fragile state she had initially thought he was trying to help to administer first aid. But when she felt his hands touch her breasts and then move down her trousers she felt a nauseous wave of realization and began fighting back.

Unfortunately, her assailant only became more violent, raining a series of blows on her already fractured skull. Screaming and crouching into the corner of the lift, she tried to use her hands to protect her blood-drenched head, but King continued to hit her, even severing the tip of one her fingers in the process. It was only when she pleaded with him not to harm her unborn baby that the beating stopped and he ran off – curiously, it can be revealed – to attack a second woman that night with a brick. But the damage was done and while she was able to stagger to her flat to call for help, she soon miscarried the three-month-old unborn child.

While she got £2,200 from the criminal injuries board and surgeons managed to stitch up her skull and sew her finger back on, she still suffers headaches and nightmares and post-traumatic stress disorder causes her to vomit whenever she is distressed. A convert to Buddhism, which has given her the strength to get over the attack, she estimates philosophically: 'His hell must have been greater than mine to have done such terrible crimes. To do such a thing you must be in hell, mustn't you?'

Thankfully, however, King's reign of terror was soon to come to an abrupt end in a surveillance operation mounted from Finsbury Park tube station in early May. The police had been desperate to try something. It was already becoming a high-profile case locally and something of an embarrassment to the police in north London. An arrest needed to be made and quickly.

The dramatic breakthrough came, it can be revealed, after similarities between the seven attacks were detected by two young PCs working on the crime squad at Hornsey police station. The two policemen, Robert Tucker and Steven Baker – who later received commendations from both the Met Police and judge for their work – had noticed how the five strangulation attacks had all happened to women leaving either Finsbury Park or Walthamstow tube stations over a five-week period. On May 6 they talked their bosses into setting up a surveillance operation from both points.

It worked like a dream and the following day, on Tuesday, 7 May, King fell into their trap. Leaving Finsbury Park tube station at 11.35p.m., he was first spotted apparently following a middle-aged woman across the road and up towards Seven Sisters, only to give up and return to the station when she jumped on to a bus. According to the official charge sheet, he had then gone to buy a bag of chips from a cafe by the station, before following a second woman, this time across the road and all the way up Seven Sisters Road and into a housing estate down Durham Road. A dark, badly lit street, it was here that he was said to have increased his stride and was 'about to accost' the woman, when a local man suddenly appeared from a side street. Not to be outdone, he is then said to have run around the block to approach the woman a second time and it is here that police claim to have arrested him with the woman 'up against the wall and he standing next to her'.

While he was not attacking her, the report says that the arresting officers found a piece of rope in his pocket, which he was unable to sufficiently explain. He was also vague and not able to give a good enough explanation for his behaviour. Later, at the police station, at some point during the early hours of Wednesday, 8 May, King was said to have confessed to the attacks. Either way, when police discovered another short piece of cord at his home there was deemed to be enough evidence to achieve a conviction and after a short court hearing the teenager was remanded in custody, first at Richmond Young Offenders Institute and later at Ashford prison.

The trial began on 5 March 1986, at Britain's highest court, the Old Bailey. It was scheduled to last three weeks but was over on 14 March, after just nine days, with the jury finding Bromwich guilty, and Judge Thomas Pigot QC, the Common Sergeant of London, ordering psychiatric reports. It had not been a particularly complicated case (the prosecution – as in the recent cases in Spain – were greatly helped with the so-called confession King had made on the night of his arrest) and King was duly sentenced to ten years in prison.

He had pleaded innocent to all of the 11 charges, which included intent to commit indecent assaults, malicious wounding, indecent assault and assault. Despite insisting throughout that he had confessed under pressure, he was eventually found guilty on seven of those counts. Through scant coverage of the trial by various national newspapers we know that on the opening day, prosecutor Mr Michael Sayers told the jury in Court Two how Bromwich had garrotted five of the woman with a length of washing line, rope or flex. In a colourful opening despatch he told the court how King had 'expertly applied sufficient pressure to make them unconscious or semi-conscious and rendering them incapable of resisting his sexual advances. The method is commonly known as garrotting.'

He continued that the attacks had all taken place at the end of the working day or late at night and added that in some cases more force was used than garrotting. 'One woman had her head smashed against the pavement breaking her nose and fracturing her jaw,' he stated. For his part Bromwich was polite and well mannered throughout. Smartly dressed in a grey Burton's suit and collared shirt, he gave his address as Buxton Road, Upper Holloway and his profession as apprentice print finisher, before formally denying the charges.

While his case was surprisingly strong (he had a broken hand, for example, on the date of two attacks and the identifications were anything but conclusive), the prosecution had little difficulty in getting a conviction and on 14 March 1986 he was led away and later pictured apparently smiling as he was driven to Aylesbury prison for his first night inside. In his summing up, Judge Pigot had described King as a 'Jekyll and Hyde' character, adding: 'Quite clearly there may well be some medical reason for his change from a quiet, diligent conscientious apprentice into something else.'

His family, who had sat in the court from start to finish, were seen shaking their heads in disbelief. Convinced of his innocence, they huddled together and cried for ten minutes after the trial. It was left to his fiancée Lynne to speak publicly to the waiting pressmen. Looking stunning in a fur coat and boots, the bank clerk told the throng outside the Old Bailey that she didn't believe he was guilty and that she couldn't wait for his release. Describing him as her 'dream man – kind, considerate and loving', she added: 'Our future looked beautiful until his arrest. It's incredible. He's not the same person I've known and loved. I can't believe my Tony can be the savage brute they say he is. But I'll wait for him.'

King's former boss Dave Hill was less sure of his innocence.

Hill – who like Lynne and the rest of King's family had, at the time, completely disbelieved the possibility that his apprentice was a dangerous sex monster – today recalls: 'I simply did not believe that he was guilty and told the police that. He didn't seem that way inclined. He had a nice girlfriend, who came in to meet him a couple of times and seemed very happy and committed to her. The police told me that people who commit rape often lead normal lives and rarely give any hints, but I was still not convinced he could be a sex monster.'

Later however, Hill, who now works for Alan Moore's Printing, in Bexley, did some thinking. And these days he is not so sure. 'I must admit now there were quite a few odd incidents that matched up after the attacks. For example he did hurt his hand one night and missed a day to come in with it all bandaged up saying that he had fallen off the bus. I believed him at the time. He had never been absent before and I didn't know he had given a different excuse that he had fallen over walking the dog to his mother and police.'

The print boss, who King has been to visit on a number of occasions since leaving prison, added that the reason given in court for carrying the type of cord he had used to strangle the women was never used in his business. 'They said that the string they found on him matched up from the printers, but that simply is not true. He didn't use that sort of string at work. That was strong cord used to pull pallets off lorries. We didn't have any although in the estate he would not have had to go far to find a bit. It was always lying around.'

Chapter Five

Prison and Understanding the Mind of a Psychopath

It is once in prison that we can finally begin to understand the tormented mind that might have driven the former 'model apprentice' to commit such horrific offences. Indeed, through a series of revealing, in-depth psychological profiles we can clearly see how King's behaviour was very much a product of his violent and aggressive upbringing.

Banged up initially in Wormwood Scrubs, the Category-A prisoner NV1294 was soon transferred to Maidstone, before spending the majority of his sentence at Grendon, Parkhurst and finally Wandsworth, often said to be the toughest prison in the UK.

Refusing to accept he was a sex offender – and continually protesting his innocence – his time inside was never going to be easy. Despite advice from prison authorities and friends alike that he would be in danger if he didn't segregate himself with the other sex offenders, he was, according to his family, adamant that he wanted to live within the main prison population.

While a brave decision, it would cause him considerable

harassment from other prisoners and ultimately prove to be foolish. It had all been fine for the first 12 months, with Tony telling fellow prisoners that he was banged up for armed robbery. But suddenly at the beginning of his second year he got the shock of his life when one day during lunch he was handed a newspaper cutting from his trial. At the bottom, crudely scrawled in block capital letters, were the words: 'GET OUT OR PREPARE TO DIE.' It didn't take long for the word to go round that he was the so-called Holloway Strangler and he was soon being threatened on an almost hourly basis. This rapidly turned to pushes and shoves and the occasional punch, which Tony could deal with, having maintained his fitness, working out in the prison gym every day, while inside. But then came the spitting and, most sinister of all (his mother claims), putting glass shavings in his mashed potato.

The final straw came a couple of months later, when two men attacked him with a knife in the showers. They had slunk up behind him just as he'd begun to towel himself off, and lunged at him from five yards. Fortunately, someone had shouted out just at the right time and he turned to face his two attackers, one white and one black. The fight didn't last long, as prison wardens soon waded in to break it up, and most importantly King managed to knock the knife out of one of the assailant's hands. All in all he had got off incredibly lightly with just a few minor cuts and bruises and after a couple of days in hospital he was back behind bars, albeit this time in the safety of the sex offenders' wing.

The decision had been made after a tearful visit from his mother, who pleaded with him to 'take the numbers' as segregation is known in prison parlance. While proud and still maintaining his innocence he realized the next time could be fatal and he applied to become subject to Rule 43, which gives certain prisoners the right to live in segregation.

While the move didn't stop him protesting his innocence it

did however lead him to start 'confronting his demons', initially by converting to Buddhism, which his mother claims helped to ease the severe stress he was suffering in prison. He also eventually agreed to attend various sex offender rehabilitation courses. It didn't happen for a while, perhaps as Lynne continued to visit him (quite religiously every week) for the first couple of years. But after a time – maybe as a result of her ending their relationship for another man, or perhaps sensing that he would have no chance of parole if he didn't face up to his crimes – he volunteered himself for the courses. The official prison records are vague as to the exact dates and details, but there is no doubt he undertook at least two courses of treatment for sex offenders, one at HMP Grendon for six months.

What is also certain is that the split from Lynne, around two years into his sentence, had a profound and painful effect. His mother believes it was the catalyst that drove him to seek help from the prison doctors. 'He was absolutely devastated when I told him that Lynne had found someone else and wasn't going to visit anymore. She told me about this new guy John Kerr and said she couldn't wait any longer for Tony. When I told Tony his world literally crumbled around him. He became extremely depressed and had to be put on prison suicide watch for forty-eight hours. I think the therapy was the only thing that saved him.'

Lynne Kerr, herself, is quite matter-of-fact about the break-up. 'I just stopped going to see Tony one day and that was that,' she recalls today. 'I told his family to tell him I didn't want to see him anymore. His mum said I'd ruined his life. I know it was a bit cowardly but I'd met John and we'd fallen in love and I was falling out of love with Tony, it was a bit of both. And ten years is such a long time to wait, I was young, only about 17 or 18 when I met Tony. It's a frightening prospect waiting all that time.'

The timid and softly spoken mother of two – who is still

happily married to John Kerr – said that after the split, Tony had not once begged her to rethink. 'He never said please come back or anything. He sent all the photos and letters back to me that I'd sent him in prison and I threw it all away. Later his parents came round for the engagement ring and I gave it to them. I gave them everything. I just wanted to get on with my life.'

Nowadays, living in a small semi-detached house in the north London suburb of Enfield, where she works part-time as a checkout girl at Sainsbury's, she adds: 'The only time I heard from him after that was when he sent me a card three years later after the birth of my first child. It just said "Congratulations on your news". It was ages afterwards and I have no idea how he found out.'

While likely he had heard through mutual friends, it is also possible that he had seen Lynne with her child, as it was around that time in September 1991 – only halfway through his ten-year sentence – that King was released after being deemed eligible for parole.

And so on 10 September 1991 – just five years into a ten-year sentence – Anthony Bromwich got a second chance. With the promise that he would attend weekly counselling sessions at his local hospital as well as liaising regularly with his parole officer, he was driven the short journey back from Maidstone prison to Archway, via a greasy Joe's cafe, near Bow, where Tony, his mother and partner Keith sat in silent contemplation over a cup of tea and a burger. Later that day the family held a barbecue in their back garden to celebrate his release and in a rare happy photograph, Tony can be seen holding a shish kebab alongside his stepfather Keith.

It was only a brief glimpse of happiness though, for the truth is, according to his mother, he was deeply depressed and found it almost impossible to get out of bed in the morning. While he had his old bedroom back and the love and support of his

67

family (his father had by now long ago remarried and was living in south London), he was a completely broken man. He was quiet and withdrawn and found it difficult to converse with people. While before he had been full of energy and loved going out with women, all he wanted to do was watch TV and sit in his room.

And, of course, he got scant help from the authorities. According to his mother there were no courses or therapy laid on for her son and the visits from his parole officer, a local woman called Freddie, hardly made up for it. 'All in all he was really down,' says his mother. 'He was like a zombie. He felt he was getting no help from the probation service and had lost all direction. He felt empty and heartbroken and had no prospects. He no longer had Lynne and had completely lost his confidence to go out and find another girlfriend. He would have loved to have gone over to Malaysia to see Irene, who had continued to write to him, but he had no money. He had no friends and told me he couldn't face being out of prison. I think all he wanted was to get back to the routine and discipline of prison, where he didn't have to think too much or dwell upon where his life had all gone wrong.'

According to one psychiatric valuation given in prison, he reached crisis point after getting his brother sacked from his job as a postman, in the most bizarre of circumstances. According to the story King gave to prison assessor Ian Wilson, he had been having sex with a prostitute at her flat in north London when there had been a police raid and both she and he had been arrested. Desperate to get out, and deemed not to have committed a crime, he used his one phone call to speak to his brother, who agreed to come and collect him in his post van, only to be reported later, and sacked for using one of HM's post vans for other work and ultimately 'causing a delay in the Queen's post'.

Unsurprisingly, this episode caused a lot of bad feeling at

home, and King practically became suicidal and desperate to find some way out. A few days later, according to his mother, the inevitable happened. Stumbling down the stairs with a look of thunder on his face, he had barked to his mother that he was going out. 'I could tell by the look on his face that something bad was going to happen. He had been saying the night before that he couldn't face it anymore. His life had been taken away from him and he seemed near to suicide. He said he felt like he had some sort of death wish. I was desperately worried.'

Unbeknown to her he had bought an imitation firearm from a market in north London and walked up the road to the nearest phone box, where a woman was on the phone. He ended up opening the door and putting the gun to her head and told her to give him her money.

While he later claimed in interviews with psychiatrists that he was doing it to save up money to visit his girlfriend in Malaysia, the real reason for the attack may have been to molest his victim. 'He apparently put his hands down her trousers and on her breasts,' insists Steve Kinchington, who holds the official file. 'But because she had initially thought he was searching her for money, the sexual assault aspect carried less weight in court.' Either way, hearing her screams a neighbour had called the police, who had been on the scene in a matter of minutes. King was still there and gave himself up without a struggle. It was 14 December 1991, almost exactly three months since his release.

Quickly charged and sent to Brixton prison on remand, he was convicted of attempted robbery with an imitation firearm at the Old Bailey on 13 March 1992. Pleading guilty, he received a five-year sentence and was immediately transferred back to the high-security prison Parkhurst on the Isle of Wight, where he would remain until the following summer.

The decision to release him in the first place in 1991 without receiving treatment must be seen as controversial at best, particularly in light of a scathing, unpublished report that clearly stressed his continuing danger to women. Dated 3 March 1992 and prepared by forensic psychiatrist John Wilkins BSc MB BS MRCPsych, at the request of Tony King's lawyers, it didn't mince its words:

> *Bromwich is a disturbed man who has a tendency to attack women. He has a psychopathic disorder and is likely to pose a menace to the public and to women in particular if he does not receive the help that he needs.*

The highly disturbing appraisal, which was undertaken at Brixton prison on 27 February 1992 while King was awaiting trial, gives, without a doubt, the best insight into his psyche. Having examined him on a number of occasions prior to this, Dr Wilkins was certainly well placed to report on the prisoner and under no illusion about his psychiatric problems. He strongly recommended that he be sectioned to receive treatment at a mental hospital rather than being sent back to prison. The five-page document, written on official hospital notepaper, pulled no punches.

> *Bromwich has suffered persistent mental health problems since he was a child and his delay in development, his neurotic symptoms, such as enuresis or asphyxia, and his difficulty relating to his classmates, suggests a development of a personality disorder and/or severe neurosis. Moreover, his sexual problems indicate that this disorder has continued into adult life . . . Bromwich is a young man with severe disorders, whose problems and feelings of low self-esteem have led him to violently assault women. Some of these attacks were serious and included death threats.*

Strong words; the psychiatrist then attempted to tackle the complicated reasons behind King's severe personality disorder. It began appropriately with his difficult upbringing, and stressed, in particular, his violent father, his late-diagnosed dyslexia and the problems he had relating to his fellow pupils. It then went on to analyse the sexual problems that began to emerge during his engagement to Lynne. It noted for instance that there was 'a substantial amount of domestic violence between his parents' and that he and his siblings were regularly attacked by their father 'who apparently had mental health problems, although it is not clear the exact nature of these problems.'

Undertaken over a long prison interview – in which King spent most of his time in tears and staring at the floor, it continued:

Without doubt, it took [Bromwich] a long time to start talking and as a child he was also prone to attacks of asphyxia [suffocation] when he felt frustrated as well as suffering enuresis [wetting the bed] until he was eleven years old. This led to his classmates calling him 'stinky' due to his habit of wetting himself and as a consequence studying was very difficult and he was not able to relax and enjoy school. When he was eleven he joined his brother at the same secondary school but could not keep up with the academic requirements. He was tormented by his classmates who called him 'fat', and he was soon admitted to a clinic for children with behavioural problems. After receiving treatment it was recommended sending him to a boarding school. Later at Archway School it also seems he did not mix well with his classmates and describes himself as a loner.

Crucially, the report then went on to catalogue the sexual problems which seemed to have reached crisis point during his engagement to Lynne. Noting the relationship as 'a bad relationship worsened by sexual difficulties', the report explained that Bromwich felt dominated by her and that he and his fiancée were 'not sexually compatible and that she was "anorgasmic" and could not gain orgasm.'

Pointedly – and perhaps explaining the nub of his problem – it continued: 'This gave him a lack of confidence and erectile impotence was one of the consequences. Of this she was very critical.'

Bromwich also admitted that the effect had driven him into the arms of another woman, Irene Wong, with whom he felt 'more compatible'. He added that he was 'a regular user of prostitutes and often masturbated more than once a day using legal pornography'.

The report also yielded other bits of compelling information such as his apparent affliction to the male form of anorexia, prevalent with some bodybuilders, and that he mixed extremely badly with his peers and had virtually no friends. It continued:

The overriding impression of Bromwich is of a man who has an extreme lack in self-confidence and a low opinion of himself. It is difficult for him to express himself clearly and he finds it almost impossible to establish friendships with young people, men as well as women. He has practically no friends, which seems to have been a characteristic of much of his life. Indeed the only close relationships he has maintained have been with his family and his two girlfriends.

He is clearly suffering some symptoms of minor depression and has problems sleeping. He complains of concentration problems and while he doesn't appear to have any suicidal tendencies he says he has thought about committing suicide in the past.

Finally – and crucially – the experienced assessor of psychiatric health gave his conclusions about the best form of treatment and made it abundantly clear (indeed reinforcing it three or four times) that the best course of action was a long spell in a psychiatric hospital.

I conclude by saying that Bromwich is a public threat, in particular to women, and his continuous mental problems lead to abnormal aggressive and irresponsible behaviour, sufficiently to warrant a detention in a psychiatric hospital for treatment. The fact that this man returned to his crimes only three months after he was set free (a crime that could have been much worse) tells us that setting free a man like Bromwich is nowhere near enough to prevent future crimes and it is unlikely that a longer spell in prison would prevent him from doing it again.

Without doubt, I see clearly the need of supervising cases like this. In my opinion, in the interests of public security, it would be appropriate to admit [him] to a hospital according to article 37 of the Mental Health Act of 1983 for the treatment of a psychopathic disorder that would alleviate the disturbance or at the very least prevent a worsening of his state. Bearing in mind the nature of the serious crimes of which he is accused and his previous crimes, the treatment could take considerable time and I would recommend sectioning him to a psychiatric hospital as soon as possible.

But, as we can see from the records, the prison board had other ideas and, completely ignoring the words of Dr Wilkins, sent King back to prison, initially to Parkhurst, one of the toughest Category-A prisons in the country. Justifying the decision, Prison Board assessor Ian D. Wilson wrote on 1 April 1992 that, while he agreed that Bromwich had some personality disorders they had not yet 'reached a point where they can be classified as psychopathic disorders'.

The extraordinary decision had been reached after a second interview was conducted with Bromwich, in which he strongly refuted many of the claims made by Dr Wilkins. Strikingly different from the outpourings to Dr Wilkins, it left the assessor with apparently no choice.

As he stated:

Without a doubt if there is no independent corroboration of the claims of Mr Bromwich, it is not possible to extract firm conclusions about the nature of his personal problems and the possible danger that they may imply. He is not aware of any such problem and does not value the possibility of putting himself under psychiatric treatment, nor would he be prepared to cooperate if the treatment were offered him. Therefore it is not possible to recommend his admission to a mental hospital as he doesn't fulfil the criteria as defined under the Mental Health Act of 1983.

As if perhaps to protect what he believes to be a highly controversial decision he added, definitively: 'The Regional Authority confirmed my diagnosis.'

And so once again Tony found himself isolated on the Isle of Wight, miles away from his family in London. With visits becoming increasingly erratic, he became extremely depressed. Fearing he was never going to get the treatment he needed, according to his mother, he was again put on suicide watch for some days, and spent a couple of weeks 'freaking out' in the prison hospital wing. His mother also believes that at some point during these early months he may have been the victim of a serious sexual assault, even rape. 'He was certainly very anguished and upset. While he would never admit he was raped I had my concerns,' she says.

As his former boss Robbie Graham claimed in an interview, he did indeed get raped while at Parkhurst. He said it was his first time. 'He was raped rotten when he was in Parkhurst,' says Graham. 'He was only a young lad and was attacked badly. It really affected him.'

Whether true or not (and it must be stressed that Tony himself strongly denies it), he could at least take some crumbs of comfort from the fact that, having confessed to his earlier crimes and having attempted to confront his demons, he was now apparently going in the right direction. He started undertaking a series of courses and indeed, over his last two-and-a-half years in prison achieved a GCSE in English an NVQ level one, in Sport and Recreation and a Pitman word-processing certificate.

With his dad continuing to visit on an almost weekly basis – taking the special bus laid on for prisoners' families from the Elephant & Castle in south London – and the occasional letters from his family and even from Irene in Malaysia, he pulled through, and was eventually transferred on 19 May 1993 from Parkhurst to a special sex offenders unit at HMP Grendon, in Aylesbury.

A highly praised and successful unit, his progress on G-wing and, in particular, the programme of therapy for sexual delinquents, was, apparently, rapid and profound. Indeed, on 11 February 1994, Dr E.Z. Shaban MBBCh MRCPsych, the medical official at Grendon, wrote that Tony Bromwich had been something of a model patient during his eight-month stay at the unit.

He wrote:

Since arriving at Grendon, Bromwich has shown considerable motivation and a willingness to change. He has been able to control and understand his difficulties in relationships with other people and his psycho-sexual behaviour towards women. He now knows the origin of his anger and negative feelings towards women . . . and is much more capable to communicate his feelings and emotions. He has become more positive in his relationships with other people.

More crucially the report added that King had now obtained a 'level of empathy with his victims' and that when this was mixed with 'a strict regime of self-control' it enabled him to control his fantasies about rape and sexual violence.

And the doctor concluded by saying that while he considered Tony Bromwich would need at least another six months on the programme, he might be able to be released if he continued with intensive psychotherapy, recommending the Portman Clinic in London as one such venue.

Nine months later, on 30 November 1994, just a couple of

months before his final release, the same doctor wrote another glowing report on Bromwich:

> *From his participation in this programme and the psychotherapy group sessions he has examined and started to understand the origins of his abnormal sexual behaviour and other problems. For many years he saw himself as 'deformed and abnormal'. Such a negative image, combined with his obsessive and introverted personality, results in a secretive person, who dwells on his perversions and violent sexual fantasies as a way of dealing with his feelings of anger and rejection, particularly regarding women, who he blames for his powerlessness and sense of inadequacy. In the therapy he has tackled and increased his self-respect and improved his capacity for expressing his feelings and emotions.*

But he struck an ominous word of warning, reminding the parole board, that King was 'vulnerable' and would certainly remain at 'high risk' of reoffending.

> *Without a doubt, his occasionally rigid and inflexible attitude has limited his progress, especially in the area of interpersonal contact. He maintains that he is already experiencing perverse and violent sexual fantasies. He is aware that his social isolation and his poor control over his feelings of anger are high factors of risk.*
>
> *In my opinion, while Mr Bromwich does not have any mental illness his abnormal personality makes him vulnerable. He will need support and psychological review at some point in the future.*

Just two months later, King was back out on the streets of London, and, unsurprisingly, with very little physical or mental support from the outside world. There were to be no more psychological reviews and, according to his mother, he quickly got on with his life without a second thought to his past.

Chapter Six

On to the Straight and Narrow

With a £20 handout from the prison authorities and the old clothes he had been wearing on his arrest, Tony King took the train back from Aylesbury to London. A chilly midwinter morning, he'd done a lot of thinking en route to his mother's house, where he would stay for the first few weeks of his freedom. After a joyous welcome from his mother and Keith, and an assembled band of extended family, who had come to an impromptu party his parents had held that weekend, he had reluctantly moved into a halfway-house-type hostel for ex-jailbirds on the recommendation of his parole officer.

Not a pleasant place, he had soon jumped at the offer of a room at his father's house in south London, albeit for the extortionate sum of £50 a week, despite only getting £43 a week in housing benefit and having to be supplemented by his ever-suffering mum. He stayed for nearly three months until, according to his mother, he fell out with Fred's new wife Elaine, a dance teacher, over a cheese sandwich he had made one night after getting in from the pub hungry. 'When he ended up moving out I remember writing her a cheque for £84.60 for outstanding rent, which included 60p for the cheese sandwich,' says Lynda.

Fortunately for Tony, however, he had by then found himself a new girlfriend, who agreed to put him up at the flat she was sharing with her best friend in Lewisham, south-east London. He had met Carol-Anne Collins while being interviewed for a bar job at Beckenham golf course, and as Tony, Carol-Anne and the interviewer got on so well, he decided to give them both a job.

'Tony was a good-natured sweetheart with a nice sense of humour and I kind of fell for him straightaway,' says Collins today. 'We arranged to go out for a date and the relationship developed quickly. I was single and divorced and was more than ready to start a new relationship,' says the mother of two, who is seven years his senior. 'I had no idea that he had just got out of prison but the clues were certainly there. For starters he was living in some kind of time warp and seemed stuck in the mid-eighties with long hair down to the middle of his back and bright, colourful shirts. Style-wise he was a right mess and I don't think he had bought new clothes for quite some time.'

But Cass, as her friends know her, wasn't worried about his appearance and was more concerned about his attitude towards her two teenage sons, who she had been left to bring up after a messy divorce some months before they met. 'It was far from a settled time in my life and bringing up two teenagers, who were about 18 and 19 at the time, was proving difficult. But Tony got on with them really well and made a real effort to fit in. They took to him, too.'

Fortunately, Tony also got on well with Cass's flatmate Ray, who charged him just over £100 a week for the third bedroom of the house in Hither Green. 'He was always such a well-mannered friendly sort of guy and made an effort with everyone,' recalls Cass, who has kept in touch with Tony throughout the last ten years – and even visited him in prison in Spain. 'He seemed such an innocent bloke and was very kind, gentle and affectionate. He eventually told us that he had been in prison for armed robbery and had this plan to make a real go of his life having got out. At first, we had to constantly tell him to lighten up and relax, which after a few weeks he did.'

She had soon got him some new clothes and forced him to get a haircut and they slotted into the routine of getting the bus together to work in the morning and spending their evenings at home in front of the television. Tony began to open up about his violent upbringing and his fears, which as an older, experienced woman, she was able to counsel him on. He told her about his father and the bullying he received from his older brother David, who Cass met on various occasions, and insists is quite different from Tony.

'He tried to avoid his father and David, who is also an aggressive type, and he spent almost all his time with me, Ray and the kids. We ended up with a really happy, steady relationship and it was obvious he was beginning to become more confident within himself. We sometimes went to the cinema or the pub, but mostly we just stayed in and enjoyed each other's company, watching videos or playing cards with friends till the early hours. It was really rather normal.'

In terms of sex it was also quite run of the mill, but Cass wasn't complaining. They had fallen into bed within a couple of weeks of moving in together, and Tony hadn't disappointed. 'It wasn't electric but I can honestly say that he did not have any problems with me. We had sex a few nights a week and it was always very loving and affectionate, never perverted and he certainly never used to go out alone late at night to get up to mischief.'

Indeed, the only real clue about the private trauma he was suffering were the violent nightmares he had at night. 'He would wake up in a cold sweat extremely upset and wake me up to talk to me. He would say he had lots of things in his mind that he wanted to put right, but didn't want to dwell on them and just wanted to talk about ordinary things. I think I helped him get his head together and supported him well.'

But despite the obvious support Cass was giving to Tony, things started to cool about a year into their relationship when it became obvious that he was desperate to start a family. They hadn't long moved into a cheaper flat in St James Road, Sutton, when the arguments started. The problem was with two older teenage children already and with little money between them, the last thing Cass wanted was another baby. 'But Tony was determined and we talked about it at length, going round in circles. I knew instinctively it wasn't going to work and after one particular row we decided to take a break from each other.'

While remaining close, Tony moved into a flat of his own in Hill Park Flats in Carshalton, where he had soon landed a job as a keep-fit instructor at the local gym Pink's. With an excellent body (he worked out at least three times a week throughout their relationship, says Cass) and having completed a couple of gym courses while in prison (he also had qualifications in massage), he was the ideal keep-fit instructor and was soon a popular member of staff, not to mention his popularity with the female clients.

But despite the increasing attention he was getting from the opposite sex he was far from happy, says Cass. 'We kept in touch and dated on and off for the next six months and regularly spent the night together at his new flat or mine. He also used to hang out with Luke and Craig. But he was not happy and used to come over in tears talking about how lonely he was. He just seemed unable to make lasting friendships and spent most of his spare time working out in the gym. I had to constantly encourage him to go out to meet people. He was actually becoming a bit clingy and reliant on me and could sometimes be overpowering. In fact half the time I felt I was mothering him.'

She now realizes that the problems he was having may well have been linked with the increasing amounts of performance-enhancing drugs he was taking to help build up his body. 'He was taking steroids to help build up his muscles and it was certainly having quite an effect on his shape, if not his mind,' says Cass. 'But the way he was acting emotionally it seems quite likely that the pills were affecting his mind. I don't know how many he was taking, or what types, but I would say that they didn't have a good effect on him.'

It was also around this time that Tony took the fated and landmark decision to try and cut off from his past by changing his name by deed poll from Bromwich to King. Telling Cass that he had been thinking about it for years, he said that he wanted to cut off from his father and he wanted to try and escape his past. 'He told me he was going to do it after visiting his mum's one day. He said that he had nothing to hide but that if he didn't change his name he would always get picked up for similar crimes in the area.'

So a few days later armed with his passport and the small fee of £20 he trooped off to a local high-street solicitor to get the necessary paperwork put together. A swift two-hour procedure, once the deed poll had been signed by both himself and the solicitor, it was then signed by a court clerk and the job was done. 'Back then there was nothing we could do to stop him,' says DS Kinchington. 'Today the sex offenders register would be notified straight away, immediately setting off alarm bells. In his case he was able to get away with it extremely easily.'

Indeed, according to one of the many companies advertising to change names by deed poll on the Internet, the undertaking is 'quick and simple' and means making just three declarations:

1. Abandoning the use of your former name.
2. Using your new name only at all times.
3. Requiring all persons to address you by your new name.

'Tony insisted on all three,' recalls Cass. 'He came back in the afternoon pleased as punch with his new name "Tony Alexander King". He showed us the document and told us how easy it was to do. We took the mickey for days saying he was trying to rise above his station, calling himself "A King", but he was happy with it and that was that.'

Suspicions, however, were aroused at his gym, where Tony insisted his boss Peter Pink had to change all the rotas and paperwork to take in the new name. 'I found it really odd,' says Pink. 'It was the only time I sensed there was something serious in his past and I must say I was quite suspicious. He said it was because of his father, who used to beat him up badly and said he needed to make a break from his past. And while I had my suspicions I didn't take it further. He was obviously a loner who didn't mix well with people, but he was great with the customers and that was really all that mattered.'

And so Tony Bromwich – a.k.a. the Holloway Strangler – had ceased to be. Tony Bromwich, the violent, aggressive attacker, who had maimed the lives of at least half a dozen women, was now no more. The chapter was closed, the only evidence of his former life being a three-line letter hurriedly typed out by a south London solicitor, with a stamp from his local court. *Fait accompli* and Tony King moved on. Within days, it can be revealed, he had found himself a new girlfriend.

Chapter Seven

Here Comes More Trouble –
Cecilia, Second Love of His Life

From the minute he clapped eyes on Cecilia Pantoja, some might say his fate was sealed. A wily, streetwise woman who, like him, had come up the hard way, she had been drifting around jobs in south London for a couple of years since moving down from her home town of Barnsley, in Yorkshire. Escaping a chequered, troubled past – culminating in her losing custody of her son to her parents – she was, in the words of Tony's father, 'ruthlessly ambitious' with one main goal in life: to get rich.

Attractive with a slender physique and long, dark shoulder-length hair, she was certainly something of a catch for a jailbird of ten years like Tony. When they met she had been working at security company Barry Bros, based in Paddington's insalubrious Praed Street (often known as Depraved Street for its reputation as being a late-night magnet for kerb crawlers). A trusted key holder, put in charge of administering and monitoring dozens of security alarms around the capital, she insists that her background was carefully checked by Scotland Yard before being given the job.

But exactly how well checked must be left open to debate, as unbeknown to the firm Cecilia, as we shall see, also happened to have some impeccable connections with the UK's under-world, and heralded from a family with distinct links to organ-ized crime, including fraud, extortion and prostitution. Pertinently, she was also closely connected to the shady and highly lucrative timeshare business in Spain, in which before long, both she and Tony would be deeply immersed.

They met in a disco on Streatham High Road in the summer of 1996. A packed Friday night, Goodfellows was the sort of place you only ventured into if you were looking to cop off or couldn't afford the taxi home from central London. Gangs of lecherous blokes hung around the bar while girls slipped around the beer-soaked dance floor. It was anything but pretty. 'I spotted Tony across the dance floor,' remembers Celia as everyone knows her, then 31. 'He was very handsome and muscular and was wearing a smart blue shirt and black trousers. He smiled when we locked eyes. He was clearly quite shy so I went over and asked him if he had a cigarette and we started talking. He said I had very nice hair and I dragged him on to the dance floor, where I could see he was quite clearly uncoordinated.'

But she was prepared to forgive his jerky dance moves and it wasn't long before they were back at the flat she shared with three friends in south Croydon, and while sex, however, was not on the agenda that night, they kissed and cuddled until the early hours. She says that Tony, gallantly, didn't push his luck, and when he left the next morning she made a point of telling him that if he hadn't called by Monday night that he shouldn't bother at all.

'He was so keen he phoned me about six hours later and asked me out for a date on the Sunday,' recalls Celia, who now lives with the father of her second child David Cooze, just outside Marbella. 'Of course I agreed and went out shopping that afternoon to buy something sexy to wear.'

She chose a denim miniskirt and a tiny tan blouse top and was expecting a nice afternoon out, maybe a pub lunch, when he met her off the train at Carshalton Beeches station at 1p.m. that day. But Tony, who had also dressed up in smart trousers and jacket, had other ideas. Taking her hand he led her straight back to his flat, a small, half-decent place close to scenic Carshalton pond and by the gym where he was working as an instructor. After two cups of tea and a bit of polite chat he went for the kill, jumping on her on the front-room sofa. She remembers it well, mostly for the minimal foreplay and nervous fumbling. 'Short-lived and jerky,' she says. 'I lay back and thought of England'.

It wasn't that she wasn't attracted to him — he had a nice body from working out and was perfectly well endowed down below — it was just that he didn't know how to do it. He didn't have experience and Celia, no shrinking violet when it came to sex, was none too impressed. 'He just didn't know what to do,' she says. 'He was clumsy, too quick and needed a lot of teaching. It certainly didn't make sense a handsome man like him, and I'll admit I found it strange.'

She soon learnt about his previous engagement to Lynne (he could hardly deny it with her name tattooed on his right arm) and that he had recently split up with an older woman, who was well out of his life. But as for prison, and his past crimes he said nothing. It also wasn't long before she discovered that Tony and Cass Collins were actually rather close and it must have been a tense moment when Cass literally walked straight into his flat on their third date. 'She had a key to the flat and literally walked straight in on us,' remembers Celia. 'She looked completely shocked and quite rightly, and I straightaway offered to leave. But Tony was having none of it and got into this big screaming row with her in which he practically pushed her out of the door, shutting it in her face. I think he was making a point and I got the message.'

From then on their relationship went from strength to strength, particularly after Tony persuaded her to leave her flat and move in with him. 'I wasn't exactly in love with him, but he was growing on me. I felt he'd done the honourable thing inviting me to move in and I was prepared to give it a go. I knew he had had a tough life so far and I felt I could make it better.'

Financially solvent, he had a decent job at Pink's Gym in Carshalton, where he had a good reputation with both the boss and clients. Grossing about £150 a week (earning £5 an hour) he usually took the evening shifts and worked on either Saturday or Sunday. According to his former boss and gym owner Peter Pink, he was an excellent worker despite not mixing well with the rest of the staff. 'He was disciplined and prepared to work any hours given to him,' says Pink, who lives close to the popular local gym. 'He would do nights, Sundays, whatever he was given and was good at his job. He enrolled a lot of our new clients and even set up a computer database, which he'd learnt how to do in prison. He was working with us when he met Celia, who he quickly fell madly in love with. He was abnormally doting on her and gushed about how happy he was with her.'

Celia, however, was soon having second thoughts. 'There was a real desperation and sadness in his eyes, but he would give few clues to the reasons why. He seemed completely in awe of me, like he couldn't believe he was dating me and became quite clingy and overbearing. He said he was very happy with me and it wasn't long before he had mentioned the idea of marriage. Given his way we would have tied the knot within a couple of months of meeting.'

But Celia had no intentions of that. He clearly carried around a fair bit of baggage. While he doted on her, he didn't socialize like most normal people. He also hated talking about his past, revealing little more than he had a violent father and a mother with emotional problems. And on top of that he clearly had jealousy issues and was very paranoid that Celia was seeing other men behind his back. He hated her going out with her male friends and was particularly angry when she insisted on going on an English Civil War re-enactment weekend with some old friends. Indeed, when she got back he asked her to move out, only to back down as she started to gather together her clothes. 'He simply did not trust me, and he hated it if anyone chatted to me at a party. He once went wild when this Irish friend put his arm around me. He stormed up and demanded to know what was going on and dragged me off home. It was all quite embarrassing.'

He was also useless around the house. Completely disorganized, he seemed incapable of running his life. With little experience of living on his own nothing got done, from the paying of bills to the shopping and cleaning. Paperwork quickly stacked up and he often got behind in the rent, leaving Celia to make up the difference. 'He was like a big kid and simply hadn't learnt the steps of life, the A to Z of how to do things, if you like.'

But they managed to muddle on by, particularly after Celia pushed him to get a better job at Cornhill Insurance, in Leatherhead, Surrey. While he was only working in the post room, the hours were more regular and his pay almost doubled to around £250 a week, with the odd shift at the gym on top. And then came the news that he had been waiting for for years: he was going to be a father!

But while it should have been the happiest time of his life, Tony was far from sure about what to do. According to Cass Collins – who Tony had continued to visit frequently – he had been on the verge of dumping Celia when she broke the news to him. 'He was miserable and planning to dump her the night she told him she was pregnant,' claims Collins. 'He had been over quite a few times in the previous weeks and poured his heart out to me about how cruel she was to him and how much he missed me. They had only been going out a few months and he said he wanted to go out with me again and that he was going to finish with Celia in the next few days . . . and bang, suddenly she gets pregnant, I'm sure in part to keep him. I think she sensed he was ready to move on and did what women have been doing for years to trap men and I think he got caught. There was no doubt that Tony was a good catch for her. She was skint, while he was a handsome boy with a decent, well-paid job.'

But the pregnancy had come as a shock to everyone who knew them. Celia, who insists they had been using condoms, says she was also completely unsure of what to do. But after much discussion with friends and, in particular, her mother (who was by now living in Spain with second husband Tom Leigh) she decided to tell Tony. She had expected him to go mad but she says he was anything but angry and told her straight out he wanted the child. 'He practically begged me to have the baby,' she says. 'He said he was desperate to be a father and asked me to give him a chance. We agreed to give it a go.'

It proved to be the catalyst for some sort of change in Tony. He became more responsible by the day and even started to open up about his past. He finally told her about the third of his life he had spent in prison, despite neglecting to inform her what exactly he had been in for. He dropped it in suddenly over dinner while out with friends. Turning to her he whispered quietly in her ear that he needed to tell her something and in a matter-of-fact way he told her he had served two stretches inside for armed robbery.

'He said he had been forced to do it out of poverty and that was all I needed to know,' she says. 'By then I had met his parents and knew about the humble, depressing roots he came from. I believed him and that was that, we didn't discuss it again.'

If anyone was going to understand Tony's tragic upbringing it was Celia. Born in Chile on 12 February 1966, Cecilia Matilde

Pantoja Grez had started life on a farm not far from the capital Santiago. Inspirational times under left-wing leader Salvador Allende, her father Enrique Pantoja Plaza de los Reyes (meaning literally Pantoja Square of the Kings) ran a small printing business, while her mother Rosalina was a local hairdresser.

While not rich, they came from good middle-class stock – they were something of an intellectual family of poets and writers, one having written one of the world's earliest books on fingerprinting – and she and sisters Rosemary, two years older, and Ingrid, three years younger, always had enough food to eat. But at the age of eight, things turned sour for Celia and her family when they were forced to flee the brutal reign of the new dictator Pinochet, who had seized power in September 1973. The problems began when her father, an avid supporter of Allende, was arrested on suspicion of printing anti-government propaganda.

'He was taken away in front of me, half-naked, arms tied behind his back and his printing press thrown on to him in the back of the van,' remembers Celia, who didn't see her father again for 59 long, terrifying days, during which he, like thousands of other suspected supporters of Allende, were famously rounded up and locked into the city's main football stadium and tortured. It is now known that thousands were lined up and shot during that time and, according to Celia, her father was put up against the wall a number of times, and only saved because his wife, who had worked as a nurse, managed to make a plea for his life through the official Red Cross list.

But while he got out alive he did not escape the horrendous torture that included electrodes pinned to his testicles and such bad beatings on his feet that he became flat-footed, and it was little surprise that within a week the family had fled to Argentina, and eventually to England in January 1975 as political refugees.

Treated as some sort of hero by the English student network, everyone rallied around to help the Pantojas, who soon had a council house in Sheffield and food parcels dropped at the door. While the girls had intensive English classes, their father landed a job as a mechanic at a big glass manufacturer, Redfearns, in nearby Barnsley, and their mother got a job packing tins at a local fruit factory.

And so the family had their introduction to the north of England, which can't have been easy for the dark-skinned immigrant family, who hardly spoke a word of the language and had never seen snow before. The girls certainly didn't like it, claiming they were treated 'like dogs' at their school St Michael's primary and later Honeywell secondary modern, where they were picked on for their appearance and for not speaking English. There was little money and few friends to show them the ropes of life in England and to add to that their parents began to argue bitterly. They were soon bunking off school, led by the rebellious elder sister Rosemary, who garnered something of a reputation of a rebel. They would go off and spend their dinner money on cigarettes and sweets and mess around in the fields until it was time to come home.

Things improved a bit when they moved to Barnsley. Their parents finally began to make friends with some of their neighbours and particularly in their local pub. It started when their mother joined the female darts team and met a woman called Rita Leigh. They were soon travelling around the county for matches, sometimes bringing their respective spouses, Enrique and Tom Leigh, who also got on.

Quite different to the Pantojas, the Leighs were an outgoing, ebullient couple, who always had money and looked like they did. A curious pair, who lived in a big farmhouse a few miles outside Barnsley, according to Celia, they didn't want for much and had all the trappings of wealth such as sports cars and a stables full of horses at their house. Rita's dad had been the former mayor of Barnsley says Celia and Tom, a distinguished-looking fellow, with short greying hair was always smartly dressed and had something of the gift of the gab.

The Leighs took a shine to the Chilean family and were soon inviting them round to dinner and out dancing, as well as to their house at the weekends. Celia and her sisters used to look forward to spending the weekend hanging around in their garden and talking to Thomas, a mysterious and enigmatic fellow, who would teach them how to paint and read them stories. It was here, coincidentally, that Rosemary met and started dating their eldest son Garry.

Jobs in a raft of their colourful companies were to follow. And that is when the trouble started, says Celia, recalling how one thing led to another and her father was soon having an affair with Rita, an attractive, if somewhat brassy, Yorkshire girl, who made a decent living working as a door-to-door saleswoman for Avon perfume company. And that was when the period of relative peace ended.

Already suspicious that something was going on between her husband and Rita, who had become her best friend, Rosalina understandably 'lost the plot' when she caught them having sex on her sitting-room sofa one afternoon when she had come home early from work. But while she went crazy and threw everything but the kitchen sink at her husband, because of her Catholic upbringing she refused to throw him out. She instead chose to wage war on her rival, who continued to date Enrique, and the pair would have frequent stand-up rows and fights in the pub and street. Bricks were even known to fly through windows late at night, scalding hot water was poured over one of them, and, according to Celia, both tried to commit suicide on more than one occasion as Enrique bobbed back and forth between them.

Enrique eventually sided with his Avon Lady (they got married a few years later) and Celia still clearly recalls the day she came back to save her mother and young sister Ingrid from killing themselves by gas inhalation. It's perhaps no surprise that her mother was eventually sectioned by her husband at her local psychiatric hospital. Even though she was discharged with the help of some friends from work after six weeks, according to Celia's little sister Ingrid, she has not been the same since.

The subject of sex is also an extremely painful and taboo subject in the Pantoja family and there is sadly a fair amount of suggestion of sexual abuse. This includes the claim by Celia's older sister Rosemary (backed up by Ingrid) that their father had sexually abused her as a child. Now a successful lap dancer running her own club called the Office, in Hull, she claims that their father began to molest her soon after fleeing from Chile. Over drinks at her club, she told a series of depraved and alarming stories (most of which are unprintable) which culminated in her running away from home at the age of 12 to sleep in a local park in an attempt to escape the clutches of her perverted father.

'I was desperate to get away from that sick bastard,' says the self-confessed 'gangster's moll', who has changed her name by deed poll to Jessie Graham, to distance herself from her father. 'He made my life a misery from a young age, starting after the torture he suffered at the hands of Pinochet and when we were on the run in Argentina. It had a terrible effect on me, but when I mentioned it to my mother she just slapped me and told me to stop lying. I couldn't wait to leave home and have as little to do with my family nowadays as possible.'

The abuse had a profound effect on her, she says, eventually leading to a life as a stripper. Her lap-dancing business is one of the most successful in the country, sending 500 dancers across three continents, and she has frequently appeared on television programmes, such as *Kilroy* and *GMTV*, to discuss her profession. 'I have very little to do with my family now and I am not surprised Celia ended up with a sick bastard like Tony. I never want to see my father again. He was really sick and depraved and basically ruined my childhood.'

While Celia herself is much more hesitant to discuss the subject, the way she discovered her father was having an affair with Rita Leigh speaks volumes. It was her fourteenth birthday and her father and Rita, who was by now very much a part of the family, had taken her out shopping in Leeds to buy a new dress and later for lunch. She continues the story: 'It had been a lovely day and on the way home I fell asleep in the back only to wake up an hour or so later in a lay-by with dad and Rita having sex like rabbits in the front passenger seat. I couldn't believe it and stormed out of the car in disgust. Dad had to come running after me and apologize profusely. He even made me promise not to tell mum. He was such a bastard and I can't believe I got back in.'

After that she quickly clammed up on the subject, apart from saying that these days she has practically nothing to do with her father, who is currently living with Rita in Scotland. There is certainly no love lost for her father, who more or less forced her to leave school at the age of 16 to get work to help pay the mortgage. Starting work in the Arnold Dennis fruit factory alongside her mum just a week after her final exam, it wasn't surprising she was very miserable. Outgoing and intelligent she was naturally deeply frustrated at the menial work and in no time at all came to blows with her mother, moving out to live with friends.

She was soon dating a coal miner, Colin Winfield, with whom she moved into a council house on the Kendry estate, in Barnsley. Seven years older than her he was a hulking no-nonsense sort of fellow, who did the right thing and married her a few months after their son Kevin was born in December 1984. It brought a brief happy spell to her life until the famous miners' strike hit home the following year. Her husband was one of the first to lose his job and then rashly agreed to take in the family of his brother, when he landed on the dole. They spent their days on the picket lines and lived off Celia's paltry £65-a-week wage.

'We had meatless stew with fruit and veg I had stolen from the factory and kept warm by using any scraps of coal we could get hold of,' she recalls. 'It was horrendous and like a cauldron at home with all these angry people. All Colin and I did was fight and eventually he began to threaten to kill Kevin and the police had to be called.'

And then began the worst period of her life. Details are sketchy, but with the police apparently refusing to get involved in 'just another domestic', she claims she was so scared of being attacked she moved back to her mother's, initially without her son. Being forced to fight for custody in the courts she made a very big mistake and one night kidnapped Kevin by breaking into the house late one night. The authorities obviously took a dim view of this – and amid further allegations of non-specified mistreatment – he was eventually taken away from both parents and incredibly placed with Celia's father and Rita; in retrospect, perhaps a bad idea.

Undoubtedly the bleakest period of her life, Celia went into a downward spiral and by her own admittance considered suicide. 'The situation was killing me and I became anorexic and very run down. It broke my heart to lose Kevin. I was allowed to go and visit him a few days a week, but I was forced to eat very humble pie in the process. I became very depressed. I was in a real state and needed to get away.'

It was at this point that she moved to Croydon, south London, where she would eventually meet Tony King. She initially moved in with her sister Rosemary, who was – officially – working at a security firm. At some point, the *News of the World* claimed Celia had become a prostitute, an allegation she strongly refutes. 'Somebody has obviously said I was on the game to darken my name, but I have never slept with anyone for money, nor taken my clothes off for money,' she says angrily. 'It is an awful slur. Sure I have met a few prostitutes and have even been inside a sauna to meet a friend, who worked there, but that game was not for me. I just couldn't stand the idea of all those fat middle-aged men pawing all over me.'

While the assumption, of course, may have come from her sister's job as a lap dancer, she certainly doesn't deny that she and her family have been in various other shady business practices. These connections seem to have begun soon after her family met Thomas and Rita Leigh in Barnsley.

An interesting pair indeed, publicly Tom Leigh masqueraded as some sort of 'new-age lifestyle coach' and wrote self-help books. He was also a fully trained hypnotherapist and dabbled as some sort of artist, says Celia. 'There was a lot of mystique about him, and with all his followers I guess you could call him some sort of guru. He was certainly very intelligent and had a lot of cash.'

The truth is, I discovered, Tom Leigh made money from a series of elaborate scams, masquerading loosely under the guise of motivational books and videos. Claiming to help people identify 'their inner satisfaction and greatness through psyche energy', he has been a director of several now-defunct companies including FPW Meta Research Ltd, Futures Product World Ltd and Profile Marketing Incentives Ltd.

Frequently finding work for Enrique and his daughters in his range of suspect businesses, he would later come under investigation by the Department of Trade and Industry (DTI) and flee England to set up a series of lucrative timeshare companies with his son Garry in Spain. Both are almost certainly now millionaires.

The most colourful and best publicized of their schemes in England was an illegal pyramid scheme father and son set up from an office above a pub in a village just outside Barnsley in 1993. Called Frequency Programming World (FPW), the 'get rich quick scheme', as the DTI later described it, was making the

Leighs so much money that the company even became the main sponsor of the town's football club Barnsley FC, before being dramatically dissolved at the High Court weeks before the season began, making front-page news locally.

'It was a major embarrassment for the club,' recalls *Barnsley Chronicle* news editor Andrew Harrod, who investigated the case at the time. 'Tom and Garry upset a lot of people and were later wanted up and down the country. I remember going to their big, plush farmhouse down this long track to try and get some sort of comment from them. When I got there, there were two snarling Rottweilers in the front garden and these two big guys, who had been polishing sports cars, warned me if I came any closer they might not be able to control them. It was very intimidating.'

Furnishing the Leighs with a series of new houses, cars and, crucially, investments in Spain, the pyramid scheme also provided lucrative jobs for the Pantoja family. Enrique and his now wife Rita became directors in charge of administration and systems while sisters Ingrid and Celia were put in charge of the telesales team. Given the job of keeping the pyramid rolling, they had a team of 18 telesales staff, whose sole job was to find new punters to invest.

Describing itself as a 'computer-generated money-payout plan' – or multi-level marketing – its literature told potential clients: '*All you do is simply enter as much as you want and bank your profit. £460 clear profit for every £140 entered. No strings, no catch, no limit.*' It was the classic rip-off, where inevitably most people ended up thousands out of pocket. Such was the company's infamy that amongst others it was investigated by the *Mail on Sunday* and even debated in the House of Commons. MP Nigel Griffiths, of Edinburgh South, described it as 'a money for nothing scam', which used 'the hard sell, threats of violence and secrecy' to entice customers. A new law was later passed to give the DTI more power to shut down such schemes more quickly.

What is also certain is that thousands of punters were left out of pocket – 8000 joined in total. These included one Captain William Harris of Lydbrook, Gloucestershire, as well as – intriguingly – one big group from Keighley, where Tony King's former boss Robbie Graham lived. Recalls Captain Harris: 'It was a bitter experience. A classic network marketing con and I was left well out of pocket, while my friend who introduced me was getting cheques for £3,000. It is a great way to lose friends and suffice to say that I nowadays have nothing to do with the person who introduced me.'

Celia admits that the con probably made millions of pounds, with her father earning enough money to buy a series of new properties, including a flat in Barnsley, a detached house, Duff Cottage, in the Yorkshire countryside, where they soon moved, and two houses near Marbella on the Costa del Sol. Former neighbours of Enrique and Rita Pantoja remember how the couple, who never socialized locally, suddenly had a fleet of new sports cars, including Porsches and Mercedes, parked in the drive.

Recalls Celia: 'Initially I had no idea it was a con and started investing £30 a month. I was soon getting back £240 a month and the pyramid was growing so quickly that we moved to a plush new office and took on 18 telesales staff to find new punters. I was put in charge and things were going really well until the shit hit the fan and the DTI closed us down. I was gutted particularly as I was just about to start getting cheques totalling £8,000 a month.'

While she narrowly missed out on a fortune – albeit an illegal one – her father, like thousands of the punters, fared a good deal worse. Unbeknown to him, says Celia, Enrique was the only director left on the deeds when the walls came tumbling down in 1994 and while Garry and Tom Leigh (who was by now with his long-term partner Maureen) did a rapid and successful vanishing act he was left to pick up the pieces. It was classic revenge perhaps for losing his wife and it proved to be very costly for Enrique when

97

it emerged that the company had not only failed to put in its annual tax return but had also failed to pay any tax. According to Celia, Customs and Excise clobbered him for 'hundreds of thousands of pounds' forcing him not only to sell his properties and cars in the UK but later, his houses in Spain.

'He got badly stung when everything was closed down,' says Celia. 'While Garry and Tom were driving around scot-free in their Porsches, wearing designer clothes and Gucci watches, Dad and Rita lost everything. They ended up in court fighting the DTI, and of course they lost. It would be fair to say that they got totally stitched up.'

Moving eventually to a small cottage on the Isle of Lewis, he does appear, at least, to have got away with one bill. According to the current owner of Duff Cottage, which overlooks the now landscaped hills of the former Barnsley Main Colliery, a legal bill for £54,000 addressed to 'Mr E. Pantoja' arrived soon after he moved in. 'We had no forwarding address and only knew they had moved to an island off Scotland. I doubt very much he ever received it.'

Unsurprisingly, perhaps, the Leighs and much of the rest of the team moved to Spain and the infamous Costa del Crime. With the heat on, and naturally wanting to protect their ill-gotten gains, the Costa del Sol was the perfect place to hide out and prosper. With over 500,000 Brits estimated to be living there full-time – the majority not properly registered or paying tax – and with an extremely laid-back legal system, it was an easy place to immerse their 'moody' money and the opportunities to make more soon became apparent.

After investing in a couple of shrewd property deals and a less successful pyramid scheme ('the Spaniards were too sceptical,' says Ingrid) they, of course, plumped for timeshare, which, while not exactly a new concept, still had a big potential market with the millions of new holidaymakers arriving every year from all over Europe. Timeshare had not yet become the dirty word it is today and persuading punters to invest money in their future holidays was still a lucrative business. John 'Goldfinger' Palmer, of course, was said to have become England's 105th richest person from it, before being banged up at the Old Bailey in 2001.

According to Ingrid, who had moved into a villa with her stepbrother Garry in El Coto, Garry got talked into the idea of timeshare one night by a well-known local Costa drug dealer, known as Bon Jovi, who disappeared in suspicious circumstances a couple of years ago after one of his 'mules' importing drugs into England died when a cocaine-filled condom split in his stomach. 'Garry got up really excited one morning and started banging on about the amount of money we could make from timeshare,' recalls Ingrid. 'Everyone was doing it and he saw it as a great way to make a fast buck.'

They soon found themselves the backing of a somewhat shady developer who owned a lot of property around La Cala, and was best known for his involvement in the construction of the Costa del Sol racecourse. They started from a small office on the N-340 alongside a strip of businesses that today – suspiciously as we shall later see – includes Vibes and the Millennium Video shop. The developer, who apparently owned the freehold to the block, had soon offered them an office in his nearby seaside development called Buti Bamba, on which they could start a timeshare operation.

Calling it Ventura, the deck, as it is known in the trade, was once again a real old family affair with Garry working as the project director, his father Tom helping to write the infamously clever and persuasive literature and Ingrid pulling in the punters as chief OPC (off premises contact). Handing out an olive branch there was even a technical job offered to Celia's father (who was very useful with his Spanish) and, according to Celia, a lot of the old faces from FPW came over en masse.

But it was the senior partners and silent backers that took the criminal activities to new heights. They included Peter Utal, an infamous brothel keeper, and two Swedish gangsters, one since murdered, the other now in prison. The team were soon pulling in £50,000 a week in profit with little in the way of outlay for the clients, who were often sold a product not worth the paper it was printed on.

As is the way however, in 1996, the company was taken over by a well-connected timeshare boss by the name Jon Daniels, who also heralded from Leeds. A somewhat mythical character – known to most in the trade as JD – he and his girlfriend Tracy Roberts took over the operation, almost certainly due to the demands of the backers, and quickly installed some discipline. An aggressive, manipulative man, whose family had moved to Spain from Yorkshire in the 1980s, tensions quickly rose between Garry and Jon and it wasn't long before Celia's father had got the chop. With various side projects, including dealing Viagra and other pills (as we shall later see), Jon was very much on the make and looking to rise up the greasy timeshare ladder. He was, however, a great salesman, allegedly pulling in £3,000 at Ventura on his first day alone. Either way the company found a new edge and became increasingly thrusting.

Jon it should be mentioned had also immediately taken a shine to Ingrid and was soon hitting on her (in more ways than one it later turned out) behind his partner's back. An affair turned into a full-on relationship and they had soon moved into a flat together in Riviera del Sol, upsetting all of her family and causing numerous rows. 'Jon treated Ingrid very badly and would often beat her,' claims Celia. 'She was always on the phone to me from Spain in tears and turning up at work with black eyes. One Christmas when we were over he even knocked her over in the street in front of me and my mum. He was a nasty piece of work, moody, angry and aggressive and always looking to get his mitts in some new pies. He even had the gall to try and persuade my older sister to come out and strip for him on the Costa. It is fair to say she was disgusted.'

Chapter Eight

Suspicions Begin and the Leatherhead Attack

Back in England meanwhile, Tony and Celia's relationship had, despite numerous hiccups, stuttered on until they married in June 1997. It was two months after the birth of their daughter Sabrina and a glorious sunny day. With shades of the cheap DIY wedding of his parents, it was hastily arranged at a local restaurant with just £50 behind the bar for a buffet, and a double-layered wedding cake lovingly prepared by Tony's mum. Attended by two dozen close family and friends – excluding Celia's father, who she claims, refused to attend – the service was at Sutton register office and Tony had made a special effort to dress up, wearing his black Burton suit, with a carnation in the lapel and a bright paisley tie. It was hardly a lavish or drunken affair, but the guests had a lot of fun, ending up in a local nightclub by midnight.

Tony had given Celia a ring (not an engagement ring, but a wedding ring, that didn't even fit!) the previous Christmas, followed later by a small celebration at his mother's house. They had almost not made it though, and the previous few months had been very rocky between them, particularly after she discovered he was having an affair with a local barmaid.

It had been during the tricky mid-pregnancy hiatus, when the last thing Celia had felt like was sex. Admittedly pushing Tony away, she was far from surprised when she got the phone call from the bar girl one morning, as she sat watching daytime TV. She was frank and to the point: 'I have slept with Tony and I thought you should know,' she told Celia. And that was that. Grateful for the call and despite being angry with him she decided to give Tony another chance. In return he promised her a wedding.

But sex was still not on the agenda and their arguments got increasingly fierce. While never turning to violence – Celia insists Tony never once lifted a finger to her in their time together – they would often end up shouting at each other.

It was around this time pointedly that her ex-husband occasionally started to disappear in the middle of the night. But while she might have been suspicious, she claims she merely brushed it off as insomnia, an affliction he had suffered from since he was a child. 'It happened two or three times during the middle of my pregnancy. I would be sleeping and suddenly wake up with a start in the early hours to discover he was not there. I would think: Tony, where has he gone? and drift off back to sleep. I couldn't tell you where he had gone, but for some reason it didn't really worry me. I just assumed he couldn't sleep,' says Celia.

But more concerns were raised in February 1997, when sensationally perhaps the police suddenly turned up at their door to cart Tony off to an ID parade. While Celia insists the police did not inform her of what Tony was being accused of, she was furious that he was bringing trouble and shame to her front door. Tracked down through his mother's address in north London, the police had turned up at their house in Wonnersh Gardens late one evening, while Tony's brother David and his wife were staying for a few weeks.

'It was a frantic time and Tony was really panicking,' Celia recalls. 'There were all these hushed conversations between him and David and the police, and all Tony told me was that it was in connection with some armed robbery and that he apparently looked like one of the thieves. I even overheard him suggest to David that he "do a runner" and disappear, so it must have been serious.

'Either way, he made a point of stressing his innocence and said: "Now you can see why I had to change my name". But while I was publicly defensive of him, saying of course he didn't do it, privately I was furious and we rowed a lot. I was seven months pregnant and scared and upset that he was going to be carted off back to prison. I remember asking him to tell me the truth and was constantly saying: "Are the police going to come round again?" The fact was I didn't trust him as far as I could throw him, and now wish my intuition had been better.'

All was soon forgotten, however, with the birth of their baby girl Sabrina Rosalind King on 8 April 1997, at Sutton Hospital. It had been touch-and-go at first, when the cord got stuck around the baby's neck, but it had finally been unravelled. Tony had sat dutifully through the whole birth, holding Celia's hand, and was so excited he was visibly shaking when he picked his daughter up for the first time. Pictures document it well and back at their house in Wonnersh Gardens Tony doted over the new arrival for hours on end. Happy times indeed, they were soon making plans for their wedding, which was looming ever large.

But the wedding and the pressures around it were again causing Tony considerable stress and he was sleeping worse than ever and over the next two months would frequently stay out late and disappear at night. His brother had by now rented a small house up their street and, according to Celia, Tony had even got David a job at Cornhill Insurance in Leatherhead. 'They were getting closer and closer and always going on about fishing or football. They would spend quite a lot of time together and you could see there was still a strong bond there,' she says.

Having his brother, who was to be his best man, nearby was certainly not helping to modify his behaviour though, as his antics on his stag night prove. A week before the wedding, it turned into a complete fiasco with only Celia's friends Ian Henry and his girlfriend Brenda turning up, and Tony disappearing halfway through not to reappear for nine hours.

As Henry, aged 40, recalls: 'Celia asked us if we would go to make up the numbers, but when we got there we discovered we were the only stags. Oddly, not even his brother, the best man, made a show. Then after hitting a few pubs on Streatham High Road, Tony insisted on going to a local nightclub called Caesars, where after half an hour he got thrown out for pestering one of the bouncers' girlfriends. It was nearing midnight and we hadn't been in there for long. We were standing at the bar while Tony swanned around the dance floor flirting with various girls. He was drunk and didn't seem to care. Then suddenly we saw him in this scuffle with the bouncers by the door and that was that he was out on his arse. The whole thing was so embarrassing we didn't even bother leaving to go and look for him. The fact that he didn't get home until 9a.m. the next morning makes me wonder what he got up to that night. Actually it concerns me very much.'

The wedding night itself had also seen more erratic behaviour from Tony, when after taking large amounts of speed for the first time he had again embarrassed himself by dancing inappropriately with a stranger on the dance floor. As Celia recalls: 'Luckily I didn't see it, but my friends told me he was rubbing himself up against this one girl like there was no tomorrow.'

Pointedly, sex was, once again, completely off the menu that night. This time Tony's fault – he was unable to perform through the large amounts of drugs he had taken – they ended up going for a long midnight walk and spent the rest of the night sitting on a bench in Carshalton Park talking till dawn.

It was the first night she had mentioned the idea of Spain. Her sister Ingrid had been there for a couple of years since the FPW pyramid scheme had collapsed, and was doing well. She had a good job in her stepbrother's timeshare company now called

Timelinx and was loving the lifestyle and weather. It suited her Chilean blood and was a lot cheaper than living in London. There would always be a job for Celia, and Tony wouldn't have difficulty finding work. It was an opportunity that Celia found hard to turn down.

But Tony had no interest in moving there whatsoever. He had a decent job at home and wanted to be near his family, he told her. He had only been out of England once, on a day trip to France with his mother as a child, and he was terrified at the idea of having to learn a new language and adapt to a new life abroad.

While he had agreed to go to Spain in September 1997 for a two-week holiday (Celia bought the flight tickets from a bucket shop in Paddington that July, with money her mother had given them as a wedding present), he refused point-blank to move there. It led to frequent rows throughout that summer, which would often end in Celia threatening to leave and go to Spain on her own with Sabrina. 'I was beyond caring. I was furious with him and quite frankly was beginning to think of going on my own without him,' she says.

But he would still not budge until, somewhat sinisterly, one day in the middle of August he suddenly changed his mind. While impossible to prove, it seems highly likely that Tony's mindset had shifted when Surrey police began to investigate his links to a brutal sex assault in Leatherhead that month. Celia claims to know nothing about it and says she was merely happy that he had changed his mind. Two weeks later they were on their way to Spain, having sold all their belongings for just over £1,000. 'He came home one day and sat down and said: "I really want to go now." We had just two weeks to get things sorted out and sold all our stuff at a series of car-boot sales. It was two weeks, we had just that.'

The attack in question involved a Hungarian au pair who had been travelling home via Leatherhead station. Attacked from behind, the 21-year-old was threatened with rape before the attacker indecently assaulted her and ran off.

While King had never been formally accused of the attack, he was apparently spotted on CCTV walking down the station plat-form at nearby Epsom station, where the girl had changed trains around the same time. When this footage was shown on BBC's *Crimewatch* on 2 September 1997, police received 'dozens' of calls from people who recognized him, but when the police turned up at his address the following day he had already left for Spain.

As King's former boss Peter Pink recalls: 'Quite a few of our members recognized Tony and called *Crimewatch* straightaway, and we had two policemen knocking on our door a week or two later. I knew they were moving to Spain through my neighbour Brenda, who was Celia's best friend. I told police exactly when they had left and where they were going. I expected them to follow it up and was surprised when they didn't.'

King had just left the country (he had flown with Celia and his friend Paul Lawman, a part-time actor who came over for a week's holiday, from Gatwick to Malaga on 1 September), a day before *Crimewatch*, it appears he was already the main suspect in the case. While Surrey Police have not admitted it, sensationally, he may have actually already been brought in for questioning, going on the word of Cass Collins, who he regularly confided in. 'He told my son Luke and I that he had been picked up for an assault at Leatherhead and had to go in for questioning,' she says. 'I initially thought it must have been to do with some sort of fight, but my son Luke told me it was concerning a sexual assault on a girl. I assumed he must have been a witness, but he was very stressed out and shaken and said: "Now you can see why I had to change my name."

'He came round again straight after the interview and said that the police had spotted him via the CCTV and wanted to know if he had witnessed anything. I don't know how they got hold of him, but he was under the impression that they were after him for it.'

Amazingly, despite the growing pile of evidence against King, Surrey Police claim they were not able to take the matter further. In an apparent legal loophole, they say they were unable to pursue him because they hadn't got a positive identification from an ID parade. Despite having compiled a 'fairly strong' dossier of evidence and having his new address in Spain, the Crown Prosecution Service (CPS) refused to prosecute.

In a classic catch-22 situation the British police were told they could only extradite King if they could get a positive identification of him from witnesses, but they could only do an ID parade if he came back to Britain.

'We were stumped,' said DS Kinchington. 'Once the officers knew he had gone to Spain they cobbled together a reasonably strong case to extradite him, but the CPS disagreed. While they were fairly certain King was guilty, there was no forensic evidence to back them up. It was a classic catch-22 and the CPS frustrated them. All they could do was send a report through Interpol to Spain with his details and address and hope they kept a close eye on him over there.'

The senior Scotland Yard detective adds: 'I think they requested he come back to England for an ID parade voluntarily and I understand the Spanish police did actually go round and speak to him. But that was that. He didn't come back and had soon moved on and they lost him. In my opinion he committed the offence knowing he was going to Spain. With the flights already booked and paid for he knew he would get away with it.'

His boss, Detective Chief Superintendent Craig Denholm, who led the King investigation, was in agreement. In a press statement, he said: 'There is good evidence to suggest that Tony King fled to Spain because he knew he was wanted by Surrey Police in connection with the Leatherhead assault.'

Alarmingly, DS Kinchington adds that the loophole still exists today, meaning thousands of similar sex offenders are able to escape justice by simply moving abroad. 'It would almost certainly be the same situation if it happened again today and sadly King was one of many sex offenders all around the world who slip the net for the same reason.'

Chapter Nine

Tony in at the Deep End

And so in the autumn of 1997, Tony and Celia were to arrive on the Costa del Sol. Initially moving in with Celia's sister Ingrid and her boyfriend Jon Daniels, in their four-bedroom house in the urbanization Las Veronicas in Riviera del Sol, it had been a long, hot summer and September was still hot, often with temperatures over 40°C during the day. The tourists were still out in full force; the beaches were packed during the day and the bars heaving at night. It was the end of peak season and an exciting time to visit southern Spain with everything still open and most businesses thriving.

It was certainly that way at Ventura, where the team was pulling in tens of thousands a week with many of the staff taking £1,000 – cash in hand – and one assumes not paying tax. Things should have been rosy, but the truth was a big storm was brewing. It was down to a power struggle between Daniels and Garry Leigh, who was far from happy suddenly having him as a boss. There were constant arguments and physical threats, and things finally came to a head one night, when they ended up fighting outside a pub and Garry flattened Jon over the

108

bonnet of a car, and according to Ingrid, even punched his girlfriend Tracy in the face.

Word of their fall-out quickly got around and within days their backers decided it would be better all round if the two of them set up their own operations with Garry staying at Ventura in La Cala – and Jon setting up a separate company Lubina Sol with American Roscoe Reynolds in Riviera del Sol, where Victoria Beckham's family have had a holiday home for years.

Garry had also soon set up another murky business, known as Matterson's Cash Back, on Marbella's Golden Mile. Something of an infamous con trick, it involved providing buyers of a new car or appliance, such as a washing machine, with a 'cash back' option, in which as long as they correctly followed all the steps they could get a sizeable chunk (sometimes all) of their money back at the end of a set term, which was normally five years. It involved paying a premium on top of the price of the purchase to Garry's company, and was a surprisingly strong pull for car salesmen, among others. Explains Ingrid, who worked at the business for a time: 'It relies on punters filling in various forms every step of the way, but if you miss a step you get nothing. It runs on people forgetting to do it and an incredible 58 per cent of people fail on the first hurdle. They always say, of course I will remember to fill in the form in a year, and they never do. It is their problem and I guess it goes on the same principle that there are millions of unclaimed lottery prizes.'

There was now no doubting Garry's fast-growing links to organized crime, his partner Peter Utal having impeccable global crime connections. As well as years of experience running timeshare decks, Utal had the added bonus of some well-known and reported links to prostitution; such as his apparent stake in Stark 92, one of the Costa del Sol's most successful and popular brothels.

But it was Garry's silent backers – brought in to add some

muscle, or security, as it is known in timeshare – that was perhaps most telling of all. Ever the businessman, Garry knew that he needed the best for his fast-burgeoning business and that is where the now-infamous Dennis New, and his cohort Mohamed Derbah – a Lebanese gangster known as Mo – came in.

Running the protection rackets across Spain (and most of its islands), it was, and still is, practically impossible to set up a new real-estate business, legal or not, without their 'involvement'. Currently awaiting trial in Spain for extortion and fraud, among other things, they are said to be worth billions of pounds collectively and command huge gangs of security operatives, numbering into the thousands. With his alleged links to Islamic terrorist groups, Mo is said to be the most ruthless of the three men, while Dennis New has the best pedigree, being the former right-hand man of timeshare king John Palmer, one of England's wealthiest criminals and currently banged up in prison on extortion and fraud charges. Palmer, nicknamed 'Goldfinger' after he admitted helping melt down gold after the £26 million Brinks Mat robbery, received an eight-year sentence for timeshare fraud. According to sources, however, he and New are still closely linked and have a lot of shared investments around the world. 'Dennis still runs a number of Palmer's timeshare resorts on Tenerife,' says one fellow timeshare boss. 'And he even bought his French castle in Normandy a couple of years ago when the heat to sell got too much for Palmer.'

It was in this den of iniquity that Tony suddenly found himself immersed, starting work as a junior salesman, on a commission-only basis, at Ventura in La Cala. He did surprisingly well at first, and while, according to his mother, he didn't like the fraudulent way they were fleecing holidaymakers, he figured he would have to stick at it until he found a better job. 'He was desperate to get a job to look after his family,' said

Lynda Bromwich. 'He knew many of them were a stinking horrible lot, but he had to make money somehow.'

But just a month into the job he had second thoughts when he had 'a major scare', according to Celia, after the police raided the office, according to Tony to investigate a connection to drugs, following numerous complaints from customers. While they didn't find anything, Tony didn't like the intrusion. Perhaps because of his alleged involvement in the attack in Surrey (or perhaps this was the real reason for the raid), he was clearly unnerved and decided to hand in his notice. 'He told me he was not happy,' recalls Celia. 'The police had turned up and he was worried about getting in trouble. He decided to leave and get another job.'

After a brief stint in a local bar, serving pints, he landed a job at the much more respectable timeshare company McDonald Resorts, where again he didn't last long and then another timeshare company Dona Lola, in Calahonda, where after just three months he was sacked, apparently for taking off his T-shirt to sunbathe in front of potential clients. Despite these difficulties he and Celia had soon scraped together enough money to rent their own apartment in Los Naranjos, in Calahonda, just five minutes from the sea and with wonderful views. At £150 a month, it wasn't expensive and by November they had more or less decided to stay, with Tony officially signing on the foreigners' register (NIE) at Fuengirola police station, on 7 November 1997.

They should have been happy, but for Tony things had hardly improved since moving to Spain. The worst of it was his insomnia, which, if anything, had got worse. Now just like his mother, he could only manage to get about three or four hours sleep a night before having to get up for work. Not going to bed until the early hours, he would usually stay up late watching television and, according to Celia, pornographic videos. It was a huge battle getting him up in the morning for work and he was constantly tired. Unsurprisingly, their sex life took a further dive and Celia would be lucky to have sex with her husband once a month.

'I would go to bed knackered after a day with Sabrina, while he would sit up usually for hours watching porno films,' says Celia. 'I would sometimes find them in the video machine the next day and while straight man-on-woman stuff they were more hardcore than I could bear and didn't turn me on. The problem was he was no longer getting turned on by me. He stopped wanting to have sex and I'll admit after having the baby I had lost my drive as well. We would have sex occasionally, when he made the effort, and I would do my best to try and relieve him sexually when I could, but it is fair to say our relationship was unravelling at a rapid rate.'

He was, however, an excellent father to Sabrina, as many friends and acquaintances confirm, and doted on her all the time. Indeed, if there was one person he would drop everything for it was his daughter. He would play with her for hours every day and at weekends he loved taking her to the beach or the park.

Work-wise he was prepared to do almost anything, and took a whole range of jobs including gardening, bar work and security (in all his time in Spain he was said to have taken fifteen different jobs). He even had another unsuccessful stint at his brother-in-law's deck, which had by then changed its name to Club Class Holidays (CCH), where one former colleague and long-time friend of Tony's, remembers both he and Celia working, at some point early in 1998. As Julie Smith, now the head barmaid of the excellent Blancos restaurant in Riviera recalls: 'I was working there as a rep with Tony and Ingrid, while Celia was in the contracts and admin department. Tony seemed a really sweet guy and we got on well, but as a salesman he was really not all that good.'

It led to him being put on 'the numbers', as it is called, when if you didn't get enough sales in a month you were out. 'It involved giving him six couples, as I recall, and he was told if he hadn't got a single deal out of them he was out. And he was out,' recalls Smith, who was one of the few friends that Tony had throughout his time in Spain. 'The poor guy didn't get one deal out of them and off he went. Celia got the sack a week later after rowing with Garry about a pay rise to make up for the loss of earnings with Tony out of work.'

It was certainly the most stressful period the pair had faced and with both of them out of work and facing eviction from their new home. Celia was forced to pull in one more family favour, one she really didn't relish, with brother-in-law Jon, whose deck Lubina Sol was by then doing extremely well despite its infamously sleazy reputation. It would prove to be Tony's downfall.

A sharp well-run operation, Lubina Sol sat in pole position, next to the beach and in full view of the busy N-340 motorway that ferries millions of holidaymakers up and down the coast from Malaga airport to Marbella every year. Part of a timeshare resort of the same name, the scruffy low-rise admin block in Riviera del Sol was at the end of a thoroughfare channelling tourists to the beach from their holiday homes inland.

Just as Victoria Beckham and her family had done on many occasions since they bought their house in the area in the 1980s, the holidaymakers would stroll into the complex to buy sun creams from the handful of shops or stop for a beer at one of the cheap and cheerful bars. Once there, they couldn't fail to miss the Lubina Sol office, where Jon Daniels and his crew turned over literally hundreds of unsuspecting tourists every month.

The walk-in trade was minimal, but a team of outside salesmen, known as OPCs (or off-premises contacts) would guarantee to bring in the punters. It was a sure-fire winner (it amazingly still is) sending out a team of young and good-looking runners to chat up potential buyers on the nearby streets and hand out the infamous scratch cards. It was a clever ruse that almost always guaranteed a prize, which depending on the card could be a camcorder or £500 in cash, but in reality would always end up being a holiday, with a teddy bear or a bottle of champagne (i.e. Cava, at £3 a bottle) as a bonus. There was only one catch! To find out what prize they had won they had to come up to the office and sit through a one- or two-hour pitch on the merits of buying a timeshare.

Playing on the public's inherent greed, it guaranteed a steady flow of potential clients coming to the office, be they British, German, or best of all 'Scandies' (Scandinavians), who were deemed to have the most money and be the easiest to sell to. It is a curious psychology, with most punters – and in particular the British – believing it would be easy to sit through the 'half-cock' pitch and then simply walk away with their prize.

Or that, at least, is what the OPCs told them as they made arrangements by mobile phone for a 'driver' to swing by to give them a lift to the deck. And that is when the rest of the sales team swung into action. Running like most of the other slick timeshare operations on the coast, the dozen or so staff at Lubina Sol would quickly get into position, coming back from the bar or the roof where they might have been sunbathing to sit in front of a computer or on a phone looking busy.

The process would begin with a smiley-faced receptionist, almost always a pretty girl, who would take the winners' names and confirm their prize. Always a free holiday, in the form of a £500 voucher, they would be told that it would have to be redeemed at one of the company's sister resorts and almost certainly booked through Travelquest, a timeshare-friendly company.

Next came the demonstration on the wonders of timeshare and they would be introduced to a salesman, whose job was to sell the particular 'pack' they were promoting that week. Armed with statistics, glossy photos and a persuasive patter, he would usually distort, exaggerate, or plain lie about the resort the pack was based on.

A confidence job in the extreme, the salesman was chosen by his position in 'the line', or the rigid pecking order, which went on his, or her, current success rate. As a former salesman at Lubina Sol explained: 'This meant all the plums, as we called them – the teachers, bankers, Scandies; those with money – going to the best salesman, while the NQs (or non-qualifieds), which included people in council houses on low incomes and pensioners, went to the salesmen who hadn't got any deals for a while. It was a kind of vicious circle, but that's life.'

Having said that there were always daily or weekly incentives, SPIFFs (meaning Special Performance Incentives Fund for Future sales), which would pay £50 or £100 to the best salesman that day or week. There were also one-off bonuses of £50 if someone managed to pass on a client's credit card details to their TO (or Take Over man) who was next in line.

While it was the salesman's job to explain the logic of owning a timeshare, it was the TO's job to tie up the deal. An experienced salesman, he had to be sharp and quick-witted to keep the scam going. It was his job to talk money and go through the paperwork. Often sitting in a separate office he would usually be gentler and act more confidently and hopefully by the end of the 90-minute session he'd have a £500 deposit in his hands, with the remaining money, normally totalling between £5,000 and £10,000, coming in a fortnight.

But should the punters just want to claim their prize – and had no interest in timeshare – that could be tolerated, as there would always be another chance to persuade them when they came back for their holiday the following year. Called the 'fly-by', it would be clearly written in the terms that, usually, on the day after they arrived they had to attend a 'welcome meeting', in which the salesman's only goal was again to persuade them to buy a timeshare.

Lasting at least four hours – and often a whole day – this meeting would normally involve going off to see the resort and all the wonderful local amenities. 'If they came back in less than four hours we would be in for a roasting,' explains the former salesman. 'And we would try anything to keep them with us all day in a bid to wear them down. We would take them to the beach, the pub, wherever, it didn't matter, as long as you were with them and kept gently mentioning the idea.'

Finally after the long 'tour of duty', the punters would be taken to a 'typical' apartment – called the 'show apartment' – which was always miles better than where they were staying, they would sometimes even be allowed to spend a night there. 'They are always stunning, beautiful places, where no one ever stays,' explains the salesman. 'But it is all about the dream, and ultimately brainwashing people. You tell them anything they need to hear to fall for the ruse. Some people even promised limos and helicopters to pick them up at the airport every year. It's incredible how many people fall for it.'

The truth, if they are lucky, is a very average apartment, probably a long way from the beach, where in the small print they get lumbered with a clause enforcing them to pay up to £500 a year for 'maintenance and cleaning'. And should they not pay it, they forfeit the right to further use of the timeshare. But these are the fortunate few, and many punters, as has been reported many times on television and in the media, get nothing at all. The contract is not worth the paper it is printed on and should you complain about the £10,000 hole in your credit card, you'll probably find the company is 'no longer listed' or has 'gone bankrupt'. Tough luck, but as the saying goes: 'People coming to Spain leave their brains at the airport' and the truth is hundreds get fleeced every week.

Indeed, the figures given for the amount of money made by

illegal timeshare scams every year are quite staggering. According to the British consul Bruce McIntyre in Malaga, tens of millions of pounds are made each year. Naturally now run by gangs of organized criminals, it has become a world of real and perceived violence and with so much money at stake, discipline is essential and occasionally people get hurt.

While we should be careful not to rope all the timeshare companies into the same bracket (some offer an exemplary service and are extremely popular), sadly, many are the fly-by-night operations that blatantly flout the law. One visit to the excellent website www.crimeshare.com confirms it. Footloose and moving up and down the coast at regular intervals to evade capture, they are close-knit and protective of one another and don't hesitate to threaten investigators, police and journalists. They also have their own ways of dealing with difficult staff.

'There is nothing I wouldn't put past the timeshare world,' says former timeshare salesman Elena Ploughman. 'They are ruthless and I have heard of many people disappearing in the hills above the coast. There are certainly hundreds of bodies of people who fell foul of the timeshare crowd, both inside and out. It is a nasty world and the English are some of the worst within it.'

Ploughman, who is now studying languages at Copenhagen University, was initially recruited to answer phones on a special complaints line. 'I spent a few months at this firm basically lying, telling people that everything was fine and being sorted out, when you knew the company would be closing in a week to go bankrupt and would disappear up the coast with a new name. It was a real scam and I felt very bad about it, especially when we moved the whole company, lock, stock and barrel, taking everything from the phones to the plants.'

Persuaded by friends to come down to the Costa del Sol with the offer of a big wage and a flat, the Danish student soon regretted it. It is an experience felt by many. 'I hated the job, but when I told them I was leaving, they put a lot of pressure on me to stay. They were very nasty and later that night two heavies turned up at my flat – one was John Palmer's former henchman Dennis New, a real scary guy – and told me I had to leave or else. You knew not to mess with them and they basically stood there and watched me pack my bag and that was it, I was on the street.'

Another seasoned timeshare saleswoman, Louise Deravairere who worked for nearly six years at dozens of companies around Spain, tells a similar story. 'I have heard of quite a few OPCs who have been killed, and anyone misbehaving, causing grief for the other staff, or not paying their way, has to watch out. It was very bad in Tenerife. People would be 'disappeared', as we called it, normally the scumbags, the scrotums, the people who cause problems and that nobody likes.

'I feel particularly bad that inadvertently I might have been partly responsible for one nasty attack,' continues the Yorkshire-born girl, who had first landed a job in timeshare after seeing an advert in her local paper in England. 'It was in Benidorm back in the late 1990s, and we were sharing our flat with this Dutch boy. I can't give you his name, but he had already been done for some thieving. And then money and things kept going missing from the apartment and we reported it to the bosses a couple of times. It turned out this guy was also pissing other people off at work, coming in late, getting drunk in the day, and being generally unreliable. What we hadn't expected though was to come back one day to find blood all over the bathroom and all his stuff gone without a trace. In fact the only trace was the blood splattered around the bath. We were so angry we went back to base and told the bosses we were not going home until the place was cleaned up. A few hours later it was, everything all tidy and nice once again; just this Dutch lad gone, not to be seen or ever heard of again.

'But I guess you try not to think about things like that and just move on. It is like everyone in the timeshare world; hear no evil, see no evil, think no evil! It was typical of the nightmare world I had gotten into. There are so many people in the timeshare world that I wouldn't even have spat on if they were on fire. You see and hear of so much bad stuff happening, but of course you don't do anything, you can't do anything.

'Like a lot of people I just got sucked in, seduced by the money. You end up with so much of it and you start living the life and soon you adopt the same attitude as the rest and become almost proud of what you are doing. You tell yourself that it is fine, you are not harming anyone and you earn more money than most people ever earn, more than teachers, professionals, policemen – and cash in hand at the end of the week as well.

'It is like prostitution and you just get more and more sucked in. Pretty soon you become like a monster treating your clients like prey. You feed on them, hook them in and don't let them go for your life, you need the money and can't do anything else. I used to tell my parents and friends I wanted to come back to England. I was miserable and desperate to leave, but I just didn't know where to start, how to do it. I had wanted to come back for the last four years and was at the stage where I really envied normal ordinary couples on the street – people just enjoying their one holiday a year. I really hankered after that life and the normality of returning back to their lives in the UK, back to the nine to five, the routine. I started to crave it.

'Most of the people I worked with are desperately unhappy. They hate their jobs, they drink heavily at night, take drugs, particularly cocaine, and have destructive and often violent relationships. The timeshare crowd loves sticking their noses into their colleagues' relationships and messing them up. Everyone's screwed everyone, and the gossip flies around. It's all very incestuous and they thrive off your misery. They wind you up and get you into trouble with your partner, play mind games. They have no family values, no morals and they certainly rarely think of others apart from themselves. In that world it is a jungle out there and every man works for himself.'

Jonathan Daniels was one of the ruthless few to fight his way to the top and by 1998 his team were doing as well as anyone on the Costa del Sol. Often pulling in upwards of £50,000 a week, with tiny overheads, times were certainly good for the exclusively British gang.

But, according to former salesman Peter Moore, who the police consider was Daniels's right-hand man at the time of Rocío Wanninkhof's death, the company was anything but clean. 'JD was about as dodgy as you can get,' said Bristol-born Moore, who worked at Lubina Sol for two years. 'He was always cutting corners, doing dodgy stuff and never did anything by the book. Tax-wise I'm sure he didn't pay and sooner or later that catches up on you.'

The Gibraltar-based businessman, who now runs his own construction company, continued: 'I often saw the other side of JD's character. He always had lots of other deals going on on the side and would use his staff to do all sorts of things they didn't want to do. Put it this way, when you are in a car coming back from Estepona and you are told that there are a load of drugs in the boot for Jon, you are not going to be very happy. I was against drugs and far from happy when I found out that I was unwittingly transporting them.

'On top of that, despite all the money coming in, Jon was appallingly bad at paying his staff on time. He would always hold back money and you had to practically beg to get it. In fact he still owes me a few thousand.'

Bearing this in mind then, it was perhaps not the best place for Tony to find work, particularly when the sharp-as-a-pin Daniels insisted it would be on a commission-only basis, meaning he made nothing if he didn't sell. But his biggest problem, however, was not the money, but being given convicted crook Robbie

Graham as his direct boss, or TO.

Graham, a long-time colleague of Daniels, had worked his way up through the timeshare ranks, having started in its heyday in Tenerife in the late 1980s. Training under Spain's infamous timeshare mafia of John Palmer, Dennis New and Mohamed Derbah, he had arrived on the mainland of Spain in 1994 with something of a reputation for violence and, in particular, mistreating women. Sleazy and crude, he was the sort of man most people crossed the street to avoid and was certainly the last person you would want to work for.

But as it happened, Tony and Robbie got on like a house on fire. The relationship between them was immediately electric, according to one former colleague, adding that they 'acted like long-lost brothers'.

'We couldn't understand it,' said the source. 'There was this incredible chemistry between them right from the start. They were very tactile with each other and seemed to bond in a very unnatural way. It was like they had known each other for ages or were long-lost brothers. It didn't add up.'

Unbeknown to their former workmates, however – and after extensive research – it can be revealed that the pair *did* actually know each other, from being in prison in England in the 1990s. While not letting anyone at work know about the connection, they had actually met while serving time at Parkhurst on the Isle of Wight. Both of them had admitted as much to close friends and girlfriends, and independent witnesses in England have confirmed that both spent time at the prison in 1992 and 1993.

While Robbie admitted to two former girlfriends Louise Deravairere and Justine Daniels (Jon Daniels's sister) that they had met in prison, Tony admitted to close friend Julie Smith that they had met at Parkhurst and planned to hook up together in Spain. 'Tony told me they had met in prison,' said bar manager Smith, who employed King on various occasions. 'He said they had made a pact to come and live in Spain, but agreed not to be seen together at first. There was no doubt there was a special bond between them and Robbie had a real hold on Tony.'

But initially, at least, the relationship had its advantages for Tony. Making a good team, they were soon bringing in a lot of money for the deck. As King's wife Celia recalled: 'They were certainly good times initially and for about three or four months they did very well. He was bringing me home at least £300 a week for the house and bought us a stereo, video and new bikes. It was nice to have money and while Tony was hardly exactly happy with the work, we could at least afford what we needed.'

The problem was Tony's increasingly close bond with Graham was driving a wedge between them. Practically inseparable, Graham insisted they hung out together almost every lunchtime and evening. Calling Tony his 'long-lost brother' he would use him as his unofficial 'minder' and drinking partner and the pair would often be seen up and down the coast getting increasingly rowdy as the night wore on. Often celebrating big unspecified deals, the huge benders would inevitably find them trawling around a series of bars famous for the timeshare crowd such as Chicken Shack in Fuengirola and David's Bar in Riviera del Sol.

Mixing alcohol with cocaine – Robbie's drug of choice – the pair would often end up getting into fights with other drinkers and even with each other. As former colleague Terry Alison recalled: 'They were a real pair of psychos and were always getting into scraps. They often used to fight each other. It was always Robbie's fault. He would be charming and friendly in the day but would turn into this nasty, aggressive piece of work when he'd had a few drinks. He became the devil and you could see it in his eyes. You wouldn't want to cross those two at midnight on a day when they had got a big deal. You could end up in trouble.'

But sadly it wasn't just men who had to watch out. As one Fuengirola-based legal secretary, from Croydon recalls: 'I had been drinking with a few friends in a bar in Calahonda, when

Robbie suddenly started to get very unpleasant with us. I started rowing with him and he ended up shoving me around before turning this table full of drinks over and swinging punches at other drinkers. As usual Tony had to step in to help him.'

It was in this role as unofficial minder that Graham liked to keep Tony. Confirmed by friends and former colleagues, it meant doing a lot more than the regular sales jobs at Lubina Sol, and much to his regret, often meant throwing his weight around.

According to friend Simon Bowers, Tony was often used as a 'clumper', as it is known in the trade, to keep the OPCs in order and make a few threats to rivals and other undesirables. 'He was a big lad and a very useful tool to have at Graham's disposal. While I knew he was as soft as a teddy bear, he certainly looked the part when he turned up at your house.' His former boss Jon Daniels confirmed his role. 'Robbie and Tony certainly did a few discipline-type jobs together. I remember one bloke in particular, who pissed Robbie off, he got a right kicking from the pair of them, but mostly from Tony. It wasn't a pretty sight.'

Graham himself admitted to me during an interview in Brighton that King was a very useful right-hand man, as he put it. 'Tony was a really hard bastard. He was exceptionally strong and I saw him get hold of quite a few people in Spain. He would pick them up like they were rag dolls and throw them wherever you wanted. He did a lot of martial arts, he was bloody quick . . . really handy to have around. His main job was to look after me on various jobs, which he did 100 per cent. If anything he became obsessed with me. Tony was like a very loyal lapdog who was always extremely useful to have around.'

Chapter Ten

Robbie Nightmare

His two nicknames – Robbie Gold Card and Robbie Nightmare – summed him up perfectly. One given to his face, the other behind his back; they demonstrate well the range of opinions about Robert Terence Graham, who few would argue was one of Europe's best conmen. While a deeply flawed character, who provoked unusually strong reactions in people, in the words of one former boss, he was quite simply the best timeshare salesman around, and had it not been for an expensive cocaine habit (at well over £100 a night) 'he would probably have been a millionaire many times over'.

It was this drug addiction coupled with his psychotic treatment of women that marked him out as someone to be particularly wary of. Being a compulsive liar to boot, it certainly made him well cut out for timeshare and after a few short spells at Her Majesty's pleasure in England, the Yorkshireman moved to Spain to seek his fortune. Despite his numerous tattoos (they include a Leeds United logo on his knee, a Popeye on his chest, a Roger Rabbit and a map of Tenerife with his favourite bar Ra-Ra) and working man's drawl, he was both quick-witted and intelligent and had a nice body and looks. All in all it made for someone well equipped for tricking people out of their life savings.

He had soon garnered the nickname Robbie Gold Card for doing just that. As ex-girlfriend Louise Deravairere recalls: 'He was excellent, a complete professional, who was always able to bullshit everyone from dustman to banker. He could talk the hind legs off a donkey and always got a big deposit, often in cash. He got the nickname as when he found out that a couple had a gold card he would literally walk into the office with the gold card slapped on his forehead. He was that cocky.'

But while his colleagues would use his new nickname to his face, behind his back most could not stand the overconfident braggart, who was difficult to deal with and impossible to control. 'While to his face people called him Robbie Gold Card, behind his back he was known as Robbie Nightmare because he was so unreliable and did exactly what he wanted,' continues Louise, who lived with Graham for nearly three years. 'He stayed out late drinking and rarely got in to work on time, but because he knew he was good at his job and made a lot of money for the firm, he thought he could get away with it. It meant he would take days off and go on the piss whenever he wanted.'

Unsurprisingly this didn't go down well with his bosses who, during his first year selling timeshare in Tenerife, took the extreme and somewhat bizarre step of slapping a 'curfew' on him. Used on a surprising number of timeshare salesmen with 'discipline' problems, it meant the firm's security enforcing his bedtime and literally making sure he was at home by midnight and out of bed by 8a.m. Robbie, more than most, knew not to mess around with security and, as he tells it, he got 'roughed up on many occasions'.

It was due to the constant falling out with bosses that Graham frequently changed jobs. Either sacked or moving of his own volition, it rarely took long to land another job with his reputation for being able to sell coals to Newcastle. And he certainly wasn't stuck in Spain. With broad horizons – and having trained up in the epicentre of the timeshare world in Tenerife – he had soon ratcheted up a series of stamps in his passport. Indeed after spells in the Canaries, the Algarve and in Madeira (he is also understood to have worked in the Far East) he ended up selling timeshare in the Caribbean for a year, and always talked of going back.

But his natural home was Spain, and in particular the Costa del Sol and Tenerife, where he worked for most of the big players including timeshare king John 'Goldfinger' Palmer and his right-hand man Dennis New. It was while in Tenerife that he would develop his cocaine addiction.

One former employer, Peter Moore – who worked with Graham in Tenerife – confirms: 'He had an extremely bad reputation even then. He was always getting into scrapes and climbing off balconies to get away from the police. He always seemed to be on the run from something. Small things, he would say, stuff like getting drunk and causing trouble, but with Robbie you always thought it would be something more serious. The thing was he was such a good liar, you never knew what to believe. And another thing for sure he was the master at scamming people.'

It certainly led to frequent run-ins with the law and he found himself in court on various occasions – certainly at least once in Benidorm and once in Torremolinos, for stealing hire cars and drink-driving. Indeed on 12 September 1998 he was banned from driving at Fuengirola court after being found 'a long way over the limit', according to a police source.

A vain man, who some likened to the actor George Clooney, Graham also had an uncanny knack with women. Indeed he was rarely without a girlfriend, despite regularly cheating on them behind their backs. 'He treated his girlfriends like lapdogs and kept them in place by real and perceived violence,' said one former friend and colleague at Lubina Sol. 'He often attacked and beat them up and didn't think twice about playing around with other girls and even prostitutes. And more than anything he didn't half love to talk about it.'

His driver – who was on call for Robbie, sometimes 24 hours a day – put up with most of his crude banter because he was employed by him. But it often used to make him sick. 'He was always on about this debauchery. Don't get me wrong I like my sex, but he was into some weird stuff. Robbie would always take his reps up to the knocking shops and have two or three girls at a time.

'They would get up to all sorts of mischief, stuff beyond ordinary shagging. In the mouth, up the arse, he would even boast that they had pissed on the girls; you don't want to hear it. It was not nice and it is fair to say that Robbie Graham definitely had sexual hang-ups.'

These bizarre sexual peccadilloes were certainly sensed by women, too, and during the research for this book countless women told how uncomfortable they felt in his company. 'My husband brought him round one night after a few beers for a nightcap,' recalls one estate agent based in Calahonda. 'There was something about him that really gave me the creeps. I had heard a fair bit about him and the way he looked and leered at me, I felt instinctively compelled to go to bed early that night. In fact, I forbade my husband to bring him round again and thankfully he didn't.'

More alarming, was his reputation for attacking women. This is best summed up by the existence of an outstanding warrant for his arrest in Portugal, where he was accused of the attempted murder of an ex-lover; time and time again ex-girlfriends and friends of ex-girlfriends told of his violent behaviour.

The incident in Portugal was confirmed by three different

friends of the victim, who pleaded not to be named, and is sadly 'too terrified' to speak out against Robbie. The attack happened while Robbie was living with his former girlfriend in the Algarve in the early 1990s. According to one friend, it had followed various attacks in which he had threatened her with a knife and beaten her to 'within an inch of her life'. On the night in question, the girl, who I shall only name as Michelle, managed to seize a knife that he had held at her throat and plunged it into his groin in anger, leaving him haemorrhaging blood and close to death. Michelle – who is now married with two children and living in Fuengirola – had quickly fled the scene and gone to the police to file charges against Graham.

But while they took her claims seriously, he in turn accused her of attempted murder and, while the case against her has since been dropped, he is – according to police sources – still wanted for questioning over the incident. 'He is an evil man, who made Michelle's life hell,' said Nicky Taylor, a close friend of Michelle's. 'She has told me a few stories about him and it sounded terrifying. He regularly attacked her with knives and beat her within an inch of her life quite a few times. She is sensibly staying as far away from him as possible and doesn't want to speak out against him for fear of retaliation.'

Perhaps more chilling is the story of an earlier girlfriend Graham had brought back to Spain from the island of Guadalupe, where he had been working in timeshare for a year. The mixed-race French Algerian, known as Nora – who had long black hair and a curvy figure – had arrived on the Costa del Sol with Graham around 1998, but had disappeared mysteriously a year later after apparently receiving a series of brutal beatings from her boyfriend. 'She used to pour her heart out to me about how violent Robbie was to her,' recalls King's ex-wife Celia who got to know her well. 'She was terrified of him and didn't know how to leave him. She said he was often having affairs behind her back and didn't think twice about hitting her.

She often used to turn up at work with bruises and scars on her. A lot of people were talking about it and we were worried for her.'

Suspiciously, it was around the time of the death of Rocío Wanninkhof in October 1999 that the timeshare crowd last saw the pretty Marseille-born teenager. She left no forwarding address, and somewhat disturbingly has not been seen since. As Celia's sister Ingrid recalls: 'I saw her quite a lot that year until the autumn when she suddenly disappeared. We never found out why or where she had gone. She simply upped and left. Robbie never told us why.'

Her disappearance has certainly caused something of a stir in the timeshare industry, particularly with the rumour that her brother recently came over from France to look for her. According to an important police source, who employed Graham various times to sell his products, her brother had been into various bars asking after her. 'He was worried about her,' says one fellow timeshare boss. 'She has not been seen for a long time and quite a lot of people are concerned about her. Robbie was probably one of the last people to have seen her.'

Unsurprisingly, it was a similar story with a later girlfriend Justine Daniels, who he beat up, despite her brother Jon being his boss. He had started dating the Yorkshire girl when she was nearly six months pregnant from a previous relationship and moved into her seaside apartment just before the birth in November 1999. But while she had been initially enamoured with him (even putting Graham's name on her son's birth certificate) within six months they had come to blows and she threw him out. As Ingrid Pantoja, her best friend at the time, recalls: 'I warned Justine about Robbie, but she didn't listen to me. She got completely brainwashed by him and believed every word he said and our relationship soon cooled. The problem was he put a big wedge between us and didn't like her seeing me. She has since told me how badly he treated her, how he never paid the rent and was thoroughly unpleasant, once slapping her hard in the face as she was breastfeeding the baby. It was no surprise when she came running to me in mid-2000.'

According to Jon Daniels – who knew Graham well – he had indeed attacked his sister and smashed up her apartment when she dumped him after months of abuse. In the fight he had ripped up half her clothes and was said to have thrown her suitcase through a glass window. 'He was a real bastard to her and she did well to get rid of him,' Daniels told me over a drink in a bar by the bus station in Fuengirola. 'I shouldn't have let him get away with it, but at the time I didn't get the full truth.'

Tracking his roots back in England, we find a depressingly similar story. Unlike King though, Robert Terence Graham had had a comfortable middle-class upbringing and wanted for little. Born in Salford on 25 February 1964, his father Thomas was a manager of a local firm while his mother Alice (ironically her maiden name was Nutter) heralded from Yorkshire. After spending his early years in the famously rough urban area just west of Manchester, at some point during his early adolescence the family moved to the much more relaxed Yorkshire town of Keighley. But while decidedly cleaner and safer, it came as something of a shock to a boy who told his classmates he had never seen a cow before.

The move seems to have had a negative effect on Graham, who was of above average intelligence but didn't excel at his Catholic school the Holy Family; instead he became known as a bully, who forced other boys to go out and steal for him. 'He was a tall and stocky lad, who pushed his weight around,' says one former female pupil, who asked not to be named. 'He was very manipulative and terrified my younger brother, who was much smaller, into stealing for him. He ended up ordering my brother to steal from our parents and from other people to avoid getting a beating. He certainly wasn't the only one though and Rob could get away with it as he had a big gang and people were scared of him.'

Later in his mid-teens, Graham became something of a mod, more concerned about his image than studying. More known for his sharp appearance than his academic skills (he regularly sported Sta-Press trousers, smart shirts and bowling shoes) he left school with a few O-levels and became a scaffolder.

According to old school friends, he liked to play the rebel, always playing up his inner-city Salford credentials and in particular his love for Manchester United. He also became a regular user of drugs, as one of his oldest friends Richard Towler reveals. 'We used to hang out together, go to a few Manchester United games and generally had quite a good laugh,' says the builder, who still lives in Keighley. 'At weekends we would go up to the Northern Soul nights at Wigan Casino and take all sorts of mind-bending drugs. Robbie was always really into the drug-taking bit and I think it ended up being his downfall.'

But he had one other big pastime – women. Well sought after among the local female population he was, in the words of one local girl, 'drop-dead handsome'. 'He was always a real heart-throb at school with his highlighted hair, tasty body and cheeky grin,' says the local hairdresser, who lives close to Graham's parents today. An experienced lover, he claimed to have lost his virginity to a babysitter at the age of 13 and slept with a series of married women through his mid-teens. 'He was a real lad, who had a silver tongue with the girls from year one,' recalls Towler. 'He was a complete womanizer and always had a girl on the go.'

For this reason, it certainly came as something of a surprise to many when he settled down with a woman called Cathy from Blackburn, whom he got married to at the age of 18. A trying relationship – riddled with frequent rows over his laziness and drunkenness – they divorced, according to ex-girlfriend Louise Deravairere, after less than two years, leaving

Robbie emotionally scarred, back home, out of work and depressed.

According to Deravairere, it was this early jolt that led Robbie into his first bout of serious criminality, culminating in a prosecution for theft, burglary and stealing cars in October 1986 at Darwen court. Understood to have landed him a few months in Manchester's infamous Strangeways prison, it was here that he would end up meeting many of underworld contacts he is still in touch with today.

Either way, prison doesn't seem to have had the desired effect on Graham, as not long after being released he was once again using drugs and getting involved in other petty crime, claim old friends. He had also soon taken up with another serious girlfriend, this time a local hairdresser called Heather Parker. An attractive girl, who was prepared to try and help him stay on the straight and narrow, they fell deeply in love and he had soon moved into the small house she shared with her best friend Rita Thomas in the centre of Keighley.

The problem was he and Rita didn't get on and Graham, who liked to get his own way, was soon resorting to a range of horrific tactics to try and force her out of the house. 'He wanted me out of the house and basically bullied me relentlessly until I left,' recalls Thomas, who today works in a pharmacy in Keighley. 'He did just about everything from leaving broken glass on the sunbed, which I cut myself on, to wiping his arse on my clothes. Someone told me he also pissed on my bed.

'It was a horrific time and Robbie just got worse and worse until I agreed to leave,' adds Rita, who is now close to Robbie's ex, Heather. 'He got increasingly aggressive and started threatening me to make me leave. There were lots of mind games and I was scared of him and never understood why Heather didn't stand up to him.'

Inevitably things came to a head one night when Rita had to be up early one morning for work and Graham refused to stop making a racket. 'I had to be up at 6a.m. and he was drunk and making a lot of noise but when I asked if he could quieten down a bit he came at me like a pit bull, swearing and telling me to get lost. I locked myself in my room but he stood outside with a plate and a wooden spoon and carried on banging it all night so I couldn't sleep. He really scared me and the next day I decided to leave.'

Rita has hardly a good word to say about Graham today. 'He was a real lazy good-for-nothing sod and did not like to work. The only jobs he ever did were thieving and he spent most of his time in the pub. He was basically a pisshead and just wanted the easy life and Heather had to carry him all the time. He would do anything to get money and used to steal the rent money to go to the pub. Put it this way, it was no surprise to anyone when he ended up going to prison for burglary. It was plain and simple a lot easier to rob someone else than do an honest day's work.'

However, despite his obvious aversion to work, he and Heather moved into a house close to her sister in the village of Riddlesdon a few miles outside Keighley. Heather worked in a hairdressing salon in the village and had soon fallen pregnant, giving birth to their baby son Conor in 1988. It should have been a happy time, but Robbie was growing increasingly aggressive. Out of work, lazy and unmotivated, he preferred to draw dole and spend the day in the pub rather than earn a living to support his new family.

Never lifting a finger to help in the home, he would crawl in late at night from the pub and get into heated rows that would usually end up with Graham hitting Heather. He also began to steal from her, until after one huge row Heather decided to call it a day. Recalls Richard Towler: 'She doesn't like talking about it, but she told me that the stuff he did to her and the children was terrible. I know he was very violent and sensibly she kicked him out after just three months in the new house.'

Apparently uninterested in trying to make amends, or see his new son, Graham completely cut off from Heather and, despite appeals from friends and family, refused to pay any child maintenance. 'He has never paid a bean,' recalls Towler. 'We tried to make him see sense and encouraged him to take responsibility for his child but he simply wasn't interested. He told us all to get lost and it wasn't long before he upped and left to go to Spain.'

Luckily for Heather, when Robbie moved abroad, his parents quickly rushed to her rescue. Horrified with their son's behaviour they began to give Heather money for Conor's upbringing and, according to a friend of the family, have paid substantial amounts towards his upbringing ever since. Says Rita Thomas: 'They have been wonderful to Heather and done everything to try and make up for their son's behaviour. They have provided for him since he was a baby and often looked after him and his sister. They are a sweet couple and they don't deserve the shame Robbie has brought on them. No one can understand where he got it from, but as they say "there is always one rotten apple in every barrel".'

It is a saying that is certainly not lost on the Grahams themselves. With two other law-abiding children – one Steven, a fireman, the other, Janet, a high-flying area manager at the Halifax building society – the retired couple are almost lost for words to describe what has happened to their eldest son.

Speaking in the only interview they have given about their son, they revealed the anguish they felt as he got immersed in the shady world of timeshare as well as their concerns for the future.

Admitting that he had not spoken to his son for months, his softly spoken father Thomas says: 'Robbie went off at a tangent, lots of tangents and I really don't know where he got his criminal side from. We have never had any sort of criminality in our family, on either side. We were good, God-fearing, working-class folk from Salford. We were all hard-working and did well to get out. I don't understand Robert – where he got it from. We simply could not keep him on track. But I guess it is just random; there is nothing we can do.'

Talking at their smart four-bedroom semi-detached home on a private golf estate, a few miles outside Keighley, their world is a million miles from the sleazy life their son inhabits in Spain. There are obvious trappings of wealth, from the personalized number plate on their car to a well-clipped front and back garden with fountain and pond. Inside the house it's just as one might expect. Impeccably tidy, with comfortable sofas and tasteful decor, there is much evidence of an otherwise happy family with photos of their grandchildren and extended family on the mantelpiece. Unsurprisingly, there isn't a picture of their eldest son.

Grim-faced, but cordial and polite, they both listened intently to the latest news about the case in Spain and in particular where their son is currently living. While his mother is said to have 'completely disowned' her son, who has not been back to Keighley for years, his father has continued to see him, travelling over to Spain at least once a year under the guise of a golf holiday. Ignoring his frequent appeals for money, he refused to admit that he might be guilty of murder.

After listening carefully to the facts, he says: 'Most of the people in the timeshare industry are very dodgy. I have met quite a few of them through Robert, including Tony King a couple of times, and I must say I didn't take to them at all. There are a lot of strange people who are running away from things. It is a dodgy world.'

However for the record he adds: 'My son might have his problems but he is no murderer. My intention is to support my son in every way possible if I can. I believe he is innocent of these murders and there has been a lot of rubbish written about him.'

What he couldn't deny, however, were the number of offences their son had been convicted of in Britain over the last two decades. While he has mostly lived abroad since 1988, he has certainly seen the inside of various English prisons since then. Indeed, confirmed by official police files, he was convicted in February and September 1989, in both Leeds and Keighley, for breaking and entering, robbery and driving without a licence. The files also show that he went on to pass his driving test on 17 September 1990, but lost it just two months later on 20 November 1990 after being convicted of drink-driving in a stolen car at Greenwich court. Two days later, he was convicted again at Grays court in Essex of stealing £350 in cash.

He received various custodial sentences for these crimes, and while the Official Secrets Act makes it impossible to confirm, by his own admittance in court and to his ex-girlfriends he has spent time in Strangeways, Risley Remand, Stile and Parkhurst prisons.

According to his ex-girlfriend Deravairere he also claimed to have escaped from Preston prison, a fact that might ring true, going on an interview with a girl he dated in the early 1990s.

The girl in question is Lynda Shorter, and she first met Rob Graham, as she calls him, in the summer of 1991 or 1992, she cannot remember exactly. She had been on holiday with a mate in Tenerife's infamously seedy Playa de las Americas when he had come on strong in a nightclub and they had ended up in bed. Working in timeshare, she remembers he had the gift of the gab and money and they had a few drunken (and unmemorable) nights, before she came home. She certainly didn't expect to see him again so it came as something of a shock when the troublemaker suddenly arrived on her doorstep unannounced a month or two later.

Living at the time with her toddler son Alan in a small council house in the Basildon suburb of Pitsea, she certainly had her reservations, but he had soon moved in regardless. 'He said he loved me and had nowhere else to stay,' she recalls. 'I kind of took pity on him. He told me his ex-wife had thrown him out and he had a picture of his son to prove it. He knew how to play the emotional card and seemed like a nice guy and was definitely handsome. Even though I always felt he was just using my place as something of a stopgap, I did really fall for him and allowed him to move in.'

While initially things were fine, her former neighbour Irene Mann recalls how the relationship soon got violent and abusive. 'He was a lazy good-for-nothing creep,' she says. 'He thought he was God's gift to women and really fancied himself. The truth was he was repulsive, arrogant and patronizing and thought work was beneath him. He didn't pay for anything and spent most of his time in the pub. No one liked him around here and it speaks volumes that during the year or so that he lived here, Lynda's son went to live with his father. You could set your clock by him getting up and leaving the house at 1p.m., in his tracksuit probably going off to rob someone.'

Pointedly, she recalls his aggressive behaviour towards Lynda and in particular her dog. 'You often heard him screaming at her, and while Lynda never told me what went on behind her front door, the police were round a few times. On top of that he would often kick her collie dog in the back garden and street. You would hear the poor thing yelp. He was an aggressive man with a nasty temper. He certainly treated her badly and didn't like her going out to mingle with her friends. He kept her under tight control and expected all his meals cooked on time. She did everything and he paid for nothing. He never lifted a finger.'

While Lynda is hesitant about admitting that Graham ever raised a finger to her, she confirms his quick temper and aggression. 'He certainly didn't have any money and wasn't the world's hardest worker. He told me he was a builder by trade, but he hardly ever did any building in the year we were together. I went out to work all day at Sainsbury's to pay for food and everything else. He just swanned around and did nothing.' And then came one of the shocks of her life.

It had been early one morning when there was a sharp knock on the door and Lynda had opened it to a carload of burly policemen, who stormed in demanding to see Robbie. Despite hinting that he was a fugitive on the run, they wouldn't go into specifics. 'They just took him off into a side room to charge him. Next thing I know he was being carted away in handcuffs. It was certainly something of a shock and the next thing I heard he was in Parkhurst prison on the Isle of Wight.'

Lynda, who is now married, but still lives nearby, ended up visiting Graham in prison a couple of times, before calling it a day a few weeks after he got out. 'I never got a straight answer out of him about his crimes. What was he in for? He would not tell me anything and I thought, what is the point? I don't particularly want to mix with criminals and people in prison and I quite frankly didn't trust him any more. I knew he had this girlfriend up north with a child, and I knew he wasn't paying any maintenance. I was fed up with him and after a couple of weeks of getting out of prison, I had had enough and told him to pack his bags and leave. I'm pleased to say he did and I never saw him again.'

Back in Spain, Graham was starting to use Tony King as he used his ex-girlfriends, a relationship that certainly suited him more than King. Indeed, under Robbie's strong and overbearing influence, King was buying increasingly large amounts of drugs on top of the high levels of alcohol. It was money he could ill afford to spend and, according to his ex-boss Jon Daniels, he was also investing in packs of Viagra, steroids and, increasingly, cocaine and ecstasy. 'He and Robbie were some of my best customers for Viagra and pills,' says Daniels, who admits that one of his main sidelines at the time was importing Viagra and other 'sex pills' into Spain from Gibraltar. 'Tony would buy them by the dozen and was taking them practically every night with a cocktail of other things.' It was leading to frequent mood swings as well as wreaking havoc with his sex drive.

His anguish was certainly apparent to his mother. 'He made it clear right from the start that he didn't trust Robbie Graham and he said Celia didn't like him either,' she recalls. 'Celia herself even phoned a few times to say that she felt Tony was being manipulated by Robbie and there was some threatening behaviour involved. Tony certainly told me that Graham was a deadly and lethal person and that he was involved with a stinking bad lot. He said he had no respect for women and that he bragged about various sexual attacks and rapes. He said; I don't want him in my life but I just can't leave. It was as if Graham had some sort of hold on him. It was very strange.'

It wasn't long before he was phoning up in tears telling her that their association was putting pressure on his marriage. He told her that Robbie was demanding he came out every night – sometimes for extra work, sometimes for drinking – and that Celia wasn't having it. 'He said she had given him an ultimatum to choose between her or Robbie.'

Celia, of course, had every reason to be upset. By now living in an apartment in Riviera del Sol, she would frequently find herself at home alone looking after their toddler Sabrina, while Tony would go out gallivanting with his workmates. 'He was getting home later and later and each time with a different excuse,' she recalls. 'He would be leaving the house at 9a.m. and not coming back until 10 or 11p.m. at night, sometimes much later and he would usually roll in plastered, unable to hold a conversation, and would quickly fall over and fall asleep on the sofa. He would always have an excuse. He lost track of the time, he had ended up getting drunk with Robbie or Jon. Whatever, we had all the usual arguments. He would never tell me where they had been and was quite evasive. I would have been at home holding the baby all night. It was really frustrating and very annoying.

'But it got worse when I got an evening bar job to bring in a bit of extra money, but I obviously couldn't go until he got home because of the baby. It made me an unreliable worker and this caused tension and problems at work. It just wasn't fair, but that was Tony, he was like that.'

Disturbingly, she says it was around this time that he started to sometimes disappear again in the middle of the night, but any questions about where he had been or what he had been up to were strongly avoided and he would clam up. It got to the point where they practically stopped speaking apart from to discuss how much money Tony had brought in for his family's food and maintenance.

'Tony was drunk most of the time. If there was a bottle of whisky in the house he would finish it. I can't say he was an alcoholic, I am not a doctor, but if it was there he would polish it off. Then I discovered where all the money for the household was going when my sister told me that he was taking a lot of cocaine with Jon and Robbie. We never had a bean to rub together and he would make all these excuses like on the occasion when he said a gypsy had robbed him of a few thousand pounds.'

Things were also getting difficult for Tony at work, with Graham drawing him into increasingly murky water. Recalls one former rep: 'Tony wasn't the best salesman in the world, but his main problem was being connected to Robbie'. This was indeed the case as Robbie devised a scheme to start skimming profits from Daniels, on top of his salary. It involved using his and Tony's personal bank account details, rather than the firm's, for clients to pay into. Between them, according to sources, they siphoned off thousands of pounds every month with Tony later claiming that Robbie threatened him with violence if he told anyone. 'There was definitely some dodgy dealing going on,' recalls Daniels's former right-hand man Peter Moore. 'Tony and Robbie were working some scam but I have no idea to what extent.'

Naturally when Daniels found out all hell broke lose. He went ballistic, sacking Robbie on the spot and was rightly convinced that his brother-in-law was also involved, or at the very least knew all about it. It led to increasingly bitter arguments and, according to Celia, the pair actually came to blows in David's Bar, in Calahonda, at Christmas 1998. 'Jon felt he had been conned out of money and that Christmas I had to actually push Tony out of the house to keep him and Jon apart,' recalls Celia. 'I didn't want it kicking off in front of my mother and the kids.'

The situation got worse when Tony unwittingly revealed to Celia's younger sister Ingrid that her husband Jon was still shagging his ex-partner Tracy Roberts behind her back. It caused considerable animosity between them and, unsurprisingly, early in 1999 King found himself out of yet another timeshare job, sacked 'officially' for failing to make any sales, and with £3,000-worth of commissions unpaid.

It was a major blow to Celia, who had just started to relax and get into the life on the Costa del Sol. Suddenly the money had dried up, just like the sex, and for a few weeks Tony did little more than hang around the house and mope. Luckily, however, he had soon found himself a job as a landscape gardener, although earning a paltry 500 euros a week; it was scarcely enough to cover the bills once he'd given Celia a few hundred for Sabrina. And then, according to his mother, the pay actually went down to as little as 300 euros a week, as the company hit a bad spell, and he had to supplement his wages by washing up in a local restaurant.

Celia had, in effect, kicked him out and he drifted from job to job with no fixed abode, working at a series of restaurants, including Harbour Lights in Cabopino and Johansson's, run by a Dane, near Marbella. He claimed to be a chef, and according to one friend, was certainly able to cook. Tony would go on to work as a chef at a Norwegian restaurant in Elviria, where he was asked to leave after the manageress's husband got angry that Tony was always giving her massages after work. He soon appeared again at another restaurant, the Newmarket in La Cala, and did several months work as a barman and kitchen hand at the infamous underworld meeting point the Chicken Shack, where he would meet the likes of self-confessed gangster Dave Courtney.

Finally by the middle of 1999, he was working again for Jon Daniels, initially as an odd-job man in a new venture he had started called A Man Who Can! Advertising in the local English-speaking newspapers, it promised to find tradesmen for any type of job. According to Celia, it did well with the calls flooding in, and Tony was soon being called up to do all sorts of work here and there. He became one of Jon's most reliable workers.

But, more crucially around this time in 1999, he is also said to have landed a part-time job on casual wages as a waiter at the apartment/hotel Club Sultan in Marbella. It was here, during his regular morning shifts that he would first have come into regular contact with Dolores Vázquez, who had been the manager since the place opened in 1996. While both Vázquez and the hotel – which interestingly doubles as a timeshare resort – have strongly denied that King worked there, three different sources insist he did.

One, Tony's friend and former employer Julie Smith has no doubt that he and Dolores worked together at the Club Sultan in Marbella. 'I know two people who knew them from there. A Spanish friend, who played in a band there, said that she has seen Tony working as a waiter. Another friend, Chalkie, also told me Tony worked there under Dolores. If anyone knew, Chalkie did, as he knew Dolores and at one point was even considering investing in the Club Sultan.'

Even more persuasive is the evidence of one timeshare boss who had employed Tony and was living two blocks from the Club Sultan at the time. 'I used to go to the Sultan every morning for a coffee on the way to work and Tony, who I already knew fairly well, used to serve me. There is no question that he and Dolores knew each other and worked together.'

On top of this there are further rumours that King worked at

Dolores' house as a part-time gardener. As Celia recalls: 'Tony was doing a lot of gardening jobs at the time, many through A Man Who Can!, and there has been a lot of talk and speculation that he was working at her house. Unfortunately, it is impossible to prove.'

But there are other likely links as well, none stronger than the fact that Vázquez's on-off lover of ten years Alicia Hornos – Rocío Wanninkhof's mother – was working as a cleaner at Lubina Sol at the same time as Tony.

While many people I interviewed claimed that they had seen Dolores Vázquez at Lubina Sol, the likelihood of the pair coming into contact is indisputable. What is also certain, meanwhile, is that Tony King would have come into contact with Hornos's daughter Rocío, aged 19, who not only occasionally turned up at Lubina Sol to help her mother clean, but who worked as a babysitter/childminder at the Club Sultan for at least one summer. It is likely that he would have taken a shine to the attractive and bubbly teenager, who was both sexy and flirtatious. But did they ever speak? It is impossible to say.

It is also impossible to say for certain where Tony King was working in October 1999, the month of Rocío's death. Strangely neither Celia, her sister Ingrid, nor any of his former colleagues can place exactly where he was, although it seems most likely that he was back working at Lubina Sol, or at the very least for Jon Daniels. He was certainly back on good terms with Daniels, who had kept him in regular employment throughout the year, and was still incredibly close to Graham.

He was also still living with Celia at their apartment in Riviera del Sol; even though the relationship was under great strain. One thing that everyone was sure about was that his behaviour on the night of 9 October 1999 was undeniably strange.

Chapter Eleven

The Innocent Teenager, the Guilty Stepmother

By all accounts, Rocío Wanninkhof was a normal, happy teenager. Living in a quiet housing development above La Cala de Mijas, she was both popular and had a promising future in teaching. The youngest of three children, she was attractive with long blonde hair and typically dark Spanish eyes. Add to this an hour-glass figure (she was 1.65m tall and weighed 58 kilos) and it was little surprise she was rarely without a boyfriend.

Born in Mijas, the half-Dutch, half-Spanish 19-year-old had mostly been brought up by her mother after her father Guillermo had returned to Holland, to live in Rotterdam, in the mid-1980s. Despite the split, however, she had grown up into a well-balanced and intelligent girl, who spoke several languages including Spanish, Dutch and English. Always keen to get on, she would frequently take weekend and holiday jobs (including working with her mother occasionally at Lubina Sol) and for a time, worked as an au pair to British businessman Cliff Stanford, founder of technology company Redbus Interhouse (he later offered a £100,000 reward to help find her killer).

She had recently begun a teacher-training course at Malaga University and, like most students of her age, at the weekend she liked to party. Saturday, 9 October 1999 was no exception. Having spent the afternoon with her boyfriend Antonio José Jurado Trujillo, who also lived in La Cala, she was heading home at 9.30p.m. to shower and change for the Fuengirola carnival – a ten-minute bus ride from her home – when she mysteriously disappeared.

Just a few weeks away from her twentieth birthday, she had left Antonio's house near the roundabout on the main N-340 highway to take the short uphill walk – perhaps little more than a kilometre – to her house in nearby La Cortijera. She wouldn't take long and had arranged to meet up with a group of friends at the carnival not long after ten, possibly firming up arrangements on her mobile phone as she walked.

But about halfway up the lane that continues on to the Costa del Sol racecourse she was attacked and killed. It would have been approaching 9.45p.m. and already dark when she met her killer between the two developments of Limonar (meaning Lemon Grove) and Los Claveles (carnations).

Little more than five minutes later and she was lying mortally wounded, having been stabbed eleven times, eight times in the back.

Naturally anxious when her daughter hadn't returned by the early hours of the morning, her mother Alicia decided to go and look for her. She couldn't sleep and about midday on the Sunday she decided to go out with a friend to look for her. She was soon joined by Rocío's, boyfriend Antonio and his friend Raúl, as well as other close neighbours.

A few hours later, early Sunday afternoon – about 500 metres from her home – she came across what every mother must fear finding when their child goes missing; her shoe and a pool of blood by the side of the road.

Police were on the scene within minutes and secured the area with tape. They soon confirmed that the trainer was one of Rocío's and five metres from the road they found a tissue with her blood on it. From there a trail of blood led into nearby scrubland suggesting she had been chased in a blind panic uphill, until just over 12 metres away they found the chilling evidence that confirmed she had almost certainly been stabbed to death. In a slight depression at the top of a slope they found a deep pool of blood, which suggested she had bled to death for two to three hours.

Nearby was another small trail of blood, 53.35cm in length, which strongly hinted that someone had later returned to pick up her body. Police were certain she had been dragged to a car; her blood having been mixed with dust making it lumpy. Tellingly, where the blood ran downhill there were tyre prints over the bloodstains.

It was extremely ominous and within hours the whole of the urbanization – and thousands of people from those nearby – were on the streets and hunting high and low for her body. Indeed over the next month teams of searchers covered around 75 square miles as far as the inland village of Tolox.

Friend of the family and former neighbour John Leech, who owned a bar on her estate, remembers well the anxious four weeks of waiting before her body turned up in Marbella. His pub, Tony's Bar, was just two doors up from Rocío's house in La Cortijera and his daughter had known the missing teenager since they attended school together.

'She was a normal, fun-loving Spanish girl, very attractive and always friendly,' recalls Leech, who has lived on the Costa del Sol for nearly 20 years. 'She used to come into my bar with kittens she had found and beg our regulars to take them in and give them homes. She was a real sweetheart and wouldn't have harmed anyone. None of us could understand it.'

The Londoner – who by coincidence often did odd jobs for Graham and King – recalled how for the next four weeks the

Guardia Civil organized search teams to scour the nearby woods and hills for her body. 'Every Sunday we all went out in our thousands looking for her,' recalls Leech, a stocky bear of a man, who is still clearly cut up by the death. 'We would all meet up by the nearby Mijas fairground and go off into the woods in a different direction each time. I used to dread finding her and with teenage daughters of my own was finding it hard to sleep at night.'

And then on Tuesday, 2 November 1999 came the news that everyone had been expecting when the body of the 19-year-old was found on waste ground up the coast in Los Altos del Rodeo, in Marbella. Exactly 32 kilometres from the spot she had been killed; she was found in the grounds of a tennis and social club in long grass that was inaccessible in the extreme. It certainly begged the question, why her attacker would have risked driving such a long way up a national highway that is always regularly patrolled by police, when he could simply have disposed of her body in thick, unvisited mountain undergrowth just a few kilometres inland?

The body had been dumped rather than buried and was already in an advanced stage of decomposition, which experts described as 'exceptional' for the amount of time it had been left. Indeed her body had all but turned into a skeleton and was even mummified in parts. Despite reports that she had been set alight, the experts first believed that she might have been kept in water, before putting it down to the amount of rain there had been that month. Either way it meant she had to be identified by dental records, and in particular through her wisdom teeth and fillings.

But it was the way her body had been left that really interested the investigators. Naked, apart from a bra, her legs had been deliberately pinned open by the attacker after dumping her, probably in an attempt to make it look like she had been raped. Next to the body were a trio of bags that had been filled with her clothes to add to the rape scenario. The truth was, they soon discovered, she had not been raped at all. Indeed, from tests of her pubic hair and remaining skin it didn't even appear she had been sexually assaulted. Even more bizarrely, the clothes in the bag were in an almost perfect state. The blood-stains had not deteriorated and there was neither mould, nor insects and they straightaway decided the bags had been dumped there much more recently. It was proving to be the most baffling of cases.

Pathologists soon established that the cause of death was from the first stab wound to her chest, which was near to the heart. It was a deep and violent stab, which would have certainly immobilized her and probably punctured her lung leading to death. There were further stab wounds in the fourth left rib, one in the eighth, one in the ninth vertebra and one in the left shoulder blade. The tenth left rib was actually fractured by the knife meaning that the knife was extremely sharp and approximately 1.15cm wide by 2mm thick. Other stab wounds were in the neck and in the lung area and the pathologists believed that she suffered an attack in the face as she was bleeding near the teeth.

They concluded that it must have been a 'very violent' attack for various reasons. First, it is rare to see bone actually fractured by a knife wound, and second, the fact that she had been repeatedly stabbed in the back, while she was probably still and already unconscious, shows a significant loss of control. This, according to the investigators, suggested a crime of passion and that the attacker had certainly intended to kill the girl.

As John Leech recalls: 'It was a terrible, terrible day and being my daughter Jessica's birthday, it is one we will never forget. The whole of Mijas went into mourning and when they brought her body back for her funeral a few days later there were literally thousands of people present. Her body was laid to rest in the tiny chapel in La Cala and a mourning bell sounded throughout the day. It was very moving.'

But Leech, who still lives in the area, was amazed, in particular, at the slack way in which the murder site had been sealed off. According to him, anyone could have walked on to the crime scene in La Cala the night after her disappearance, and picked up gory souvenirs. 'You could pick up cigarette ends and perhaps more alarmingly drop them,' he claims. 'There was no one guarding it and because it wasn't covered when it rained the following day half the evidence must have been washed away.

'It wasn't as if the police hadn't been warned. The forecasters had been predicting rain for days and fittingly the skies had darkened considerably on the day after she disappeared. God knows how much evidence was lost, but the whole operation seemed distinctly shambolic and badly organized.'

It was an inauspicious start to one of the most bizarre and protracted – some might say amateur – murder investigations ever seen in Spain. Falling under the remit of the Guardia Civil and not the National Police – as it had taken place in a town of under 30,000 inhabitants (Mijas has 10,000 residents) – the investigation would be headed by Capitán Fuster and the murder squad in Malaga, with a local office under Juan Ramirez in nearby Fuengirola. It was to be the beginning of a five-year investigation that would look into around 500 individuals and end up charging three.

Naturally, perhaps, the finger first pointed, as it so often does, to Rocío's loved ones and, in particular, her boyfriend and her father. Guillermo Wanninkhof would be the first to come under suspicion. An ordinary guy from the Netherlands, who had worked on the Costa del Sol in 'a variety of jobs', he had apparently returned to Holland in something of a hurry in the middle of the 1980s after falling out badly with Rocío's mother. The police straightaway thought there might have been a drug connection. Predictably, of course, there was a suggestion that he was involved in the famously burgeoning drug scene that has its focus in the Dutch capital Amsterdam. But after a few weeks of digging, the rumours appeared completely unfounded. 'It was rubbish,' says Leech. 'He was a lovely man, a real gentleman and in no way linked to the crime world. They were back to square one.'

Next up was boyfriend Antonio Trujillo, who had been dating Rocío for nine months, having met her the previous year. The son of a taxi driver, he was said to have had a heated row with Rocío culminating in her storming out of the house on that fateful night. But according to sources, it was little more than a lovers' tiff (later he said he was too tired to go the carnival and had gone to bed soon after she left at 9.30p.m.) and it was certainly the first time he had let his girlfriend walk home alone. Indeed, they were said to be 'very happy together' and were even planning to get engaged the following February.

It didn't stop the police, however, putting a great deal of effort into investigating the youngster and he was questioned several times, and even had his phone tapped. Later, in court he stated, somewhat comically, that the police had actually insinuated that he might have gone up to his bedroom, and then jumped off the balcony without being seen and followed her up the road to kill her.

Frustrated again, the police started to look into a series of known paedophiles and other dangerous criminals living on the Costa del Sol. Their long list, it can be revealed, included one Tony King, who had arrived in Spain in 1997. But somehow, somewhat inexplicably – particularly in light of the fact that Rocío's mother (and indeed often Rocío) had worked at Lubina Sol since 1996, therefore at some point alongside King – the police never came looking for him.

'We never understood it,' said his sister-in-law Ingrid Pantoja. 'The police asked questions all over La Cala and even came into David's Bar, in Riviera del Sol, which was practically next door to where Tony and Celia lived. Had they knocked on my door or Celia's, I'm sure we'd have said something. We were both quite suspicious of Tony and his behaviour at the time.'

But while they had every reason to be suspicious of King – whose movements on the night had been bizarre in the extreme – somehow, the two sisters talked themselves out of it. 'At the time we thought we were going crackers,' recalls Ingrid. 'We had various conversations with several different people about whether he could have been involved or not, but somehow we didn't take the matter further.'

Their fears had first surfaced at 'a girlie night' at Ingrid's Calahonda house on Friday, 15 October 1999 when Celia had arrived preoccupied with worry about her husband. In total there were six of them: Ingrid, Celia and their close friends Justine Daniels (Jon Daniels's sister and, later, a girlfriend of Robbie Graham), Jane Maynard (it was Jane's birthday), Amanda Lewis and Sarah Bell, who worked part-time as a nanny for Ingrid.

As Ingrid recalls: 'It was a couple of days after the disappearance of Rocío and posters had already gone up around the area, and in particular in Lubina Sol, where Rocío had often turned up to help her mum clean. It had been on the television and we all knew about her. Celia had just suddenly come out with it, how she was really worried that Tony had killed Rocío and she was thinking of going to the police. She said he had been out that night and had acted really suspiciously. We all talked about it. How strange he had acted around then, but somehow we came to [the] conclusion that he couldn't have done it.'

Their concerns centred on the fact that King had come in late (by Celia's reckoning between 11p.m. and 1a.m.) and after having a shower, gone straight out again. Not talking to his wife, who was already half asleep in front of the television, he

151

spent much longer in the bathroom than he normally would, and when he was finished, changed into new clothes and left without saying a word.

Celia thought it was suspicious. 'I remember him coming in at some point in the evening,' she recalls. 'He went straight to the bathroom. I could hear the shower going and him washing himself. I can't remember the exact time, but I know we didn't talk – we rarely did at that point – and he went straight out again wearing, as I recall, a black shirt and jeans. I remember thinking it was strange that he had gone out so quickly again after having a shower and I got up to look in the bathroom expecting to find his dirty clothes all over the floor, as usual, but there was nothing. The bathroom was spotless. He had completely cleaned up after himself for once, and left no clothes lying around. It was strange and it made me wonder what was going on here?

'The next thing I knew I was woken up at about 2a.m. (in her official transcripts she says 3a.m.) and the phone was ringing from my friend Jane, whose car Tony had borrowed earlier in the evening. She was quite anxious and concerned that her car had not come back and she needed it early in the morning for work. She pleaded with me to try and track Tony down, but the problem was I had no idea where he was and said I'm really sorry, you know what he is like!'

Police believed that the reason that King had asked to borrow Maynard's car was that having punctured two tyres on his white Ford Fiesta while trying to move Rocío's dead body he needed to borrow another one to finish the job. While Maynard (a.k.a. Hills) confirmed to me that King did indeed borrow her car, a blue Ford Fiesta, that night – bringing it back in a bad state at about 4a.m. – she was unable to say at exactly what time he came round. 'I really can't remember exactly,' Maynard told me. 'You will have to look at the court transcripts. An hour or so is a small period when you are talking about four years ago.'

What is more certain is that a few days later he showed his sister-in-law Ingrid the two punctured tyres in the back of his Ford Fiesta, which he had already got two new tyres for. 'They were completely shredded to bits and I mean knackered,' says Ingrid. 'I could see right through to the strings and the rims were completely destroyed. It was incredible. I don't think he meant me to see them, as I recall I just happened to see into the boot, when I put a bag in or something. He gave me some half-cock reason for them and it really made me think.'

The police also took particular interest in that part of Ingrid's evidence – and indeed, spent a long period of time trying to track down the white Ford Fiesta, which Tony had bought from a fellow timeshare salesman Nigel Bateman in March 1999, and eventually written off over six months later in a controversial crash in Torrenueva. It has never been found.

Whatever, the state of the tyres and the mess in Maynard's car were the main topics of discussion that Friday night at Ingrid's. 'We got to talking about Tony that night and really got ourselves into a stew,' recalls Ingrid. 'Jane had certainly been very suspicious, particularly with the state he had returned her car in. She started putting two and two together about how he had borrowed her car and brought it back dirty. With me having seen the shredded tyres from his car, we became like detectives. We were really suspicious, but somehow after an hour or two decided that Tony couldn't have done it, somehow he was too sweet. He wasn't that way inclined.'

The suspicions were, however, to return the following morning when Maynard turned up unannounced at around 9a.m. 'She was really worried about the whole thing and wanted to go to the police,' recalls Ingrid. 'I remember it well. It was a Saturday and Jon's day off and she got us out of bed to talk it through, and again for some reason we talked ourselves out of it.'

As Celia concludes: 'We all basically came to the conclusion that there was no hard evidence and after a while they calmed me down saying he couldn't have done it. They told me not to be silly, "he's not like that", "it could not be him", he is so calm and lovely with the kids, it's just not his way. They talked me out of it and made me feel I was being stupid. We didn't discuss it again, and then a few months later they pulled in Dolores Vázquez for the murder and life moved on. While subconsciously I might have had my doubts, on the surface I didn't give it a second thought.'

The Guardia Civil, of course, didn't have this luxury. Constantly reminded by the public and media that Rocío's killer was still at large, as 1999 drifted into the new millennium they came under increasing pressure to make more arrests.

It was, in fact, almost a year to the day of Rocío's death that they finally arrested the former lesbian lover of Rocío's mother. Swooping in on the evening of 7 September 2000, the Galician-born 50-something-year-old was taken to Mijas and then Fuengirola police station for questioning. The arrest had certainly been for show and she had emerged from her house, El Retiro, in La Cala de Mijas, to dozens of blinking cameras, before shouting to a neighbour to keep an eye on her elderly mother as she was led to a police car.

After two days of interviews she was formally charged and sent to Alhaurín de la Torre prison (where King was also kept) to await the trial, which began the following year.

On the surface it certainly seemed that the police had got their man and unsurprisingly, it took the case to a whole new dimension. The Spanish press went rabid and suddenly La Cala de Mijas was once again swarming with journalists. The line being touted: that in a jealous rage Vázquez had stabbed to death the teenager after being dumped by the dead girl's mother. The tabloid press (which in Spain happens to be television rather than print) went on to run a series of TV documentaries about Vázquez being 'cold, demanding and violent', not to mention the fact that she was a lesbian!

The police investigation had taken around ten months, and involved a female detective living undercover in La Cala digging around for the truth. And while the police could find no forensic evidence against Vázquez, they managed to build up an impressive body of evidence to point the finger at her.

Her trial in September 2001 at Malaga's Supreme Courts of Justice proved to be one of the biggest Spain has ever seen and was covered across the country's front pages and main news bulletins throughout its two-week duration. It ended in a conviction and a 15-year sentence for the hotel manager, who had effectively brought Rocío up as her own child.

The facts were thus: María Dolores Vázquez Mosquera had met Alicia Hornos Wanninkhof at the end of 1981, while she was going through a trial separation from her Dutch husband Guillermo Wanninkhof, who worked in the same hotel as Vázquez. Alicia would occasionally stay at Dolores' house to get away from allegedly violent attacks by her husband, and the pair had soon launched into a steamy affair and had fallen deeply in love. It had naturally caused all sorts of upset when the Dutchman had discovered his wife's infidelities particularly with another woman and after a series of angry rows the pair decided to proceed to divorce. He had soon returned to Holland, where he has since found a new partner, while Alicia stayed on in Spain and the following year, when Rocío was still only two years old, Alicia moved into Vázquez's house, renting her home out to a Swedish family.

Their relationship went from strength to strength and in 1988 the pair had moved into a large, detached house just yards from the sea called El Retiro, in La Cala de Mijas, with Alicia claiming to have contributed some 15 million pesetas (or approximately £60,000) towards the 70 million cost.

The court heard that by the early 1990s they had become a well-established lesbian couple, with Dolores – or Loli, to friends – taking up the role of fathering the two children. It was a job she took with apparent relish, being both compassionate and authoritarian, and Rocío's children took her surname and were said to look up to her. But by the middle of the 1990s their relationship started to cool, amid allegations of infidelities (in particular the accusation that Dolores had had an affair with a cousin in Santander).

By 1995 the pair had all but split and Alicia and her two children moved to another smaller house nearby. But while Alicia went back to dating men, and one local man in particular, she and Dolores stayed in touch and throughout 1998 and early 1999 were said to be dating again. The problem was, while Dolores was completely in love with Alicia and desperately wanted her to move back in, Alicia was far less keen. Continuing to date men at the same time, she was crucially said to be under pressure from her daughter Rocío to keep her distance from Vázquez.

The prosecution's case hinged on the fact that Rocío and Vázquez had become sworn enemies of each other in Rocío's final year. Describing it as a crime of passion, prosecutor Mr Montijano claimed that Dolores had killed Rocío, believing she was the stumbling block against her rekindling her relationship with Alicia. 'She blamed Rocío for their emotional problems,' stated Montijano, adding that Dolores believed it was Rocío, who was stopping Alicia from moving back in with her.

It was with this in mind that the two of them were said to have crossed paths at 9.40p.m. on the night of the murder. While Rocío would normally have crossed the road to avoid Dolores, whom she avoided like the plague, on this occasion, the prosecution claimed, she was unable to do so and an argument ensued. It led to Dolores first hitting Rocío in the mouth and then taking out a knife, which she was carrying for self-defence, and stabbing her fatally as she tried to run away.

The prosecution continued that after dragging the body out of sight of the road, Dolores left it for a few hours before returning at 2a.m. to move the body to Marbella, where she dumped it at a place she knew well and made it appear to have been a sex attack.

In total the prosecution had over 30 pieces of evidence to put to the jury over the two-week trial that began on 3 September 2001. Collectively it made for a very convincing case.

First of all the prosecution tackled the motive and the fundamental claim that Dolores had good reason to want to kill Rocío. This hinged around demonstrating that they were sworn enemies and the contradictions between the claims of Vázquez and Rocío's family couldn't have been more pronounced.

Indeed, while Dolores claimed in court that they had a good relationship and that Rocío 'not only admired her but wanted to be like her', those close to Rocío painted a very different picture. Her sister Rosa, for example, was in no doubt. While she admitted that she herself looked up to Dolores 'like a father', she claimed Dolores simply did not get on with Rocío. She added that Rocío would have nothing to do with Dolores, and admitted that while at first she didn't believe that Dolores could have been guilty, with time, she became convinced of it. 'As far as Loli was concerned, the reason that Alicia would not come back to her was the fault of Rocío,' she said. 'It is possible that this provoked revenge against the family.'

Rocío's best friend Alicia Perez Garcia, who had known her since she was nine, confirmed that Rocío would always cross the street if she saw Dolores coming the other way. She added that Rocío had told her that she 'didn't like' Dolores, nor the sexual relationship she had with her mum. She also explained how when Rocío came home to find Dolores' car parked outside her house she would ask her friend if she could hang around at her house until her mother's lover had gone.

Finally, Rocío's mother Alicia confirmed that Rocío had indeed been against her moving back in with Dolores and was particularly against 'the lesbian aspect' of their relationship. In an emotional, but convincing performance, she claimed that despite her daughter's protests she had no intention of living with her again anyway. She explained why, going on to paint a picture of Dolores being 'possessive, violent, dominant and jealous'. And added that she was a complete disciplinarian and after one beating from her stepmother, Rocío told her prophetically that 'Dolores is going to kill me and you are not going to do anything to stop her'. She also recalled how on one occasion Dolores had started cutting Rocío's hair viciously without her permission and another time how she had kept her grounded for three months because she had bad grades at school. She concluded by saying that Rocío hated Dolores and blamed her mother for having to see her at all.

Finally, to cement the fact that Rocío and Dolores were enemies, the prosecution introduced a tape recording of a phone conversation held between Dolores and a friend, five months after the murder, in which Dolores clearly admits that Rocío hated her. While Dolores had earlier denied that Rocío hated her in court, it proved to be damning evidence.

There were numerous other bits of evidence, however, that helped to convict the lesbian hotel manager. These included psychological reports which showed that Dolores had 'a quick and explosive temper', with the prosecution giving a few examples, including a time in the Canary Islands, for example, when she had apparently sent a man to hospital after he annoyed a friend of hers.

Later a psychologist from Alhaurín prison described Vázquez as a compulsive person, who relies on other people for emotional support. 'Two elements which she has in common with violent delinquents,' he added. While he admitted that she did not have any mental disturbances, there was certainly evidence of a jealous personality. Another psychologist, who had attempted to get friendly with Dolores while working for the police, gave a profile of the accused being a 'cold, demanding and occasionally violent person'. Bizarrely, Dolores denied knowing the woman.

Vázquez was also apparently caught out lying on a couple of crucial issues. The first time hinged around her alibi that on the night of the murder she had been at home all evening looking after her elderly mother and the two-year-old daughter of her niece. This was, however, proved to be untrue when the chef of her local restaurant, Oasis, came forward to claim that she had in fact come into his restaurant after 11.30p.m., sweating and agitated, to buy tobacco. Wearing cycling trousers, a sweatshirt, and a bumbag, she had told the chef she was out of breath as she had been out for a run to 'clear her head because her mother had been very restless'. A shame-faced Vázquez was forced to admit that yes, she had been out to buy cigarettes as she did every day, but that she was 'not at all agitated'.

The waitress Encarnación Lozano added that Vázquez's reaction when the body was found was decidedly 'strange' and that she believed that she was putting on an unusual act at times, and wasn't surprised when she was arrested.

A further sensational claim by the chef that she had seen flames coming out of Loli's chimney on the night of the murder – suggesting she was burning evidence – was later apparently contradicted by other members of staff, who said that it had actually been a few months later, when she was cleaning the chimney.

But the hotel boss was proven to have lied a second time, however, when she insisted that – despite police evidence – her car had not been used or lent to anyone in the days after the murder. This apparent discrepancy came about when seven days after Rocío's death on 16 October 1999, a red Toyota Celica was seen driving slowly around the scene of the crime. According to a police report on the incident, the car had finally come to a halt and someone had got out to survey the scene, before noticing four policemen, and quickly getting back in the car and driving off. The policemen noted there were two youths in the car and took down the car registration. It turned out to be Dolores' car. But when they asked her if she had lent the car to anyone she said 'no' adding that it had been broken down and in the garage on the day in question.

This was later proven to be a lie as not only did the garage confirm that her car had in fact only come in to be fixed more than a week later on 25 October, but other witnesses saw the car working at that time. It was one of the main discrepancies in her bid for freedom.

Perhaps more damning, however, was the evidence of her cleaner, a Ukranian woman, Tetyana Kozmukhar, who said she had seen her boss stabbing a 'missing' poster of Rocío in her house, shouting 'problem, my problem!' While, in court, Dolores claimed it was a spoon or fork and not a knife, the cleaner was, unfortunately, unable to remember the exact day it happened, or whether it was before or after her body was discovered.

Further evidence, strongly denied by Vázquez, came from a witness who said the accused had told her that when she went out running she always carried a knife as a weapon of self-defence in case of attack. Another witness told how the day after the murder he had spoken to Vázquez at a wedding and she had told him that she was tired and had hardly slept because her mother had kept her up half the night. The jury's attention was also drawn to the timing of a series of phone calls that Vázquez had made and received on the evening of 9 October, and in particular, that none had taken place at the time of the murder.

More convincing still was the intriguing fact that there had been family connections with the tennis and social club, where Rocío's body had been finally dumped, some 32 kilometres from her home. Confirmed by the owner of the club, it emerged that Rocío's uncle Jesús and his brother-in-law Serafín Ruiz, had been interested in renting the venue some months before the murder. The pair, it turned out, had actually visited the club on several occasions to discuss the possibility of renting it as it had become available that October. While unwilling or unable to give any reason why they had wanted to rent it, the owner was able to prove the connection by providing a phone number he had written in his diary for Jesús, in Jaen, where he lived.

The Guardia Civil claimed to have thoroughly investigated the two men, saying they had cast-iron alibis, and came to the conclusion that the body was dumped at the club to try and put the blame on them. The theory went that because the pair had something of a reputation as 'womanizers' and the fact that Rocío's body had been left in a position that suggested she had been raped, it was a deliberate ploy to get them accused.

Later, after the trial – in easily one of the most shocking bits of police work ever seen – it emerged that a report that supposedly showed that a fingerprint of Serafin Ruiz was found on one of the black plastic bags found at the crime scene was suppressed by the Guardia Civil.

The report by the force's fierce rivals, the National Police, was allegedly not admitted to the court proceedings because, according to a police source, it contradicted the findings of the Guardia Civil and 'would have caused confusion'. And then, in a bizarre cover-up attempt, the National Police came out to deny that the report – saying that the fingerprints coincided on 14 counts with those of Ruiz – officially existed, despite the fact that it had been printed in the Spanish media. A spokesman insisted that the report was sent to the media in a private capacity and that it 'did not follow the scientific method that is essential in any report issued by police sources, nor did it go through the normal procedural route. For that reason it has been repudiated.' He was backed up by forensic police in Malaga and by National Police HQ in Madrid. But the smell of intrigue still remains.

More importantly in the case against Vázquez, however, was

the evidence of a clairvoyant, Marisa Sevillano. In easily one of the strangest aspects of the trial, Sevillano claimed that just weeks before the crime Vázquez came to her consultation rooms for a reading and told her that a daughter, or a son, was preventing her getting back with the person she loved. She claimed that Vázquez then referred to 'Rocío' by name and that her 'hatred' towards her was 'of great intensity'. She said she had only come forward after seeing Dolores being arrested on television, and chillingly recalled that during the session Dolores had told her that the person she was in love with (i.e. Alicia) would later 'cry tears of blood'.

It left the jury and public gallery aghast, and as emotive evidence goes, was incredibly convincing. The only problem was that the prosecution had no forensic evidence linking Dolores to the crime scene after apparent fibres from Rocío's clothes found in her house were rejected. It gave her defence a major lifeline and they spent hours picking apart each aspect of the prosecutor's evidence.

Her barrister Pedro Apalategui made it clear that his client had always maintained her innocence and that the Guardia Civil had made numerous mistakes, including not allowing a lawyer present at her initial interviews. He pointed out that there were no fingerprints on any of the bags used to transport the body, that there was no proof of any fibres on the body corresponding to her house, and that in a whole year of having her phones tapped there was not a single incriminatory conversation recorded.

He summed up by saying that the case was being investigated by 'amateurs' and that it was only being instigated due to the strong media pressure to find a culprit. He finally went on to plead with the jury not to convict Dolores on the 'flimsy' evidence the prosecution had put forward.

But his appeal fell on deaf ears and on 19 September 2001, seven out of the nine jurors found her guilty of murder and six days later she was sentenced to 15 years in prison.

However, during an appeal against the sentence at the High Court of Granada on 1 February 2002, Vázquez's lawyers argued successfully that there was not a 'sufficient motive' to find her guilty. They argued that the evidence was 'too general' and not concrete enough. Furthermore, they pointed out that under Spanish law (article 24 of the constitution) a jury was not allowed to find a verdict on a case based on mere contradictions and suppositions.

The judge, Augusto Mendez de Lugo, agreed and annulled the guilty verdict ordering a retrial in Malaga the following year with a new jury and a new judge. Meanwhile, the prosecution was sent off to find better evidence to convict and a few weeks later Vázquez was given bail for the sum of 30,000 euros, having served a mammoth 17 months in prison.

The differences of opinion between the supporters of Dolores and the family of Rocío couldn't have been further apart. On one hand, her sister Elvira said it was good news and pleaded that the next trial be by a professional tribunal of judges and not a jury, to prevent it becoming another 'circus'. On the other side, the family of Rocío was devastated. After fainting, having heard the news, her mother Alicia said pointedly: 'They didn't catch her with the knife in her hand, but she definitely lied. The jury had 39 pieces of evidence against her and Dolores Vázquez is the murderer of my daughter. I will not rest until justice is done.'

Her sister Josefina Hornos was even more direct: 'Justice sucks! How can they use a jury and then not trust its verdict? It is a joke.'

Even the original judge Fernando Gonzalez Zubieta had a few words to say. In an unprecedented statement, he was reported to have said: 'I gave my all in that case and they have turned round and beaten me with a stick. I don't take it personally. I did what I should have done and followed all the rules of a jury trial. I wish a lot of luck to the colleague who takes over the next trial.'

Chapter Twelve

Life Falls Apart

While the wheels of justice were grinding, and then stuttering, to a dramatic halt in the case of the People versus Dolores Vázquez, Tony King was having a fairly spectacular life crisis of his own. Indeed just three months after the death of Rocío Wanninkhof in October 1999, his wife decided to walk out on him to move to a mobile home on a camping ground known as Calazul, in Mijas Costa.

It was to be the start of the most shambolic year of his life and, according to his mother, would regularly bring him close to a nervous breakdown. Celia was, however, in no doubt that she had made the right decision. 'I had been wanting to leave him for nearly a year, but quite frankly had been too scared to make the leap,' she says. 'We had talked about it a few times and I'd told him how having a trial separation would be good for both of us, leading our own lives, finding new partners for a while, but he wasn't convinced.

'He said he still loved me and didn't want to break up, but I knew it was for the best. We were living separate lives. I had my friends and he had his. I hardly saw him and assumed he was having an affair. We hadn't had sex for months and I had started to find pornographic videos in the tape machine.

'He had become an insomniac staying up all night, apparently watching these films, and never made an effort with me in bed. To be honest I had gone off sex anyway. I had the baby to look after and we were clearly leading separate lives. I had had enough of his behaviour and with Tony pretty much giving me almost no support, either financial or emotional, I was ready to move on. I guess it is entirely possible that his strange behaviour on the night of Rocío's death might have been the catalyst that finally helped me make the decision. I am sure, subconsciously, it did.'

While Celia was soon openly dating new boyfriend David Cooze – a former timeshare salesman from south Wales – Tony rapidly went off the rails. With no money coming in and nobody supporting him emotionally he had soon been evicted from the apartment she had left him rattling around in, and had spent a few months moving around the area like a nomad with no fixed abode.

Initially sleeping in his car and on the beach, he even spent a couple of nights under his former house in Riviera. As his mother recalls: 'He only told me the full truth later about living rough on the beach and in cars, but I knew he hardly had enough money to eat, and he once admitted to me he hadn't eaten for three days. He had a broken heart, but while I would get furious with Celia and curse her, he would always say it was not her fault.'

For a couple of months he managed to get a grace-and-favour flat through yet another stint of work at Lubina Sol, but by March 2000 he had been evicted after falling out with owner Roscoe Reynolds's girlfriend.

And then things got worse when in the same week he had a near fatal car crash on the N-340 motorway, near Torrenueva, in which he controversially, as we shall later see, drove his white

Ford Fiesta off the road and into a 12-foot deep embankment, from which he had to escape upside down.

The car was, quite naturally, a write-off, but somehow King managed to persuade his estranged wife to help him retrieve a bag from the wreck which had his passport inside. Massively shaken and with cuts and bruises all over his body, she took pity on him, and allowed him to come and stay in the spare room of her mobile home for a few days. This had soon turned into weeks and it was no surprise – with his continuing inability to get proper work and his erratic behaviour – that she had kicked him out by early summer.

It was perhaps inevitable that the only person he could then turn to was his best friend Robbie Graham. By then going through a difficult time of his own – having been kicked out of the house he was sharing with Justine Daniels in Balcon del Mar – he was living in a borrowed tent in the same campsite as Celia. Somewhat bizarrely, he invited King to stay.

As Graham admits: 'Tony was absolutely shot to pieces because he felt he had lost his daughter and his wife. It was all he cared about. He got really depressed and would tell me about all his problems and if he was pissed up he would start crying. He was desperate for someone to help him and I agreed to let him move in. It was anything but ideal, but he had nowhere else to go.'

Celia certainly recalls the comical situation of her husband and Graham living in this bright orange tent just a few hundred metres from her home. 'They became like a pair of dossers,' she recalls. 'They looked like down-and-outs and became scruffy, unkempt and smelly. They simply let themselves go and it was obvious they were both doing quite a lot of drugs and were incapable of holding down any sort of job. They drank so much beer they both got fat and would spend a lot of time in local bars cadging drinks and cigarettes. It was almost funny until I discovered they had been breaking into my home taking my food and money, while I was out.'

But by then Celia had both physically and emotionally moved on and was spending the majority of her time with her new boyfriend David, who works in real estate in Marbella. Living at David's house in Alhaurín, she had soon left the campsite for good, and arranged for Tony to keep the tenancy at the mobile home on the agreement that he paid all the bills.

But Tony was once again incapable of raising the sufficient funds and had soon been evicted, leading to yet another spell living in his car and wherever he could find a bed.

By late 2000, however, he had landed on his feet again in the mountain town of Coin, where he would later be accused of murdering Sonia Carabantes. In part due to his wife and daughter's move to nearby Alhaurín, the main reason appears to have been a new girlfriend, a high-flying PA at one of the coast's most successful estate agencies Interealty in Marbella.

It is unclear how the two had met, but she had soon set him up – like a toy boy – in a small house owned by friends behind a local slaughterhouse on the edge of town. Known only as Shelly, the busty English girl, who was in her late thirties, had been brought up in Spain and lived nearby with her mother and grandparents. A single parent with a daughter about the same age as Sabrina, according to Celia, she would come up to the small country house for regular sex sessions when she had a spare moment.

An educated and intelligent girl she was earning good money on the coast and was certainly another good catch for Tony, who was practically incapable of holding down a job. For a time things went well and the couple even went out for dinner with Celia and her new partner Cooze. But as per usual, Tony pressed the self-destruct button when he borrowed his new girlfriend's car to go out one night, got drunk and ended up crashing it into a tree behind La Cala golf course. 'It was a complete write-off,' recalls Cooze. 'She went ballistic. She needed it for work and was not about to give any sympathy to a drunkard, with no licence and no idea how to drive. As far as she was concerned that was that and she not only gave him his marching orders, but she got him kicked out of the house she had set him up in.'

However, Tony had by now started to make friends in the pubs and bars around Coin and nearby Alhaurín where he had luckily garnered something of a reputation for being a nice guy. He was also becoming popular with the large ex-patriot female crowd, with his well-honed body and all-year tan. This was reflected in one of the local English papers, *El Sol*, when it named him 'Hunk of the Week' with a big picture of Tony grinning at the camera on page 3.

According to acquaintances at the time, he always seemed to have a woman on his arm (causing some to suspect he was a rent boy) and, in particular, he dated a Finnish girl by the name of Heidi. 'It only lasted for a month or two,' says friend Simon Bowers. 'But he told me how he shagged her upside down, inside out and senseless.' While details of Heidi, who went back to live in Helsinki, are slim, he also managed to get a bit more stability in his life when he landed another regular job as a barman and occasional kitchen hand at the Chicken Shack pub in La Cala.

There, Julie Smith, who would become his boss and later close friend, said: 'He was a big emotional guy, who would often end up in tears. He was always very tender and tactile and was very protective of his family and friends. A lot of people complained about him being so quiet and not finding it easy to have a laugh with him, but when you got to know him he was incredibly sweet and supportive. He was always extremely good with his daughter Sabrina and would bend over backwards to help us. And I'll tell you another thing: he was an excellent worker.'

It was through the Chicken Shack that he would also find himself another good place to live.

Chapter Thirteen

My Year with the Costa Killer

Elena Ploughman couldn't have asked for more in a flatmate. Tidy and attentive, the British barman, whom she had met through her job as a waitress at the Chicken Shack, was also a dab hand in the kitchen and bent over backwards to ensure that she was happy. It was just as well. Stuck up a dirt track, without a car, in the middle of the Spanish mountains, Tony King would often be the only person she would talk to, let alone see, for days on end, and she soon got to know him as a brother.

Trusting him implicitly, the attractive Scandinavian, who speaks fluent English, had no qualms about wandering around the house in her underwear or sunbathing topless in the garden of the house that was some 20 miles inland from the Costa del Sol. While she insists there was never a physical relationship between them, she would often end up cuddling him on the sofa watching TV and occasionally fell asleep with him in the double hammock strung up on the terrace outside.

It was a close friendship, and while her friends keep telling her how lucky she was having lived with a 'sex monster', Ploughman still strongly believes that she was in no danger and is far from convinced that King is a murderer. 'I always thought he was the sweetest, nicest man and there was no way he would dream of betraying my trust and making a move on me,' says the Dane, over coffee at a bar near her home in Copenhagen.

'We lived completely out on our own in the mountains with only the goats and the bread man passing once a day,' she recalls. 'We couldn't get a telephone and we had to pick up our post from the post office in Coin. There were many days when Tony was the only person I saw, let alone talk to, and I trusted him with my life. He was a real gent and appeared to be every mother's dream son-in-law. He was always so kind and attentive that I never got a hint of what he was up to when he went out. I knew a lot of people down on the Costas who got up to bad things, and you never thought he was one of them.

'He certainly never lifted a finger to hurt any of his friends and he was lovely to his girlfriends and particularly his daughter Sabrina, who used to come up and stay most weekends. He obviously had a deeper, troubled side, and if he is guilty I pray he can get the help he needs to get better.'

It is about as far as she will go on entertaining the idea that he might be a murderer. Even when pushed about the possibility of him being a sex attacker – and chillingly King was linked to a handful of vicious sex attacks (although none proved) during the period they lived together – she still doubts that he was involved. 'Of course it makes my blood curdle to think that just hours before he would return home and stroke my hair on the sofa, those very same hands might have been strangling and sexually assaulting some poor victim,' says Elena, who now lives in her native Denmark. 'But I still don't believe he was doing that stuff. I wish I had grilled him good and proper about his movements and perhaps picked up on some of the clues, but sadly I did not.'

The 30-year-old, who is studying languages at college and hopes to become a translator, had first met King in late 2000, when they worked together in the Chicken Shack pub – for many years, until its recent closure, an infamous but welcoming haunt on the Costa del Sol for much of the English underworld. An amiable sort of bloke, who worked in the kitchen as well as the bar, she had initially thought he was gay with his penchant for skintight T-shirts and shorts and a squeaky effeminate voice.

'We used to rib him about his shorts and called him "the gigolo" and "the stud" because he always seemed to have these older women falling for him. He certainly had quite a few older girlfriends. He would occasionally bring them into the Shack for a drink but would never introduce them. There were three or four of them, and we really felt that he might have been hired as a gigolo on some occasions, as the women were so rough.'

She soon discovered that he was living close to her in Coin, where she was sharing a house with her fiancé, Douglas Craig, a Scottish builder, whom she had been preparing to marry in the summer of 2001. She and Tony immediately struck a chord and he started to give her lifts to and from work. He also happened to get on well with Douglas, who often had small part-time jobs for the barman around the area and soon he was being invited round in the evenings to have a drink, watch television and occasionally stay the night.

She noticed that King did not like to talk about his past, and was certainly still very much in love with his wife Celia. 'I guess we took pity on him as he was clearly living a pretty tough hand-to-mouth existence, often sleeping semi-rough in his car or even out in the open,' recalls the pretty Dane, over dinner at a restaurant in Copenhagen. 'He never had any money and things came to a head when he got kicked out of the flat next to the slaughterhouse. It was a grotty place anyway and he was miserable and said he was being driven insane by the screaming of pigs day and night. I can't remember if it was me or Doug who said it, but we offered him our second bedroom for just £200 a month, which he jumped at.'

However, tragedy was soon to strike, when two weeks later Elena's fiancé was killed in a head-on collision with a lorry on the dangerously windy mountain road leading up to their house. Completely devastated, she believes it was thanks to Tony King that she was able to pull through. Often the only person around to comfort her through the long and painful dark days that were to follow, he refused to leave her side as she sat in floods of tears, incapable of getting out of bed.

Cuddling her for hours and frequently lying beside her in bed as she tried to come to terms with the tragedy, she credits him with helping her pull through and avoiding a long-lasting depression. 'He hardly left my side for the first few days and was very supportive,' recalls Elena. 'If I was crying he would always come over and comfort me with a hug and a chat. He really cheered me up and I thank him to this day for that.'

The pair grew increasingly close and Tony was devastated that the following year Elena decided to return to Denmark to further her education. 'He was pleasant company, a fantastic cook, and surprisingly tidy around the house. While his room was a bit of a mess, he made a real effort to keep things tidy. He was also a delightfully attentive father to his daughter Sabrina. He used to spoil her rotten, giving her sweets and little presents, like dolls, and he certainly didn't seem to harbour any bad feelings towards her mother Cecilia.'

She remembers how they would often fall asleep lying next to each other in the double hammock on the terrace of the house they shared, and sometimes on the sofa. 'We often used to have a cuddle but there was never any sexual connotation to it and he never once tried anything on with me. I certainly didn't hide my femininity and never felt I needed to cover up with him. He would often massage my neck and shoulders and would frequently caress and stroke my hair while we were watching television.'

But looking back now, she admits there were various clues, which hinted at his darker behaviour. 'For example,' she recalls, 'he would often disappear for days on end and when he went out at night he would rarely get back before four or five in the morning. I would hear him come in at the crack of dawn and would occasionally find him still awake sitting on the terrace staring into space when I got up for work at 8a.m.

'He would appear to be in some sort of trance and it was impossible to get a word out of him. He would just stare into space in his own bubble, completely phased out. It was very strange and I assumed he might have taken some sort of drug and realized it was best to just leave him and he would normally spend much of the day in bed. A couple of times he would come home in the same clothes two days later absolutely reeking of booze and dirt. I would ask where he had been and he would just say: "Down on the coast". He would refuse to open up more and I'd simply assume that he had pulled a woman, or had ended up sleeping rough or in his car. One time he was gone for three or four days and I had begun to get worried about him. Perhaps he went to England but he wouldn't let on at all.'

More alarmingly, however, one night in August 2001, he returned with cuts and bruises on his face and body. 'He told me he had been in a fight and that he had been drunk and didn't really remember why it had happened or who came off worse. But he was a big guy, and knowing what the English are often like down here when they are drunk, I took his word and forgot about it. Now I wonder what he had really got up to that night?'

Elena also recalls how he started to suffer from repetitive nightmares while living with her. 'They started about a month after Douglas died. He would wake up in the middle of the night screaming and I would run through to his room to find him lying in a cold sweat and totally freaked out. He would be thrashing from side to side, which was really quite scary, but when I had woken him up he would say he didn't remember anything. I would get him a glass of water and we would sit and talk until he had calmed down.'

She also recalls his collection of porn films, which he kept in a drawer in his room. 'He kept them in one of his bedside-table drawers, but God knows why because he didn't have a video to watch them on.'

She adds that he always used to brag about driving up and down the coast drunk. 'He was really proud that he could get home with ten pints inside him. He would always drive me about to work and to the shops as I couldn't drive and didn't have a car and he loved to point out all the places he had crashed and come off the road. There were plenty of trees and walls, believe me. It is why I can almost believe that he really did kill Sonia Carabantes by accident as he claims. When he says he reversed into that poor girl coming home from the carnival in Coin this summer, I can really believe it. His driving was bad at the best of times, but when he was drunk it was appalling and it is amazing in a way that he didn't kill anyone else in his cars.'

Furthermore, to this day the Dane, who left Spain to start a degree in languages in October 2001, still finds it very hard to reconcile the public image of the sex monster and the man she knows. 'I still can't believe he murdered those two girls for sexual reasons,' adds Ploughman, who has seen Tony a couple of times in 2002 and 2003 when she returned to Spain for holidays. 'He was just not that way at all. I can honestly believe these allegations he recently made about his friend and former boss Robbie Graham controlling him and using him to commit crimes in Spain. I just don't see Tony as a murderer. Yes I can see him as a sex criminal, who needs to be locked up and given the treatment he deserves, but I just don't see him as a murderer and I really don't want to believe it. To me Tony will always be the charming, smiley Englishman, who helped pull me through one of the worst experiences of my life. And maybe having him that close was the best place to be with Tony – for many of his friends and family he will be' remembered as anything but a bad and evil man.'

Naturally devastated when his flatmate and closest friend Elena went back to live in Denmark in October 2001, Tony King was extremely fortunate when another saviour arrived in the shape and form of Leeds pub owner Simon Bowers. They had met in the Chicken Shack pub earlier that year after the affable Yorkshireman had arrived in Spain in June 2001 and got a part-time job playing drums in the pub's resident band Shack-attack.

While a competent drummer – who had played with various groups, including T'Pau and Jools Holland – he was a landscape gardener by trade, but had decided to sell his business in Leeds after being convicted of drug dealing and receiving a heavy fine and suspended sentence.

He and his wife Janine (and son Jonathan) had planned a fresh start in Spain and purchased a small bar on the main street of the scruffy, but rapidly expanding, mountain town of Alhaurín el Grande. King, who was always behind the bar on Simon's regular jam sessions, lived nearby in Coin and the pair quickly hit it off. Both keen fitness fanatics, with a similar sense of humour, when his bar the Bowers Arms finally opened in November that year, Simon didn't hesitate to offer Tony a job as barman (with the occasional role as cook and bouncer).

For Tony, the timing could not have been more perfect with the work at the Chicken Shack just ending as the bar was closing for winter. Simon saw his opportunity and told King there would be a job for him and somewhere to live, at the bargain price of just £150 a month. He was soon working six days a week on a proper contract. According to his mum, Tony was overjoyed. 'He sounded happy for the first time in years,' she says. 'Simon had been a godsend and seemed to genuinely care for Tony. He didn't just use him like Robbie Graham did and they appeared to have a healthy relationship.'

A typically English joint that felt more appropriate in Fuengirola than the mountain village of Alhaurín, the Bowers Arms served up a warm pint of bitter and, of course, Guinness. The day of Tony's arrest, a sign outside read: 'Sunday Roast – the full works, roasties, Yorkshire pud, the lot.' King fitted in perfectly and liked his new accommodation, which he shared with the Bowers and another lodger, Sinead, who also worked in the bar. They were soon winding down at night playing backgammon and smoking marijuana together and the Bowers were extremely happy with the new addition to their team.

'He was tidy, thoughtful and sensitive and bent over backwards to make an effort,' recalls Bowers, who has since been forced to move back to England after the bar was shut because of paperwork wrangles by the local authorities in a backlash against the Brits in Alhaurín. Keen and able, King ended up being a bit of a jack of all trades, doing just about everything in the bar from knocking out the odd few *tapas* to bouncing out troublemakers. 'He was a fantastic worker. Not great with timekeeping but he could do just about anything thrown at him and when it came to keeping undesirables out he was ideal for the job,' says Bowers.

Tony was to work in the Bowers Arms for much of the two years leading up to his arrest. He also lived with the family for 16 months, apart from a six-month spell, when they fired him for continual lateness, largely due to his frequent late nights.

The Bowers were undoubtedly some of the few people Tony King completely trusted in Spain. And while he never told them the exact reasons why he had been in prison (as with Celia, he said he was in for armed robbery), he did open up about his horrific upbringing and the cruel treatment he received from his father. 'He didn't say much about his father except he hoped he would never see him again, but he often mentioned his brother, who he said used to beat him up.

According to Bowers, these earlier experiences spurred King on to build up his physique. In a bid to make himself less vulnerable he got heavily involved in weight training, using 'a range of powders and pills' to help boost his muscles. 'He told us he had sprung up from a ten-stone weakling to a sixteen-stone hulk. He took up judo and tae kwon do and also entered competitions as a powerlifter. He took his fitness very seriously and claimed he could have become Mr Universe had he really worked at it. We took it with a pinch of salt.'

He also used to like to talk about his sex life, and in particular boasted about his past conquests, reveals Bowers. 'He often used to talk about this Malaysian girl Irene, who was apparently a right goer in bed and forced him to work on his stamina. She clearly made a long-lasting impression on him.'

And as for claims by the police and the media (also backed up by his last girlfriend Mariluz Gallego) that King was impotent, Simon snorts with laughter. 'That is crap. He often had different women over the 16 months he lived with us and I can tell you the sex sessions were usually loud, long and physical. He always made a big racket and was very aggressive in bed. One time he was so physical he made the whole double bed collapse and you could tell what a relief it was to finish with all the noise he made.'

Bowers is also adamant that Tony King was never a wife-beater – and in fact his behaviour towards women suggested, if anything, the complete opposite. While he now admits that he was perhaps trying to cover up his sex problems, King was always extremely protective of any female drinkers who came into the bar. According to Bowers, he would get angry if any of them talked about being hit by a man and would rapidly eject any man, who came on to a female drinker too strong.

He was also devastated with a rumour that went around town

that he had broken up with Celia because he was a wife-beater. He was so upset, in fact, that, according to Bowers, he went down to the coast, and personally brought Celia up to Alhaurín to come to the pub to deny it was true. 'She did it apparently without any hint of coercion or aggression,' recalls Bowers, adding that she certainly had no qualms about letting her estranged husband spend the weekend with his daughter.

Physically, however, he did sometimes go too far. 'Sometimes I don't think he knew his own strength. He was a big strong boy and few people would want to cross him, and let's face it he didn't have any problems landing a job as a bouncer at Vibes nightclub for a few months. I think he was also quite often used as a hired heavy for the odd outside job, if you know what I mean. Certainly at the bar he had few qualms about throwing his weight around when needed and I saw him literally pick up and throw out at least three people while he worked there. On one occasion after he had given this drunkard a thick lip in the street outside the bar and we had to caution him, he said to us: "You have no idea what I am capable of." Nowadays I wonder if he was trying to tell us something.'

It is this phrase that made Bowers rethink his opinion of King after he was arrested in the summer of 2003. While still describing him as one of his 'best friends' – and extremely defensive of the Londoner – the publican admits that King clearly had deep emotional problems. While he says he was generally mild-mannered and gentle, he clearly suppressed his feelings and was tightly wound like a spring. Complex and often withdrawn, on the one hand he was a doting father to his daughter Sabrina and on the other a self-confessed insomniac who would regularly stay out all night.

Bowers recalls how in the evenings after work, King would always sit on the sofa at home with the television on, drinking his favourite tipple, brandy, and smoking cannabis, which was clearly something of a serious habit. Unable to sleep till four or five in the morning, while the rest of the family would turn in at around midnight, he would go off gallivanting, as Bowers puts it. 'He would say he was going off to all sorts of things and places. He particularly liked going to the Spanish carnivals. They really interested him. He used to go on his own, not normally coming back until the very early hours. I think he liked the large crowds, the excitement, and the ability for him to be anonymous in them. Perhaps it meant he could slip away unnoticed at the drop of a hat. He loved the big festival in Malaga, the one in Fuengirola, the one in Marbella and, of course, the one in Coin, which he had been to for about four years in a row.'

Sometimes, perhaps more sinisterly, according to Bowers, he would say he was going out 'rabbiting', walking out with his air rifle under his arm. 'He did that a few times a week for quite some time, not coming back until 3 or 4a.m., not once with a rabbit I hasten to add. We would hear him creep in and go to his room and go back to sleep. He did it for months until one day the local police picked him up and seized his gun. They brought him round all shamefaced to check that he really lived with us. It turned out they already knew him, as he had been pulled in over the illegal dumping of a Volvo car. Anyway, this time they brought him round and told us they had caught him on a country road with a torch and the gun. I think it had even freaked them out. But surprisingly they did little more than fine him for using a gun without a licence. After that he still went out, but said he was going down to the coast, sometimes later admitting he had been shagging, although goodness knows who and he was always very careful what he said about it. But you knew he had usually been up to something sordid.'

Most illuminating of all, however, was his apparent homosexual side. A former dancer in gay clubs, Bowers is convinced that Tony was struggling with his sexuality and almost certainly slept with a series of men while living in Alhaurín. 'Janine and I are pretty sure that he slept with two or three of the local gay men when he was drunk. He had the demeanour of a gay man, with his rippling muscles, tight clothes and high, poofy voice. The way he minced around the bar, his giggle. I have met a lot of gay men through work in England in gay clubs and I really felt he only slept with women to cover up his homosexual side.'

He added that there was one man in particular, who used to come into the bar and flirt with Tony. A handsome but very camp Spaniard called Miguel, and according to Simon, a lot of people thought the two were having a fling. 'The word certainly went around Alhaurín and this guy used to come into the bar, until one day Tony started acting very strangely regarding him. I think Tony had finally heard what the local gossips were saying – something that Miguel, as I understand it, tried to encourage – and was embarrassed. Either way, when Miguel next came in Tony got really angry with him, took him into a corner and told him never to come back to the bar.'

Simon's wife Janine recalls another local man José Antonio – better known by the nickname Coco – who once came into the Bowers Arms and cried on her shoulder about his relationship with Tony, who apparently lacked affection for him. 'He was gutted,' recalls Janine. 'He had completely fallen in love, after he ended up giving Tony a blow job one night. They had bedded down for two or three days after that, but Tony had suddenly told him to get lost. He was gutted and beside himself.'

Later, according to Bowers, José Antonio phoned up a live chat show on Antenna 3 in Valencia to declare his love for King. In an embarrassing episode – in which Simon and his wife Janine were studio guests – Coco phoned the chat show from his house in Alhaurín to tell the live audience that he and Tony had been lovers, and he and Janine then had an on-air disagreement about whether or not his relationship with King had just been a one-night stand. 'It was really cringey and weird,' says Simon.

It might have been due to these sexuality rumours that by the middle of 2002 Tony King had apparently settled down with a local cleaner, known as Mariluz Gallego. A mother of three, they had met when the friend of Janine's had taken over the cleaning duties at the Bowers Arms earlier that year and straightaway got on. According to Bowers, the pair loved flirting with each other and Tony enjoyed practising his Spanish with the petite Andalusian, who was two years his senior. With three children to feed, and apparently with a lousy ex-husband who paid no maintenance, she immediately saw Tony as a potential candidate as a boyfriend. She had seen how he doted on his daughter Sabrina, and he straightaway got on with her teenage daughters and young son Adam. Indeed, he seemed anything but a dangerous man and one night after she had stayed behind after work for a few drinks the pair had ended up kissing. Within a few weeks they had started dating, and Mariluz was to become a frequent overnight guest at the Bowers home.

While far from beautiful (she was fair, rather short with a plain, careworn face), Tony believed he had found himself something of a soulmate and, according to both Bowerses, opened up to her about his life, in particular telling her about his time in prison and how he had changed his name. He also got on well with her children, particularly the youngest, Adam, whom he would regularly take to the park to play games. 'Mari was a real sweetheart and really fell for Tony,' says Janine Bowers. 'It was a nice coupling as we all got on very well and enjoyed having her around. Tony seemed very happy with Mari and they were soon inseparable.'

Indeed, by early 2003 Tony had moved in with the cleaner who had a grace-and-favour flat inside the grounds of the Emilia Olivares school, through her father, who was the former caretaker there. One of a pair of compact, three-bedroom flats that literally sit right next to the school playground, it was the ideal arrangement for Tony, who was having problems with his landlord and employer Bowers over his constant lateness to work.

According to Celia the arrangement made them even closer and she had even thought they might get married. 'He and Mariluz seemed really happy together, and Mariluz often said how good Tony was with her children,' she says. 'I was not at all worried when Tony took Sabrina for the weekend. Sabrina saw it as having two mummies and two daddies. She liked Mariluz and by then Tony and David were getting on fine and we occasionally went out as one big family.'

The move also happened to be particularly timely as by February 2003 the barman had found himself out of work at the Bowers Arms, his employers fed up with his constant lateness. 'We both liked Tony but we had to let him go,' says Simon. 'We wanted him to get to work at 10 or 11a.m. to open up for the lunchtime session, but he was always at least half an hour late, unsurprisingly having often not gone to bed till 5a.m. or 6a.m. There were no hard feelings, however, and Tony took it well. In fact we stayed on good terms and he continued to come into the bar for social visits.'

Bringing yet another chaotic spell for King, he worked at a series of restaurants and nightclubs, in particular working as a bouncer at Vibes nightclub in La Cala, through a contact of the Bowerses'. 'He really looked the part and seemed happy there,' says Simon. 'The girls would literally fall at his feet he looked so smart and handsome in his tuxedo with his hair greased back. I think he enjoyed himself.' He also worked at a couple of gardening firms, one in particular run by an English couple, known only as John O'Connell and Gwen, in Benalmadena. A hard worker, for the first time in years he would be up and out of the flat he shared with Mariluz at the crack of dawn, to go off doing gardening jobs up and down the coast.

But this all came to an end in July 2003 when, under controversial circumstances, he was sacked, apparently for making a crude remark to a woman when handed a hot dog at a barbecue. Fortunately for Tony, however, his old employer Simon Bowers was prepared to take him back. 'He came back really upset one day and said he had been sacked for crashing the gardening van into the roof of a car park. I felt sorry for him and told him he could have his job back and he certainly started to make a real effort to get in on time.'

By now the middle of summer, it was Tony's favourite time of the year – the holiday season, when many of the Spanish towns have their local carnivals. According to Simon, the barman seemed abnormally upbeat about things and was clearly enjoying life. Going out most nights of the week, he would regularly attend the fiestas scattered around the Malaga province in his blue Mazda, usually drunk. Coming back with tales about the crazy, drunken nights of excessive partying, Simon knew he was in his element. By the middle of August, King had already had a couple of nights at the big carnival in Malaga, plus visits to the events in Benalmadena and Casares. Next up was the festival of Coin, a town that Tony knew extremely well.

Chapter Fourteen

Sonia Is Killed, Tony Gets Pulled

The evening of Wednesday, 13 August 2003 could not have been more pleasant. The record-breaking heatwave that had wreaked havoc in Andalusia throughout June and July, taking hundreds of lives in the process, had already subsided and in the mountain village of Alhaurín there was a lovely cooling breeze.

It was 10.30p.m. and Tony King and his girlfriend Mariluz were sitting down on the terrace outside the Bowers Arms having a few drinks with owners Simon and Janine and a few of the regulars, when Tony suddenly stood up and said: 'Right, who fancies going to the *feria?*'

Referring to the carnival in Coin – which was just a short ten-minute drive inland on the windy C-344 to Ronda – the barman was clearly crestfallen when he discovered that no one was interested. He had talked about it for weeks and had hoped he could persuade his boss, or at least his girlfriend to join him on the festival's penultimate night.

'You could tell he was disappointed,' recalls Simon Bowers. 'He had been really excited about going and had mentioned it a couple of times during the week. He had been the previous few years and kept telling us what fun it was. But both Janine and I were tired and had to get back to our son Jonathan.'

Sadly for Tony, Mariluz was in a similar boat. But she had another perfectly good reason not to go with her boyfriend. Having been working in the bar since early afternoon – and having drunk a skinful – he was already pretty inebriated and in no fit state to navigate the pot-holed and badly signposted road up to Coin. After ten minutes of trying to persuade her to go she drew the line and hissed at him to stop. 'The last thing she wanted to do was go to the carnival,' recalls Bowers. 'She was tired, having been working nights in a bar for the last week and she wanted to relax on her night off. She told Tony he was far too drunk to drive her there anyway and that was that. Half an hour later they wandered home, with Tony clearly pretty cheesed off.'

The next time Bowers saw his employee, teenager Sonia Carabantes was dead and Tony's behaviour the next day, he now realizes, was suspicious in the extreme. It transpired that after getting home and watching television for a couple of hours (his girlfriend having gone to bed) Tony decided to go to the carnival. The next morning, clearly still inebriated and with a hangover, he arrived at work an hour late covered in mud and, somewhat tellingly, sporting a series of nasty cuts on his hand and neck.

'He had not slept at all and came straight to work with mud all over his shoes and trousers,' recalls Bowers, who normally opened the bar with Tony in the mornings. 'He was so filthy I ordered him into the loos to have a proper wash down and told him to take off his shoes for a clean.'

The weirdest thing, however, was his left hand, which was swollen and had small cuts all over it. 'It was horrible and looked like he had punched a brick wall and I made a joke about feeling sorry for the other guy, but he insisted he hadn't been in a fight and said, quite rightly, that if he had hit someone he would have used his right, not his left hand. He then made up this cock and bull story that he had been in an accident on the way home. That he had been driving along pissed out of his head when he lost control of the car, which spun around and hit something. He said he wasn't wearing a seatbelt and that the force of the crash had sent him tumbling forward into the stereo and that is how he had hurt his hand.

'Of course I knew it was rubbish and said so, but he refused to change his tune. I also quickly noticed that he had one or two visible scratches on the back of his neck, which made both Janine and I assume he had had a fight with Mari, having got in from the pub the previous night.'

Either way, the barman's temperament and behaviour changed dramatically over the next few weeks and he became oddly withdrawn and started to drink more heavily. According to Simon he became distant and seemed to have something on his mind. It made him erratic at work and when he started arriving late again, Bowers was once again considering sacking him. 'He was not the same person after that night. He started acting quite weirdly and was drinking a lot more alcohol, in particular before his normal shift started at 2p.m. He was finding it hard to communicate and he didn't seem at all happy. To be honest he seemed a little confused, like his mind was somewhere else.'

His girlfriend Mariluz Gallego had also noticed the change since the morning he had stumbled into the house before heading out again. She had also seen his muddy clothes and the scratches on his body, but when she had asked him what they were from he had given the same excuse that he had had a car accident. 'One of my daughters told me she had heard him get up in the middle of the night to go out and when he reappeared at 8a.m., he was in a real state. He had scratches on his body and what looked like blood on his clothes. He told me he had

had a car accident while out buying some cigarettes. I simply didn't believe him, but what could I say?'

Suspicions were also aroused at his ex-wife Celia's house when two days later he went to pick up his daughter Sabrina for the weekend. It was his usual Saturday visit and he would have Sabrina until Sunday afternoon, when he would return her to the semi-detached three-bed home, which sits alongside the N-340 motorway, just beside the castle in Fuengirola. Celia had been out doing a Saturday job at a bar in Torrenueva, but her boyfriend David Cooze was at home to let him in. He recalls how, on the surface at least, King was his usual chatty self when he turned up in his blue Mazda on the dot of 1p.m.

'He seemed completely normal apart from the fact that he had this big bandage on his hand and cuts and scratches all over his legs,' recalls Cooze. 'But when I looked closer I could see about 20 in all and they were already going crusty. Anyway I invited him in for a drink and asked him what had happened and he told me he had been in a car accident, which I remember thinking was odd unless he had crashed his car in the middle of a bramble field. He told me he had been drunk and rolled it into a field and somehow knocked his hand in the process.'

But then, while King was helping Sabrina to get her stuff together, the estate agent started thinking. 'I was puzzled how if he had really rolled his car into a field, why were there no dents or scratches on the roof? Why hadn't it collapsed? So I asked him and he quickly replied that he hadn't rolled the car he had actually spun the car a few times and sort of clammed up. And I remember wondering how the hell he could have cut his hand like that spinning the car around. And anyway, you wouldn't end up cutting your legs so many times that way. It simply didn't add up!'

Later that night the Welshman, who grew up in Swansea

before moving to Tenerife to work in timeshare in the 1990s, saw an item on television that got him thinking. 'Celia and I were both sitting there, in fact, when this small news item came on about this teenager being missing. I'd already told Celia about the strange accident that Tony had had in Coin that night, and we both looked at each other and did a double take. Could Tony have been involved? And decided no and kind of put it to the back of our minds.'

A few days later, however, the same thought came up again when the body of the 17-year-old was found. 'But again we ended up dismissing the thought, as the police announced they were seeking two youths from Coin who were out with the girl that night.

But when on 2 September 2003 it was announced that DNA from the murder scene matched with the murder of Rocío Wanninkhof in 1999, the couple started to really worry. It wasn't, however, until an article appeared in the Costa del Sol's most comprehensive ex-patriot publication, *Sur*, in English the following Friday that they decided to take action. Informing its readers that police were seeking someone who may have a cut or bandage on their arm, Cooze was adamant they had to do something. That newspaper article would prove to be the catalyst that led to Tony King's capture.

As Cooze explains: 'The bandage on the arm was the main thing, but knowing that Tony had lived close to Rocío when she died in 1999, I put two and two together and told Celia we had to go to the police.'

Tony's past, as it happened, had already been at the back of his mind after a friend of Celia's had revealed that Tony had been wanted over a sex attack in England just before he left for Spain. The friend, Brenda, had been staying with the couple for a fortnight's holiday when she blurted out that she had seen his face on *Crimewatch* in reference to the sex attack. 'While Celia had somehow shrugged it off, as not true, or whatever, it had really got me thinking and I remember on the Saturday at a friend's barbecue telling Celia that I was sure he was guilty.

'We talked about it all weekend and Celia was understandably worried about the implications for Sabrina and for us, if it turned out to be true. But eventually on the Monday, Celia agreed to try and investigate Tony's real past in Britain and she got a number from a friend, who had an uncle at Scotland Yard.'

And so on 11 September 2003, Cecilia Matilde Pantoja took the brave decision to phone up Britain's police headquarters to try and discover the real truth about her husband. She remembers the conversation well. 'I asked to be put through to the crime hotline and told them my name was Cecilia King and that I was married to a Tony King, who had changed his name from Tony Bromwich by deed poll. I gave them his exact date of birth and said he had told me he had a criminal record for armed robbery, but I was suspicious it might have been for something else as two girls had been murdered in Spain near to us. Was there any chance he could have done it? I remember feeling terrible that I could be shopping a man who was completely innocent, but that was that and I gave them my mobile number in Spain and they promised to get back to me as soon as possible.'

But by the middle of the following day Celia had heard nothing. 'I was getting very agitated so I called Scotland Yard again and asked what was going on? And they simply told me to phone Crimestoppers, which I did straightaway. But again I got this man who didn't seem very interested. I told him the circumstances and stressed the point that two young girls had been murdered. After a long while he eventually came back and told me he couldn't tell me anything. I got angry and just begged him to tell me was there any way Tony had killed those two young girls and all he would say was, 'listen, he is a violent man' and I should contact my local police force in Spain. He wouldn't tell me what he had been inside for in England and that was that. It was very frustrating.'

Luckily, Celia decided to persevere and the following day, 13 September, she asked a neighbour if she had a number for a discreet local detective, who might be able to help. After a quick phone call the neighbour came back and said a friend in the National Police force in Fuengirola would call her in a couple of hours. That detective's name was Manolo and after a quick call he came round that evening for a formal interview.

'Thankfully, at least someone was taking me seriously,' recalls Celia. 'He was very efficient and asked all about Tony and what I knew about his past. I told him how we had married in London in 1997 and moved out to Spain soon afterwards and rented a small flat. I told him that he had changed his name by deed poll because no one would give him a job because of his connection to armed robbery and he asked for the paperwork for his change of name.

'I went on to tell them how I had thrown Tony out after he became erratic and started taking drugs and about the car he was driving on the night of Rocío's murder. They told us to act as normally as possible and said they would try and trail him and see if they could check if there was a DNA match.'

Five days later on Thursday, 18 September 2003, Tony was dramatically arrested as he entered the apartment he shared with Mariluz Gallego in Alhaurín. It is a day that neither Celia, Simon Bowers, nor Mariluz Gallego will forget for the rest of their lives.

Celia had heard the news via the television. As she recalls: 'The kids had gone to school and I was tidying the house, when I saw the newsflash on Antenna 3. It was the middle of the day and the police had arrested a *Británico*, with the initials T.A.K in reference to the two murders. My stomach literally dropped and I almost fainted thinking, my God, I hope they have got the right man, but at the same time praying it wasn't him. An hour or two later the detective phoned me with the news that his DNA had matched up and told me I had done the right thing. But it didn't matter, I felt physically sick. My world was spinning and I felt terrible. All I could think about were those two poor girls and poor Mariluz, who had been arrested at the same time and what she would be going through.'

Mariluz was indeed going through hell. Kept for almost the whole day at the police station for questioning, she would soon find herself shunned by the town, evicted from her flat and generally treated like a leper. She recalled how the police had arrived at her flat and quietly told her that they had the proof that he was the assassin of Sonia and Rocío . . . or at the very least involved in some way. She told me how the police had arrived while Tony was out doing an errand and how they had spent the best part of half the morning holding them at the flat, before taking them both to Malaga. 'It was terrifying,' she recalls. 'There were around a dozen of them swarming around the flat, looking everywhere. They wanted to know everything and went round the flat with a fine-tooth comb looking for clues and eventually carted off six bags of clothes, including underpants and various cigarette butts.'

Naturally, she was soon released, and had gone on to give an exclusive TV interview for money in which she described Tony as a monster, saying she never wanted to speak to him again. 'I still can't believe I've lived with a killer without knowing it,' she said. 'He was my knight in shining armour and I give thanks to God that my daughters and I are alive. This has hit me like a jug of cold water and I have ripped up all our photographs together and don't want anything to do with him.'

Privately, however, she still had her doubts. Talking to me at the flat in Alhaurín from which she has now been evicted, the mother of three said: 'I just can't believe he did all that. He was always so good to me and the children. I'm far from convinced and wish someone could please tell me the truth.'

Simon Bowers also had his doubts. Despite being convinced that Tony was guilty of the murder of Sonia Carabantes, he is convinced that others were also involved in the death of Rocío. He had heard the news also via the television while entertaining friends at home over lunch. 'They didn't give a name or anything, but I knew straightaway it was Tony,' said Bowers. 'They soon gave the initials which confirmed it. We'd certainly had our suspicions about him and just felt sick as dogs to think about those poor dead girls.'

It was King, however, who was made to feel literally as sick as a dog, as he had interrogation after interrogation in a row and was grilled for more than 20 hours.

Chapter Fifteen

I Did It, No I Didn't

According to press reports, Tony King had confessed to the two murders within a couple of hours of arriving at the National Police headquarters in central Malaga on 18 September 2003. Actually untrue, King had only finally 'confessed' some two days later on 20 September, after the courts had ordered that he was transferred into the custody of the Guardia Civil in Fuengirola, who were in charge of the investigation. Furthermore, while it is impossible to confirm the exact times of his so-called confessions, they are certainly controversial in the extreme if, as King claims, he was tortured.

Confirmed by both his mother and lawyer, King claimed to have been slung in a cell and made to lie on the floor with his arms painfully clamped behind his back. Given no food or water he was told he was 'a dog' and given round-the-clock beatings. According to his mother, he had phoned her in tears just two days later to tell her of the 'physical and mental torture' they had used in order to extract a confession out of him.

She says: 'He was extremely upset and couldn't stop crying. He told me they had forced a confession out of him by yelling and screaming at him from the minute they got him in the cells. He said they stuck a paper bag over his head from midday until 10p.m. and made him lie on the floor like a dog. He said it was hell and that they were kicking and punching him in the face and round the head and calling him a pig and a dog. He said he didn't know what they were going to do to him. They had handcuffed his arms behind his back the wrong way, so it was agony, and he said he felt dizzy and sick from the pain and couldn't stop shaking.

'Then when they finally stopped and gave him some food he said they put half a packet of salt in it so it was inedible. He said it was impossible to swallow, and he was so thirsty he could hardly talk. He said he finally gave up and admitted to the murders just to make the agony stop. He obviously regrets this now.'

King would later claim in court that the police deliberately handcuffed him with his hands facing outwards after he told them he had back pain. Saying they would only release the handcuffs when he confessed, they screamed and shouted at him until he cracked.

Naturally, the police deny that any mistreatment or torture took place while King was being interviewed. They claim that he was treated as well as any other prisoner and that King had no complaints at the time. Either way, they had the 'confessions' that they needed and it wasn't long before the highly damaging statements trickled out to the Spanish, and then English press.

Indeed, on Tuesday, 28 October 2003, in something of a bizarre move, Fuengirola court, which was dealing with the death of Rocío Wanninkhof, released the transcript in which King allegedly confessed. In the long, rambling statement, King is apparently heard to admit that he had stabbed the teenager to death after she had struggled against his sexual advances.

In the sensational transcript he is said to tell how, on the night of 9 October 1999, he had been at the house of his friend Robert Graham, on the Balcon del Mar development, in La Cala having a few drinks (both beer and vodka) and smoking a couple of joints. At approximately 9p.m. he said he had left the house in his white Ford Fiesta and soon crashed into something, bursting two of the tyres. Typically, as he only had one spare he had then made his way back to his house, where he asked his neighbour Jane Maynard if she could lend him her blue Ford Fiesta in order to go back to get his car repaired. Using her spare tyre he was able to fix it, before returning it home and going back for her car. It was then, however, after he had picked up her car, that he saw Rocío walking home alone from La Cala.

'I didn't know her, although later I found out who she was,' he is alleged to have said. 'She was attractive and I wanted to touch her bottom. So when I saw her turn into a very quiet street I decided to do the same. I overtook her and then stopped and got out of the car. When she came close I thought that if I took out my knife I would be able to scare her into coming behind a wall so I could touch her. But when I held the knife to her throat and told her to come with me she pushed me and tried to run away, and because the knife was very sharp I ended up wounding her in the throat. I didn't expect that to happen; it took me by surprise.'

He continued that he had then grabbed her around the waist and covering her mouth with the other hand so he was able to force her down a terraced slope. 'The only thing I could think about was getting away as everything had gone wrong,' he said. 'I only wanted to touch her; she was young and I thought she would be afraid and would do everything I told her to. I never imagined she would struggle with me. I told her if she kept still I would leave her alone, but she never stopped struggling and screaming. So I stabbed her; I don't know how many times. I remember three but perhaps there were more. The last time was in the back and she fell to the ground and stopped screaming.'

Next, in an attempt to conceal the body, the barman said he had dragged her into deeper undergrowth by the arms, hair and eventually the feet and admitted that because her shoes may have come off he then pulled her along by her trousers, which also came off.

Once hidden out of the way, he panicked and fled in the car he had been lent. But before he got home he decided to turn round and go back as he realized that he had left the knife at the scene. Then he put Rocío's body in the boot, and drove up the N-340 motorway until the Elviria junction, where he turned down an unsurfaced road until he came to a plot of waste ground, where he dumped the body.

It was at this point then that he claimed to have molested the body. 'Rocío was wearing white knickers and a blue top that had got torn in the struggle so her breasts were uncovered. I touched her body but I didn't stay long in case I got caught. I covered her with branches and left.'

He said he had then gone to the beach from where he threw the knife into the sea and carefully washed himself. He then returned the borrowed car and threw everything that might have blood on it into a rubbish bin en route. On getting home he took off his bloodstained clothes, put them in a bag, had a shower and went to bed.

He continued: 'I tried to lead a normal life after that, but I was terrified. Lots of people were looking for Rocío and the spot where I had left her body was easy to find. I chain-smoked and never stopped drinking.'

It was about a fortnight later when he decided he needed to hide the body in a better place. Insisting that nobody helped him, he undertook the job on a wet, rainy night when his wife had gone out with her sister. After cutting up two black plastic bags, he fixed them together with adhesive tape and placed them like a carpet in the boot of his car. He then put the body on top and drove up the coast for 'a long time' until he found the right spot to leave it.

Indeed, it wasn't until he had reached the other side of Marbella, some 30 minutes later that he found another unsurfaced track, which he drove along before turning right beside a fence. It was here that he lifted the body and dropped it over the fence, before – he claimed controversially – he had set it alight. 'It was difficult because it was very heavy and when I went back to the car to see whether I had left anything I saw a can of petrol. So I decided to set fire to the body so that there would be no clues anywhere. I then went to the beach, washed myself and went home, but before that I threw my anorak and plastic waterproof trousers into a container.'

Around the same time, the judge in the Sonia Carabantes case, in Coin, also took the decision to release a 1,500-word transcript of King's alleged confession to the media. It made for further sensational reading, with the barman apparently confessing among other things, that he had apparently molested her dead body and enjoyed pursuing women like a 'hunter'.

In the alleged confession taken on the same day, he apparently said: 'When I approach women I feel like a hunter, a conqueror who has taken his prisoner or target. I have no interest in sex with my partner and am not able to achieve orgasm. I have difficulties having sex and that is why I stalk women. I bother them and touch them. I've suffered this problem for years. Stalking women, touching them and then, while I pleasure myself, remembering how my victims once walked, how I approached them and intimidated them – that motivates me more.'

He continued: 'I am mentally ill and touch girls when they are dead. When I see the girls' families I feel terrible. I apologize to all women. I am disgusting.'

But, in the released confession he claims that the death of Sonia was, in fact, an accident after he ran her over drunk on his way home from the carnival in Coin. He explained: 'It happened after I got in my car after leaving the fair and reversed at top speed like I always do. I realized I had hit something so got out and saw Sonia lying on the ground bleeding. I felt terrible because I didn't have insurance to drive. I didn't know what to do and lost control and hit the car and possibly Sonia as well. She was badly injured and couldn't stand up. But she was still alive and groaning so I picked her up and rested her against a parked car. But she was too badly injured so I panicked and put her in the boot. I was very drunk. I began to slap her to try to bring her round. She showed no sign of life and I got out of the car, shouting: "What on earth am I doing here?" I returned to the back seat and started hitting her harder, violently. That's why there was so much blood.'

In the alleged confession – in which he can apparently be heard being physically sick on a couple of occasions – he then revealed how he had driven the dead body of Sonia towards Monda, where he had finally found a dry river bed and buried her under some big rocks and boulders. But first he admitted that he couldn't avoid the temptation to molest her. 'I know I am ill because I was touching her breasts and the rest of her body,' he was reported to have said.

While the so-called confession naturally gained numerous tabloid headlines his lawyer Adrian Broncano quickly came to his client's defence, insisting the alleged confessions were given to the police under a great deal of pressure. He also hinted that his client might have been suffering from some sort of psychiatric disorder, which made him claim responsibility for things he had not done.

He also drew attention to the various contradictions such as the alleged burning of the body, which had definitely not been burned. On top of this, King had claimed to have stabbed

Rocío in the stomach, although forensic reports had established that she had been stabbed in the chest and in the back.

But it was the words of Robbie Graham, and not Tony King that were to really rock the somewhat cosy and up till then straightforward inquiry, when he suddenly came out to claim that King had only killed Rocío with help and under orders from Dolores Vázquez.

The amazing claim was made in a series of interviews, one with me, after his memory had apparently been jogged in a highly controversial hypnotic session with police in Madrid. First appearing in the British press, Graham alleged that Vázquez had helped his friend kill the teenager and then paid him £800 to remove her body. Likening the relationship to that of Moors murderers Myra Hindley and Ian Brady, Graham said: 'Tony King had met someone even sicker than him.'

In the new evidence, Graham claimed that on the night of the murder in 1999, King had actually turned up at his house unexpectedly between 9p.m. and 11p.m. with a puncture and acting frantically. Graham – who admitted that the pair were good friends ('he was my kind of guy') – said he had a look on his face that he had never seen before. Wild-eyed and incoherent, he said King had half-confessed to the murder, before Graham asked him to leave.

'He was in a very strange mood, talking about his wife and his problems and starting to tell me that he had grabbed this girl and thought that he had killed her or left her unconscious.' A week later over a beer, however, he claimed King had poured his heart out and admitted all the gruesome details of the murder and how the girl had been stabbed twenty times in the back.

By now living in Brighton (having reportedly fled Spain for fear of retribution), Graham rambled at length about the apparent connections to Dolores and how on the night of the murder King had turned up at his apartment with her in tow.

'The police knew he had an accomplice,' he said. 'They knew it was a woman, but the woman has already been in jail and they had to let her go.' He went on to claim that Tony was basically hired to do it. 'It took him about a week to tell me this. I didn't really believe him when he came to my house on the night of 9 October 1999. He was terrified like he had been pushed over the limit. He was shaking, his eyes were black . . . Absolutely black. He was gone. He came to me because he had nowhere else to go. He came to me because he was terrified and didn't know what to do. I was his boss and he thought I would know what to do in any situation.'

He then claimed to have told him he couldn't help him on this occasion and told him to go away. But a week later after a few beers he claimed King confessed to him what had happened on that night. 'He said he had been hired to do a thing for this woman, who was the lover of the mother of the victim. He told me the name of the woman was Loli or Dolly, which I never connected to Dolores Vázquez at the time as I didn't know her. He told me he had been paid to hurt somebody. He told me he got 150,000 pesetas, which was about £800 at that time just to assist and drive a car.

'Anyway,' Graham added, 'there is no way that Tony could have got that body to the place she was found without that woman taking him to that site. Whether she paid him first and then he did it, or she went with him, I don't know. But I believe she went with him. I believe she stabbed the girl, maybe after Tony had given her a bump. But Tony said she had got out of the car to let the girl get in and then when they dragged her out of the car he couldn't stop the woman stabbing her. He said she stabbed her about twenty times.'

Graham – who had moved to Sussex after his then-girlfriend Louise Deravairere paid for his ticket – claimed, however, that at the time he had not been convinced his friend was telling the truth as he took many drugs. 'He was a bit of a fantasist, like a

Rambo character, and I was not sure if any of it was true. But now I believe he was very heavily involved and I believe on that night he met a greater evil.'

The claims, which also appeared in the Spanish press, were naturally quickly met by a strong and aggressive rebuttal by Vázquez's lawyer. While she threatened to sue the newspapers as well as Graham, the police quickly made a statement saying that they had by no means discounted Vázquez from their inquiries. 'The case is still open and Dolores Vázquez is still under investigation,' said a spokesman for the Guardia Civil definitively. Adding salt to her wounds, the Minister of the Interior, Angel Acebes, then praised the exhaustive investigation of the Guardia Civil against Vázquez and added that he believed the evidence they had presented was more than enough to convince the prosecution to go to trial.

Either way, it is impossible to know the motives for Robbie Graham to suddenly come out and mention this key information, when earlier in interviews on Spanish TV and in the *News of the World* there had been no mention. While he insisted it was down to the voluntary hypnotic session he had undertaken with the Guardia Civil in Madrid, others – including his girlfriend at the time, Deravairere – told me that he was a hypnotist himself and had never gone under.

One thing is for certain, it created a huge element of doubt in the case against King who, unsurprisingly, used Graham's statement as ammunition to come out fighting. Indeed, a few days later on 13 November, he went on to give a completely different statement to Judge del Rio at Fuengirola Court. In a record 12-hour session, which didn't end until 11p.m., King sensationally denied he was guilty and blamed Robbie Graham for the murder, saying it was ordered by 'mafia bosses' who ran the timeshare world on the Costa del Sol.

Pleading for extra protection for both his daughter and for himself in prison, the barman gave, by all accounts, an impassioned performance as he told – in tears – how he feared for his daughter's life, having revealed 'the truth'.

One thing is for sure, Fuengirola had seen nothing like it for years, with over a hundred journalists and photographers crowding around the ugly, three-storey court when King had arrived under police escort from Alhaurín.

A pleasantly hot autumn day, the crowd more than doubled with locals who had come out for a look at the man the whole of Spain was calling 'a monster'. Sadly, there was to be only one brief glimpse of King, who shuffled in like an old man in a heavy overcoat, looking like he hadn't slept for weeks. With no journalists allowed inside (it was a 'closed court session', for all that that is worth in Spain), by late afternoon the majority of photographers and locals had left, with just the very hardy sticking it out until the impromptu press conference from the various lawyers on the court steps around midnight.

When King's full statement was released a few days later it certainly caused a sensation. After talking about his tortured upbringing in England and his arrival in Spain in 1997, King completely contradicted his so-called confessions, saying he had been ordered to come round to Graham's house between 6 and 7p.m. on the night in question because 'something important was going to happen'. He said that after having some beers and smoking some joints, Graham had received a flurry of phone calls, which wasn't normal because it was his day off. He said that most of the calls were taken in private in the next-door room and when he finally asked him what was going on, Graham told him he needed to borrow his car.

He recalled that they had soon been joined by a third party (later identified as Peewee Bachour) and that Robbie had gone outside to talk to him for around a quarter of an hour. He said that when Graham came back in, they took some cocaine before going out to discover that his car, the white Ford Fiesta, had a flat tyre. Graham pointed out that he actually had two punctures and told him to go off and borrow his neighbour Jane Maynard's car, which he did, only to get back some time later to find Robbie high on cocaine and – bizarrely –'dancing backwards like Michael Jackson'.

King admitted that he had also taken some cocaine and drank some red wine that night, but that he hadn't overdone it because Robbie had told him not to get 'too comfortable', because he was expecting a call and they would then go out and do the job.

He said they had eventually left in Jane's car, first going down to a pub, Harvey's Bar, in La Cala to buy some cigarettes, then parking up by the side of the road leading up to Rocío's house, where they sat and smoked a joint.

It was then, while they were sitting in the parked car that Robbie suddenly pointed to the left and said: 'Look there's a girl I know; I'm going to have a laugh with her'. It was, of course, Rocío, and King recalled how he had seen this young, attractive girl, with long hair and dark clothes walking up towards them, before Graham started the car up and drove past her in the direction she was walking. King claimed they had pulled up beside the road on a rough track and switched off the lights. 'Graham laughed – he seemed in a good mood – then he said: "Now I can see her coming up the road. Don't worry I've just got a surprise for her." Robbie told me to sit and wait. He walked towards the girl and she stopped. They talked and gesticulated; she seemed nervous and Robbie pointed towards where his car was. But she said "No" and started to walk off. It was then that Robbie hit her in the face and pulled her hair, calling her stupid and saying: "That's what you get for causing trouble." I saw Robbie holding a knife at the girl's throat and then she pushed him and he injured her.'

According to King's statement, it was at this point that he had rushed over to try and stop Graham from injuring the girl any more. Trying to restrain his boss, while the girl also fought to get away, he soon found the knife turned on him. 'Robbie had lost control,' he recalled. 'I went towards him and shouted: "What the hell are you doing you crazy bastard?" I pulled his shirt so he would let her go, but he turned round, threatened me with the knife and told me to keep out of it, that I didn't know what it was all about.'

Graham had soon stabbed her again, this time from the front, and ordered King to help hold one of her legs, which he admitted to doing, pulling her trousers off in the process. By now the girl was nearly dead, and Graham had dragged her further into nearby waste ground, where King claimed to have seen him stabbing the girl viciously in the back.

He continued that Graham was talking to the girl saying: 'Now you won't be able to tell anybody,' and then told King he was a traitor. He recalled how he then jumped in the car alongside Robbie and had driven at top speed along the N-340 as far as Riviera del Sol. 'I stopped there and smoked a cigarette, but Robbie kept insulting me and telling me we had to go back to clean it all up.'

According to King, he agreed to go back to help him move the body after he threatened him with his daughter's life. 'I'm not the one who could lose his daughter,' he said. They had then driven to the murder spot, where King claimed Graham gave him a cigarette, which he later discarded on the ground nearby. He continued that they had then put the body in the boot and that Robert had then driven towards Marbella, turning off in an area with a lot of bushes. They took some more cocaine and then took the body out of the boot.

In a further sickening claim, he said Graham had first played with the girl's body as if she was a puppet and then pretended she was talking 'as if he was a ventriloquist. He even danced with her,' he said. After that Graham covered up the body with leaves and the pair went to the beach where they cleaned both themselves and the car, before returning it and then going home. Scared and sickened by what had happened, he claimed that Robbie had told him not to worry and 'that there were a lot of sick people that killed girls'.

He said that after showering and changing his clothes that were covered in blood, he had told his wife he was late because he had had car trouble. He also recalled how the next day his neighbour Jane Maynard had asked him what had happened to her car, that things were missing, including a mat, and that it looked like there was blood in the boot. She asked what had happened and he told her that he had hit a dog and apologized and agreed to clean up the car.

He continued that around two weeks later on a rainy night, Graham had turned up at his house, with some beers and dope. After discussing the news that was by then all over the television, he told Tony that they would have to move the body. Graham told him not to worry and took out a big black plastic sheet and said there was a special place where he could take Rocío's body to burn it. King refused to go with him and Graham said: 'Don't you dare go against me, because you could lose your daughter.'

After a long and heated argument King eventually agreed to give him his car keys and Graham was gone for about four hours and didn't get back until 1a.m. 'He said that he had driven a long time, that he used my jacket because it was raining and that he had torn it on a fence when he threw the body over, but not to worry because he had burned it.'

King went on to blame the murder on Graham's connections to the Costa del Sol 'mafia' and in particular Lubina Sol, which he claimed, like many of the other timeshare companies on the coast, was merely a 'cover-up' for other, illegal, activities. He claimed that individuals at the company were involved in all sorts of gangland activity including robbery, drug dealing and blackmail. 'Graham told me that in those circles they were also dealing in ecstasy, jewellery and luxury cars. They've got businesses in Russia and Prague. They're pure Russian mafia.'

He admitted he had worked for Lubina Sol and claimed that he had been asked to do many jobs against his wishes. There were a few he had managed to turn down including one in which he had been offered 300,000 pesetas (£1,600) to deliver a suitcase to a car park in London without 'seeing anything, hearing anything or remembering anything'. But he said he rejected the job because he was afraid he would quickly get pulled in because of his criminal record in England.

While his claims as a whole initially seemed a little far-fetched and the Spanish media was duly sceptical, the judge, María Jesús del Rio, didn't hesitate to alter Graham's status from a witness to being 'a possible suspect' and ordered him to appear 'for further questioning' as soon as possible.

Graham, however, had little intention of coming back to Spain and had already fallen foul of the judge's orders when he had failed to appear to give evidence on the day before King. Perhaps sensing that King was going to blame him, I discovered that he had sent a fax to the court, via his friend Franco Rey (who had by now become his unofficial spokesman), saying that he was unable to attend because of 'financial reasons'.

He had, in fact, had no such financial problem and in a panic had told his girlfriend Louise Deravairere that he had 'to flee' somewhere that Spain didn't have an extradition agreement and had subsequently taken a lucrative timeshare job in Egypt, where he believed he would be safe.

But the Spanish courts were not going to be beaten as easily as that and, according to reports, the police were ordered to track him down immediately. Indeed, in one of the more dramatic episodes of the case an 'international manhunt' got under way with an eight-strong squad of Guardia Civil apparently soon tracking him down to a hotel in Cairo only to discover that he had moved on the day before.

Reports were vague (and information from the police non-existent), but it seemed apparent that they were not to give up.

With both Louise Deravairere in Brighton and Franco Rey – a long-time collaborator with the Guardia Civil – in regular contact with Graham, it appeared they would find him.

There was certainly increasing public pressure for his capture with new reports coming out daily about his connections to other disappearances on the Costa del Sol. In particular, was the case of María Teresa Fernández, aged 18, who had gone missing in August 2000. It emerged that police were investigating a series of sightings of the timeshare tout in the girl's home town of Motril, which was very close to Nerja, where Graham had occasionally lived. According to reports, detectives were said to be carefully checking Graham's bank account records and mobile phone movements around the time of the teenager's disappearance. 'They are taking the sightings extremely seriously and desperately want a break,' said a police source.

The case was rapidly turning into something of a farce. And in terms of drama, Graham's close friend Franco Rey was proving to be a real master. How the Spaniard in his late fifties had got to know Robbie Graham was the subject of much speculation among the Spanish media, but what was undeniable was his dramatic fall from grace.

For Franco Rey's real name was, in fact, Juan Gey Vicente, and he had once been one of the main stars (the 'third most important' in his words) in the disastrous BBC flop *Eldorado* in 1992.

Taking the role of Dr Roberto Fernández, he had previously had a few small parts in British soap *Eastenders* and *Howard's Way* among others. But *Eldorado* (which was ironically filmed at a studio in Coin, where Sonia Carabantes lived) was his big chance. Set in Los Barcos, a fictitious Costa del Sol town not dissimilar to La Cala, he was perfect for the role with his deep swarthy tan and pidgin English. He had moved to Spain from England (where he had run a chain of opticians) and assumed he had hit the big time, with a contract said to be worth nearly a £100,000 a year.

Lapping up the adulation of fans and loving the media attention, it had certainly come as something of a disaster for Gey (pronounced 'gay') Vicente, when the soap opera was dramatically scrapped by Alan Yentob after only a year.

Things went rapidly downhill for the actor, who like Tony King decided to change his name due to homosexual connotations and also, according to close friends, to avoid national service in Spain. Thrown on to the dole and losing his wife, who divorced him to move back to England, he turned to various stimulants and went into a deep depression. Scrabbling around doing any work he could get, he even worked as a tour guide, taking tourists around the defunct studio set, which still exists today. And, by his own admittance, he was only rescued from this ignominious job when the dole office found him a job as a police interpreter with the Guardia Civil in Mijas. While it was a badly paid job – helping translate for unfortunate tourists, who might have been robbed or worse, say, sexually assaulted – he soon found a good way to make money on the side, by selling the information to the British and Spanish media.

Obsessed with the rapidly burgeoning crime scene on the Costas and with increasingly large numbers of Britons going to Spain for holidays as well as to live, he started making thousands a month from his exclusive 'tips' to papers like the *News of the World* and the *Sun*.

He had soon set himself up as a 'fixer' for interviews and 'undercover investigator' – which led to a long and lucrative partnership with Roger Cook's documentary team, as well as the likes of the so-called 'Fake Sheik' Mazher Mahmood among others, at the *News of the World* – and above all he fancied himself as a journalist.

I had met this curious fellow the day after Tony King's arrest. Attempting to take over a round-robin interview with Simon

Bowers, Tony King's former boss, he was mostly ignored by the British press pack, which had turned up en masse that day. We'd had a beer, and with his good police contacts with Mijas Guardia Civil – and in particular his 'close friend' Juan Ramirez, who had been in charge of the Wanninkhof investigation – I said I could employ him on a few stories I was doing for the British newspapers. He seemed happy and our little arrangement bore fruit for both of us for a time.

But things started going wrong when he hijacked an interview I had set up for Spanish television with Robbie Graham in England. Using Rey as an intermediary, he suddenly insisted that the TV station in question would allow only him to do the interview and I begrudgingly agreed to pay for his flights, accommodation and just about everything else, only to discover countless complications on getting any remuneration once the interview was screened on prime time a few weeks later.

Ultimately, however, the interview (for which I finally got paid some four months later) landed Gey Vicente in hot water, with questions being raised about the appropriateness of a police translator making money as a journalist on the same case. Unbeknown to me, it also emerged that he had later put Graham up at his home for a week for further interviews.

Their relationship had undoubtedly got too cosy, and Judge María Jesús del Rio duly summoned him to explain how he could justify helping the police with their investigation and at the same time cash in with the media. It was an awkward moment, which he somehow managed to wriggle out of.

Alarmingly, it didn't prohibit him from continuing to work for the Guardia Civil – and in particular on the Tony King case, in which there were many more English witnesses to be interviewed. He was getting increasing amounts of work and incredibly even bragged about using the Guardia Civil's in-house canteen as 'his office'. Indeed, on one occasion he summoned me there to meet him and investigation chief Juan

Ramirez and then demanded to know all my information without letting me ask a single question. On another occasion he boasted how pally he was with everyone, including the barracks' chef, who had proceeded to knock out one of the worst meals I have ever eaten in Spain.

He was also the key (by his own admission) to arranging for Robbie Graham's cloak-and-dagger appearance in front of the judge to answer further questions in December 2003. In yet another bizarre chapter in the case, he boasted how he had single-handedly managed to persuade Graham to come back and face the music. Claiming to have stumped up the £1,000-plus airfare from Egypt, he controlled the whole week-long visit and even put Graham up at his Fuengirola home.

It led to undoubtedly one of the strangest sessions in the case with the judge and lawyers being made to take a ten-minute walk from the court up to the Guardia Civil's Mijas barracks at the last minute. Because of 'safety reasons' (although apart from a pack of journalists nobody knew Graham was back), Gey Vicente insisted Graham would be questioned only at the police station, leading to the comical scene of the said lawyers walking up the hill hotly pursued by around a dozen confused and irritated journalists.

In the two-hour session, after which Graham was whisked away by Gey via the back door, the timeshare tout once again denied any involvement in the case and reiterated his story about Vázquez paying King £800 to do the job. He also completely denied ever going to Motril and somewhat amazingly was allowed to leave the country a few days later totally scot-free. 'He says he is completely innocent and stands by his story that Tony was paid to kill the girl by a lesbian friend, Dolores Vázquez,' Gey told me later. 'As for this investigation in Motril in 2000, it is ridiculous as he wasn't even living on the Costa del Sol.' Although how Gey was so sure of this we'll never know.

The next major instalment in the case was not to come until well into the New Year after I had sent a letter to King in prison asking him for an interview for this book. In it, I asked how he was getting on in prison and amongst other things if he was happy with his lawyer Adrian Broncano Campus? I had little idea that his reply – dated 4 March 2004 – would cause the massive outcry that it did.

It certainly didn't make sense, as the claims he made in that letter to me I later found out he had already made twice before – to his mother and the family of Rocío Wanninkhof – in the intervening months. The crux of it was that, at last, he was levelling the blame at Dolores Vázquez, as well as Robbie Graham.

As I said, he had already told his mother in a six-page letter in January that he had made the breakthrough after 'realizing' that he had been hypnotized on that fateful night in 1999. He said this had come about after spending hours trying to work out why he had claimed to set alight to Rocío's body when forensic reports stated clearly that it hadn't been set alight. In the letter, exclusively accessed for this book, he wrote:

It is funny, but I have always known that there were things wrong with these memories, but I could never see what they were. I saw myself pour five litres of petrol on her and set fire. That was the clearest of all my memories and yet there was no fire at all! Now I realize that my first testimony, which I believed was made accurately, was wrong in every important detail.

The intriguing claims – which he had also made, I later discovered, in a letter to Rocío's family on 2 February 2004 – hinged around Robbie Graham hypnotizing him on the night of the murder, in order to make him a 'scapegoat' for the crime. While on the surface it sounded a little far-fetched, in many ways it could have been plausible that he might have gone round to Graham's house, where he was given some sort of 'hallucinogenic' drug (he claimed LSD), and then put into a hypnotic trance.

He wrote:

Robbie said he wanted to try it on me and I was curious and agreed to do it. He went and got four tablets and a small torch and asked me to take the tablets, which like a mug I did. Then in the dark room he was flashing his torch, talking to me. He was having a laugh at first then got serious. I can remember the point where I could still make him out in the flashes behind the torch, but could just about realize that he was talking, but hearing it differently as if through a long tube stuffed with socks so I could not actually understand the words.

It was at this point where some people came to Robbie's flat. I know these to be Dolores Bazgues [sic], Peewee from the Millennium Video Shop and a middle-aged Spanish man who would have been shorter than me, but built like a barrel, with a bigger belly than chest. I never said any of this when I made my second statement because I had not seen through the hypnotism.

He then went on to claim that there was proof of the hypnotism, based on a series of tests the Spanish psychologists had done on him to find out about his state of mental health. During one test where his brain was hitched up to a monitor to look at its patterns, he heard a doctor exclaim in surprise that the pattern was of someone dreaming. 'This was of course impossible when I was wide awake and the only way you can be awake and show sleep-dreaming is if you're in a state of hypnotism.'

Then in a further, perhaps more outlandish claim, he said that Graham had hypnotized him again three months later in order to get him to kill himself by crashing his white Ford Fiesta on a dangerous bend on the N-340 motorway. He said on the night in question he had left Robbie's apartment in Fuengirola feeling 'heavy and ponderous'. He wrote: 'Every atom in my body and mind was tingling and everything was moving strangely as though there were frames missing from a film.'

In a dramatic fashion, he recalled driving to a petrol station where he filled up the car before cutting a small hole in the petrol tank with a knife and then driving off down the motorway at a 'mad speed'.

He wrote:

'I can remember the crash site clearly. I hit [a] big green bollard with two arrows, which was shattered as if I had aimed for it! It was the one place to crash where you could practically guarantee someone would get killed, as there was a 7–8m drop down a storm drain which my car went down, upside down. The whole place stunk of petrol and only having my safety belt on and turning off the engine as soon as I knew I had hit something saved my life.

The other letter to 'Mrs Wanninkhof and family' (to which this book has also had exclusive access) gave considerably more detail about the night in question. First, apologizing for her daughter's death and for his first two testimonies, he went on to list in detail what he claimed had happened on the night of her death. In the letter, dated 2 February 2004, he blamed his earlier confession on 'police pressure' and 'the mental and physical cruelty' he had received at the hands of his father from an early age, which made him easy to bully into doing things. He wrote:

With my past I believed I would be convicted anyway and also felt sure that the police would not beat me if I confessed. Confessing also insured [sic] that no one would hurt my own baby who is precious to me.

Of those alleged to be involved in the murder, he blamed five people: Dolores Vázquez, Rocío Wanninkhof's uncle Serafin

214

Ruiz, Robbie Graham and brothers Peewee and John Bachour from the Millennium Video shop.

In his letter, he claimed that Robbie had told him about the 'special job' two days before going round to his house on that Saturday in October 1999 and after drugging and hypnotizing him, Robbie opened the door to let in Vázquez, Ruiz and Peewee, who had earlier brought round some cocaine.

I saw Peewee introduce the woman as 'Dolores' and the man as 'the girl's uncle'. Peewee was the go-between and was speaking Spanish and English. Dolores was wearing tight pale blue jeans and had a lilacy [sic] coloured jumper with a few thin white stripes across the chest and upper arms. She had a big black ladies bag over her left shoulder that was about 30cm high, 40cm long and 6cm thick. It had a broad black strap that was about 4cm wide and seemed to be fastened to the bag by something gold and circular in shape. I thought it was unusual that when she was wearing the bag it hung to a height that was almost tucked under her arm. She talked with her thumb through the strap. I was sent out to the balcony while they talked so I can't tell you what they said.

The only thing that is confusing to me is that when I came back into the living room Dolores and Peewee were no longer [there] and when I went to the car with Robbie I don't remember seeing them in the car, although they must have been because once Robbie had gone down and attacked your daughter, cutting her throat and stabbing her, I know that Dolores and the man were definitely in the car because I saw them. I know that I was told to pick Rocío up and put her in the car . . . this is when I noticed Dolores. I turned around because she was talking to Robbie and I definitely saw Dolores stab Rocío over the back seat of the car . . . and I am one hundred per cent certain that this is how and when Rocío died. I was just set up to be the scapegoat. I swear on my daughter's soul before God that what I have been saying is the whole truth.

King then claimed that after dropping Rocío's uncle off at

Camping Calazul with a bag of Rocío's things, they then drove to Elviria, where they dumped the body, before Dolores drove off in her 'small, dark red car'. He said Robbie then drove them to the beach at Lubina Sol, where Robbie made him believe that they had thoroughly cleaned the car, before he was told to take it back to Jane Maynard's house.

He would also claim in this letter that he had been 'forced' by his solicitor Adrian Broncano not to mention Dolores Vázquez under any circumstances until the day of the trial. Calling him a 'dirty lawyer', he claimed, quite outlandishly, that Broncano had told him not to mention her at all during his second testimony in an attempt to get Vázquez off. These were serious allegations that would lead to him getting a new solicitor Javier Saavedra, particularly after he wrote to the College of Solicitors (on 7 March 2004) with the same claims.

He wrote:

Adrian put immense pressure on me to implicate the timeshare mafia instead [of Dolores]. He told me to write an account of the murder with only Robbie Graham, telling me that everything to do with Dolores should be used 'only' at the time of the trial, which would not be for some years to come. He would not let me speak about Dolores at all. He kept telling me she wasn't important and that if I did what he told me it would get me released from prison.

It is now plainly obvious that the way he manipulated me not to mention Dolores and the way he tried very hard on TV to discredit Graham's hypnotism session (where he said I never killed Rocío, but Dolores did) that the only person to benefit was Dolores.

The letters had certainly put the cat among the pigeons, leading me to immerse myself deeper and deeper into the seamy Costa del Sol underworld in a bid to try and verify their claims. While I quickly discovered that Graham had indeed been close to a Peewee Bachour, and that he might have been a hypnotist, going on the claims of his ex-girlfriend Louise Deravairere, most of the time I met a wall of silence.

It seemed that as long as I was investigating King's links to the murders it was fine, but as soon as I began asking about Graham and Vázquez, people clammed up and didn't want to know. While just about everyone I had spoken to earlier in the timeshare world believed that King might well have been helped, suddenly nobody wanted to go on the record, or indeed, talk at all. At Graham and King's old office, Lubina Sol, in Riviera del Sol I had a particularly nasty incident. Approaching a spotty young man with various tattoos and his ears and, bizarrely, nipples pierced, I asked what he could tell me about the pair. With his girlfriend by his side and his daughter in a pushchair – the sun beating down – the words couldn't have been more sinister. 'I don't give a fuck what Robbie Graham or Tony King did,' he barked menacingly. 'I don't care if they killed ten girls, whatever, I'm not fucking telling you anything about them and if you don't fuck off now I'll put a bottle round your head. In fact get in your car and fuck off back to your own country, or you'll end up like the last journalist asking questions round here – with a glass in his face.'

That journalist happened to be one Nigel Bowden, a seasoned hack, who had worked the Costa beat for over two decades, since realizing that a career in marine biology was somehow evading him.

Having spent the last six months going through a messy divorce he was initially hard to track down for a bit of background. But when I finally got hold of him, it proved to be very revealing. He told me that I should be particularly careful with the timeshare world. He had been investigating the likes of John Palmer and Dennis New and many others in the coast's timeshare business for the previous ten years and had certainly had his fair share of threats and attacks, including a particularly nasty glassing incident in 2002.

The attack in question had happened when he started asking too many questions about a Liverpudlian timeshare gang that was operating in Miraflores just around the corner from Lubina Sol, near Riviera. He had been having a beer in the 24-hour Bar, in nearby Cabopino when his attacker suddenly came up and said: 'Fuck off, get out of this bar. I hate journalists.'

Not having a clue who the spotty, street-fighting Scouser was, Bowden had stupidly (he now admits) told him he was minding his own business and would leave when he felt like it. 'It was a bad mistake as the next thing I knew a beer was poured over me and a second or two later this guy shouted "Oi" and when I looked round he smashed this pint glass around my face. It caught me over the left eye and if I hadn't flinched backwards I would have probably lost an eye. I was rushed to hospital and had 19 stitches.'

Alarmingly, he said it was just one of a handful of attacks from the timeshare crowd. 'I have had my ribs broken, my face smashed and have scars on both my hands from attacks. I have had a hundred stitches in all. All from timeshare scum, who are the nastiest bunch of people you will ever come across. It's very cut-throat down here and there are literally hundreds of timeshare gangs making fortunes from other people's misery. I have to be very careful as I might get murdered for saying too much. Getting beaten up is a constant worry. The timeshare crowd will smack you first and think later. Be careful.'

With this in mind, when former Lubina Sol boss Jon Daniels – who had initially been helpful when asked about his former employee Tony King – had quickly clammed up and told me in threatening tones not to call him again, I knew not to try.

There were vague threats coming from other sources though, one via Franco Rey, who told me that the police were not taking too kindly to my new line of questioning. I discovered I was not the only one getting threats and one seasoned Spanish TV reporter, who had been digging around in Vázquez's past for the last year, told me she had received a number of chilling threats to her mobile phone, telling her to 'leave the Vázquez case'.

Things got nasty again when I started making enquiries about Peewee Bachour and his family at the Millennium Video shop in La Cala, which I was told from reliable sources had strong links to drug dealing. Next to Vibes nightclub, where King had worked as a bouncer, and the strip of businesses where Celia's family had first got their foothold in the timeshare world, it had, according to police sources, already been busted once for dealing drugs from the premises.

According to the sources, the Bachour brothers and their father George, a Lebanese businessman, were well known to local police for their activities. Indeed, Peewee (Pierre to use his real name) had been convicted of drug dealing and spent some time at a young offenders' institute in Malaga. 'They were being watched by the Guardia Civil for quite a long time,' said the source. 'The National Police were also involved. There was some sort of dealing going on from the shop and the videos were really just a cover. They were busted but are still apparently quite big distributors and have good connections on the Costa del Sol.'

I decided to take a visit to one of their two video shops in a scruffy backstreet in Riviera del Sol asking to speak to Peewee. He was not there, but a small, rough-looking Liverpudlian girl with a harelip told me I'd catch him at the other branch. But when I went into that shop, next to Vibes nightclub, the following day, a red-haired girl told me he no longer worked there but she could give me his mobile number.

I dutifully called the number I was given while sitting out in the sun eating some lunch in the cafe outside Vibes nightclub (which doubles as local English station Global Radio) to ask what he made of King's claims. He first of all told me his name was not Peewee, but Pierre, and he worked in real estate, before finally admitting that his family owned the video chain – but only for the last three years and the business was previously called Gogglebox! He didn't seem too interested in talking and when I mentioned Tony King's claims he said aggressively: 'That bloke is mad. He does not know what he's on about. He's a psycho and we weren't involved.' Click. And the phone went down.

I figured that was the end of that episode and I settled back into my lunch, before suddenly noticing a trio of girls, one of them the red-haired girl from the video shop, standing at the doorway of the cafe looking threatening and staring at me. I managed a half-smile, before another of the trio came over and told me in a sharp Scouse accent: 'If I were you I'd get the fuck out of here, before my boss arrives. Go on, get lost,' she spat, adding: 'We don't want scum like you round here!' I looked more closely to see it was the very same Liverpudlian girl with the harelip I had spoken to a day before. She was sneering and looked quite evil. I took my cue and didn't hang around.

It was around this time that I discovered Tony King had been attempting to get in touch with me by phone from prison, and, later, letter. His mother had told me he intended to write and typically, one weekend when my phone was off, he left a message on my mobile phone saying he would try again. It also turned out he had attempted to send me a letter on 4 March 2004 to my address in London, but unknown to me that letter had been intercepted by the prison authorities and passed on to the police in Fuengirola.

The first I had heard about it was from a jovial Franco Rey on the phone at the end of March. I hadn't heard from him in months and suddenly he was asking cryptically if I had received any letter from King in prison? And more importantly had I sent one to him? He told me I could be in big trouble if it was true and said he was 'trying to find out' if there was any truth to the rumour that we had been corresponding.

A week later he was positively gleeful when he phoned me up to tell me that I should turn on the radio to listen to the news about the so-called 'scandalous claims' King had made to a British journalist. It was soon on the television and all over the newspapers and I suddenly found myself in the eye of the storm. On the front page of many of the Spanish national papers, including *El Mundo*, I was being called by every news organization to give an interview to explain my findings. Referring to me as Tony King's 'English journalist friend' (and implying I was some sort of mouthpiece), it led to the judge going to Alhaurín prison to discuss the claims and I was also told that the judge was going to summon me to hear my evidence. It was anything but pleasant and I did my best to ignore it, refusing all requests to talk.

Above all it was upsetting and highly suspicious that it was making such big news now, when the claims of King's letters were anything but new. As they had indeed been made in three previous letters written from his prison cell and despite the authorities monitoring all his letters (I was told that every single one was passed to the police), for some reason someone had picked on mine, leaking it to the press. I took it as some sort of warning.

There was certainly little in the letter that hadn't already been written in his previous letters. In the letter to me, which was published word for word in some publications, King once again reiterated the reasons he had sacked Broncano and went on to say that Rocío had died in Jane Maynard's car and that four people were involved.

Practically the only things that were new were that he was now claiming that Peewee's brother John was monitoring the movements of the girl and that he had been told to 'smoke a cigarette and throw it by her body' so he would implicate himself. In the letter, which I only finally received somewhat comically six months later, he also claimed he had seen Dolores stabbing Rocío in the back seat. He wrote:

Robbie was driving; I was in the passenger seat; Rocío's uncle was sitting behind Robbie and Dolores was behind me. Dolores was talking over her shoulder to Robbie while she was half over the back seat where Rocío was and she was stabbing her.

A few days later the judge herself went to Alhaurín prison to clarify the claims and in the session, that again made headlines, King confirmed many of the points he had made in the letter and corrected some of the more confusing ones. He reiterated that he was indeed now blaming Dolores and Graham, insisting he was a scapegoat and that he was being framed. He claimed that Graham had been the first to stab the girl some three times at the initial scene, while Dolores did the rest in the car. He said he had been given four tablets of LSD that night and that he hadn't seen Dolores again until he saw her on television when she was arrested a year later. He also said that he had always blamed Dolores for the crime, well before his second statement, and had told Luis Miguel, the psychologist at Alhaurín prison, perhaps seven or eight times that in reality the murderer was Dolores Vázquez.

Through his new solicitor, Saavedra, he also offered to undertake a lie-detector test and pleaded to be regressed by hypnosis in a bid to try and remember more detail from the time in question. 'It was four years ago and there are things that he doesn't remember,' said Saavedra, a highly experienced lawyer, who had previously represented a host of famous Spaniards, including singers Isabel Pantoja and Ana Obregon. His request was, however, turned down.

Chapter Sixteen

Did He Really Do It?

Of course, whether found guilty or not by the Spanish courts –
and it was inconceivable that he would ever get off – the fundamental question must be did Tony Bromwich really go from
being the Holloway Strangler to Tony King, the cold-blooded
murderer of two teenage girls?

It is a question that has haunted me for much of the year it
has taken me to write this book – and it will continue to haunt
me for years to come. While I feel the evidence is stacked
heavily against Tony King in the murder of Sonia Carabantes
(there is too much direct evidence to put him there), I have
certainly had major doubts from the beginning about his exact
involvement in the murder of Rocío Wanninkhof.

There have been various theories about what happened on
that night in October 1999. One that it was a drug deal that
Rocío stumbled across, another that the teenager knew too
much about the business going on at Lubina Sol, another that
she disapproved and planned to go to the police about a brothel
that her uncle planned to open in Altos del Rodeo. There is
even one that suggests that the trio of King, Graham and Jon

Daniels were re-enacting a bizarre homosexual fantasy, which involved the killing of a girl.

While mostly far-fetched, there are certainly too many discrepancies and coincidences about the sole prosecution of King that night. And we mustn't forget that a woman – Dolores Vázquez – was properly tried and convicted of the murder before later being exonerated.

With too much evidence on others, and no clear motive for King murdering the girl – the sexual one lacking credibility due to Rocío being neither sexually assaulted nor raped – there will always be doubts. None more strongly than from the dead girl's family who have always insisted Vázquez was to blame – and indeed continued with their own costly private prosecution even after the judge announced the case would be solely against King.

My own theory started to firm up after getting to know one key witness in the case. A long-time timeshare salesman, Louise Deravairere, knew two of the key protagonists, Robbie Graham and Tony King, extremely well. Indeed, she lived with Graham for two-and-a-half years and was with him on the day of his initial arrest. She was deeply in love with him and even persuaded her family to pay for his airfare back to England, where he stayed with them for almost three months. She knew Graham intimately and unlike the vast majority of people I came across in those early months of the saga, was the one person who remained supportive of Graham, forever putting forward his side and trying to defend him.

Despite having endured constant infidelities and numerous physical attacks from him – at least one leaving her in hospital – she continually backed up his story to me (via a series of bizarre late-night phone calls), as well as to police and, later, journalists from the *News of the World*.

But the pretty, mixed-race Cheshire girl eventually broke

down a couple of months later to reveal what she claimed had really happened on the night of Rocío's murder in 1999.

Over a series of long-distance calls, and later heart-to-hearts in her home town of Brighton, she slowly told me exactly what Graham had told her about the night in question. This is what she claimed.

Her concerns about Robbie's involvement that night, began on the day that they first heard the news of Tony King's arrest in August 2003. At the time she and Robbie had been staying in the Hotel La Ermita in Nerja, since they had done a 'midnight flit' from his apartment in Calahonda, owing 3,000 euros in rent. Robbie had got the news in a phone call to a colleague Jeremy Stokes around mid-morning and came straight back to the suite they were sharing on the second floor of the hotel. He was in a real state and quickly burst into tears.

'His reaction was very strange,' she recalled. 'He came in and threw himself on to the bed crying like a baby. He said Tony had been arrested and kept repeating: "He did it, I know he did it." I didn't know what he was talking about at first, but as soon as we put the news on and I heard the name Rocío mentioned the hairs sprang up on the back of my neck.

'I knew straightaway that Robbie must have been involved. He'd frequently been on about this local girl who had gone missing some years earlier. He told me her name was Rocío and her mother had been a cleaner who they worked with at Lubina Sol. I didn't know anything about the case as in 1999 I was nowhere near the Costa del Sol, but Robbie had soon filled me in. It was all quite strange and as time went on he would tell me more and more about her death, usually bringing it up when he was drunk or stoned.

'A couple of times he hinted that he knew a lot more about the death than he had let on. He also said there were things I would not believe that he had done. I'd say what? But he would clam up and just say: "things". It was actually quite irritating.'

She went on to recall how the day after Sonia's death they had got a phone call from King, much earlier than normal at 9a.m., saying he had been in a car accident and asking for Robbie's advice. Louise had picked up the phone in bed and quickly passed it to Robbie, who had taken it in another room. Talking in a low voice he had come back to bed 15 minutes later and told her simply: 'Kingie's been in another accident.' And that was that until Louise went to pick Robbie up from work two days later at Lubina Sol, to find him engrossed deep in conversation with Tony King at the downstairs bar. 'They were talking about his car, which was parked outside, and he seemed desperate to get a part, a hubcap or a light-bulb cover, or something like that,' said Louise, who had straightaway started to play with Tony's daughter Sabrina. 'Tony seemed quite flustered and there was a tension in the air and I'm now sure they were talking all about the murders.'

It was a Sunday and Louise recalled how they had ended up going out to a favourite restaurant, Tropicana, in La Cala and while she played with Sabrina on the beach nearby the pair talked in whispers. 'But as soon as I came back into earshot they would clearly change the subject and talk about football or something. But I managed to catch a fair bit of it anyway, in particular the two of them talking about Rocío. It was all quite suspicious,' she remembered.

So it was particularly alarming to see her boyfriend collapsing in tears on the news of his friend's arrest. 'He was completely on edge in a way I had never seen him before,' recalled Louise. 'He was crying and in a really weird way kept trying to condone Tony's behaviour, without saying what had happened. I kept saying what did he do and how do you know? But he would stop short from telling me.'

But that evening after they had gone out for a few beers at a bar called Big Al's and Robbie had scored two grams of cocaine, he sat up and finally told her the whole story. 'A good part of me didn't want to know,' said Louise, who had met Graham when they had worked together in a timeshare company in Benidorm in August 2000. 'But I guess he just had to get it off his chest and I was the only person he could trust. I had stuck with him for two and a half years, the longest relationship he'd ever had, through constant bullying and beatings and I guess he figured I would stick with him through this.'

Talking over a coffee at a restaurant near her work in Brighton she continued: 'He had never mentioned Dolores or Tony in connection to the murder before, but now he was suddenly saying that Tony and her had done it, and the police would come for him next, and I kept asking him: "Why?" And, "How do you know? How do you know?" And eventually it all came out.

'First of all he described it like he was not there, saying Tony had turned up at his house at 4a.m. in a real state saying that Dolores had stabbed the girl, that she just went crazy "stabbing and stabbing and stabbing". He said that Dolores had paid Tony to help, but that it had got out of hand and she ended up stabbing Rocío and Tony could not stop her. He claimed she had started hitting Rocío to get at her mother or something and then Tony said she went mad and started stabbing her. When Tony turned up at Robbie's house terrified, she was in the car and Robbie told him there was nothing he could do.'

Sensing Louise was still holding back, perhaps in an attempt to cover up for her ex-boyfriend, who by this point had gone to work in Egypt, I gently pushed her to reveal more. After nearly five minutes of silence, in which she smoked and stared into space, she suddenly blurted out: 'She did it, she did it', adding, quite clearly terrified by the significance of her allegation: 'I can get in trouble with the Spanish police for not saying anything. I had to give a statement and I lied to protect him. And now it doesn't matter any more, they have let him go and he is walking around Brighton scot-free and he knows where I am and he'll know that I have spoken to you.

'I'm scared and can't understand why they have released him and given him his passport back. I was hoping he would be charged and taken to Alhaurín prison to await trial like Tony. I thought they had enough [evidence] without me having to say anything.'

By now sobbing quietly, she continued to allege: 'Robbie told me that Dolores was having an affair with the girl's mother and that it had gone pear-shaped. The idea was to hurt the mother by hurting the closest person to her. If you beat somebody up you cause them pain for a few weeks and then the pain goes away and they can carry on with their own lives. But to really hurt somebody you go for those close to them. They wanted to kill her. That is the way minds of psychos work. Some people know where to stop and some don't.'

She continued to claim that Robbie had finally admitted he had been driving on the night of the death and Dolores was in the back of the car when they picked Rocío up. 'They knew the girl would get in the car because she knew Dolores. Robbie was driving. Dolores was in the back. Tony was sitting next to Robbie . . .' And again she clammed up, shivering into her coffee. It was, by now, nearly the end of her lunch hour and I suggested we continued after work.

Before walking her to her job as a British Telecom salesgirl, she added: 'You know Tony would not have been capable of doing things like that himself. He would not have been capable of knowing where to hide the items. He would have panicked and messed up. He needed Robbie to help him. Robbie was like his dad. He told him to do something and he would do it.'

Later, over an informal supper of pizza and beer, she came completely clean. Despite being nervous about the reper-cussions of implicating her ex-boyfriend – and re-emphasizing how dangerous he was – she alleged: 'Tony did not kill Rocío.

Yes; he helped to move the body, and yes; he was there. Yes; it was his car, and yes; he was paid to drive. But he didn't know she was going to be killed and he did not do it. He was there and he panicked and he should have said something, but he was scared of Robbie and Dolores and the power she had . . . and on top of that he had been paid to keep quiet because things went too far, further than they should have gone. And anyway Tony felt that he owed Robbie as he was always giving him bits of money for this and that. He kept him in money, in drink and drugs and paid for everything he needed. Robbie was the real instigator. Tony was only guilty of covering up the crime, not the other way round. Tony should have been released for that crime, not Robbie. He and Dolores should still be inside awaiting trial.'

Louise, who lived in Spain from 1997 to 2003, claimed Robbie told her Tony had introduced him to Dolores in a pub a few weeks before the murder to discuss the plan. 'Dolores told them that she wanted to hurt Rocío's mother and she wanted Rocío slapped around a bit. It turned out she knew she was going to the local carnival that night and Dolores would pay Tony the equivalent of about £700 to £800 to pick her up while she gave her a few slaps to scare her.

'But once in the car, Robbie said things quickly got out of hand. They were off their heads from drinking and taking cocaine when they saw Rocío, and Dolores said; 'Come on we'll give you a lift home' . . . she got in the back next to Dolores and then they stopped the car somewhere and Dolores started hitting her, but then went mad and started stabbing Rocío. He said they panicked and tried to stop Dolores and get her out of the car, but by then it was too late and Rocío was too badly hurt and Robbie had to finish off the job.

'He said she was probably already dead and argued, how could they take her to hospital? I don't know if he either strangled her or smacked her about a bit but he told me he put something – and I can't remember if it was a jumper or a jacket – over his hand to smack her or strangle her with. At one stage they were outside of the car, which was parked up not far from La Cala on the back roads leading towards Mijas and the racecourse. She was actually killed there and then they dumped her body back in the car and took it to Marbella. Robbie said Dolores told them to dump the body at a place that she and Rocío's mother used to use as a rendezvous point. The coat and clothes Robbie had on him at the time were taken off and put in bags with Rocío's stuff and they were dumped in bins somewhere out of the way on the way back.

'Robbie said that Tony was really het up, and absolutely petrified. He said he was shaking like a leaf. Anyway they dropped Dolores off and then Robbie told Tony to drop him off and go down and be seen at Cecilia's place in Fuengirola. He said Tony then got changed and came back and they drove up to Marbella to dump the body where Dolores said to dump it.'

While visibly shaken by her words to me, Louise said it was a real weight off her mind to have told someone. While, at this point, having no intention of following it up through the courts, she was merely pleased to have unburdened herself with the gory details. 'I have not been able to sleep for the last few months knowing what I know,' she said. 'It has been horrific having to put up with Robbie being out on the streets and I just hope the police in Spain will broaden their minds to realize that more than one person was involved in this case and go out and prove what really happened,' she said. 'I pray that they find the evidence to prosecute Robbie, because right now there is a guilty man walking.'

Deravairere had met Robbie Graham having fallen into timeshare after reading an innocuous advert in her local paper in the north of England. A typically dreary November day, the advert in the *Manchester Evening News* had literally jumped off the page for the attractive young girl in her early twenties. It had read 'Come and have fun in the sun!' and there was a seminar in the Britannia Hotel that weekend. 'I persuaded my friend Pam to come for an interview and three weeks later we were on our flights to the Costa Blanca,' recalled Louise.

She was certainly something of a catch for the company, based in Benidorm. An intelligent girl, she had excelled at school and after eight O-levels went on to do a BTEC in Business and Finance. Leading to a decent job in the bookmaker Ladbrokes, where she had risen to the post of trainee manager, she had eventually become a junior manager at a central heating company, based in central Manchester.

But by November 1997 she was bored and ready for a new challenge. No one could argue that the new job, initially as an OPC with Timelinx, was in any way boring. A typical timeshare set-up, she had soon become one of the best sales-women on the Costa Blanca, regularly bringing in £10,000 a week for the company. 'I'd secured my first deal on the second day and within a month was earning more money than I could ever have dreamed of,' recalled Deravairere, who had grown up in the Cheshire village of Leyland, with an English father and Dominican mother.

'I'll never forget that first payday, getting around £4,000 in cash. It was a huge wad of notes and I went straight out on a huge spending spree buying a couple of new suits, the latest mobile phone and the best champagne I could find. I obviously had the gift for timeshare and on a couple of occasions made sales totalling around £30,000 a week, which being on a 20 per cent commission was a very decent earner. Put it this way I was never short of cash – I sometimes earned £5,000 a week – and was having a fantastic time.'

Garnering the nickname Lulu, she, initially at least, had no complaints about the job or her bosses, who bent over backwards to look after her. The Costa Blanca was the gentle end of the timeshare industry and it was relatively laid-back and civilized. 'Pam and I were given rooms in a lovely apartment overlooking the marina in Altea and I was soon dating one of my colleagues, a really sweet Belgian guy called Sven. After a few months I'd moved in with him and I soon gave birth to a baby girl Damilee.'

But for Lulu, Sven was simply too nice and didn't have the same ambition or tastes. While he was from a family of millionaires he didn't have the magic touch and his family refused to give him handouts. He worked as a driver for the timeshare deck, but didn't bring in much money. 'I was always the one bringing home the bacon, working ten-hour days right up to the birth of the baby. I was even back at work within four weeks of the birth, while Sven would spend half the time sitting at home. By the end of 1999 I had called it a day, which really broke his heart.'

The following year, Robbie Graham had arrived on the scene 'like a breath of fresh air'. Having spent some six months in Lanzarote working for one of John Palmer's ventures he had got his orders to take over the Timelinx deck in Benidorm. It was an assignment he couldn't refuse and in August 2000, he arrived with a bodyguard in tow, called Mark, who was as wide as he was tall.

But while Robbie already had something of a reputation for being 'someone to avoid', Louise found the fellow Mancunian dashing, successful and confident. He also took a shine to the young star of the organization, who flirted with him at every occasion. 'I won't deny I fell in love with him. He was such a hunk and very charming,' she recalls. 'He was really something of a face and had a lot more experience than most of the other salesman on the Costa Blanca. He loved bragging about his knowledge and, soon, his Salford Sausage. At first the sex was quite good and he always took me out on dates. We had a lot of fun at work and hanging out with my friends.'

But by the end of 2001 this had all ended when Graham got

new orders to relocate to the Costa del Sol. Back in the big league – where the numbers were double or triple and the transactions always in cash – Graham would be back on home soil. He had worked there on many previous occasions and had a raft of old acquaintances. He had soon persuaded Louise to go with him, despite it being a step down the ladder job-wise and initially having to hand out scratch cards again.

Things were, however, considerably better as regards accommodation, and they landed on their feet with a large three-bedroom apartment in the centre of Nerja, just a few hundred yards from their deck. But within just days Robbie's behaviour began to change. Fuelled by heavy drinking and increasing amounts of cocaine, he got more aggressive and began to attack Deravairere physically. 'Away from my friends he turned into an arsehole,' recalls Louise. 'The only people we saw were his scummy lowlife friends, many of them criminals with dodgy pasts. Probably 90 per cent of them were on cocaine and most couldn't go back to England for one reason or another. They were a bad influence on Robbie and he started drinking every night, going straight to the pub from work and not returning till late.'

But while he would frequently stay out late he always insisted Louise came to pick him up from the pub when he was ready. 'He didn't care whether it was 8p.m. or 11p.m., he wanted me at home when he called. He would go out while I got to stay cooped up at home on my own and wouldn't let me see any of the girls from work. He called them slags and wouldn't let me go to their barbecues or nights out. He was a bit of a loner and didn't like socializing in mixed groups.'

But his behaviour at home wasn't much better. 'The large amounts of cocaine and alcohol could turn him into a raging bull and he would often hit me. In fact the beatings started almost as soon as we arrived in Nerja and in our first week he grabbed me during an argument and punched me right in the face. He even tried to throw me off the balcony that night. I went to bed crying in pain and remember the next day waking up with my eye all bloodshot and bulging out and he had the nerve to ask me how I had done it, going on to announce that I must have fallen over while drunk the previous night.

'He said if I grassed him up to anyone he would get security on to me. I knew what that meant and knew that Robbie wasn't short of useful contacts in that area. But despite not telling anyone the word soon got around regardless and everyone at work knew what was going on. Quite a few of them told me on the QT what a psychopath he was and that I should leave him. One of the bosses John Wiseman told me I would never get a decent life out of him. He had always had a cocaine problem and if it wasn't for the drugs he could have been a millionaire many times over.

'There was certainly no doubt that he was spending a small fortune on the drug; a couple of grams a night, at about 120 euros a time and sometimes more. While I won't deny that I took a few lines now and again with him, it was not unusual for Robbie to get through as many as 15 lines in an evening. He was an addict and just couldn't shake it.'

But it was the violence and not the drugs that were causing the problems. 'The beatings just got worse and worse. I took hundreds of them and even ended up in hospital a few times. On one occasion he was arrested after attacking me in the street in broad daylight. It was a Sunday afternoon in Nerja and he suddenly held me up against this wall and was punching me in the face during an argument. It was agony, but luckily this girl quickly phoned the police and then took me to hospital when he ran off. My nose was bleeding and I had cuts on my lip and eye when the police turned up at the clinic.

'They managed to arrest him later that afternoon, but not until they had chased him through the streets when he jumped off the roof terrace to evade capture. They kept him overnight, and had him up in court the following morning in nearby Torrox, but while this girl, who had witnessed it, was willing to testify I had stupidly refused to press charges so they had to let him go and he came home begging for forgiveness.'

More chillingly was the night that he nearly strangled her to death. While clearly terrified of the consequence of telling the story she recalled how he had jumped on her during one mammoth row. 'We were screaming at each other and the next thing I know he was on top of me with his hands around my neck,' she recalls. 'He said I'm going to kill you and he leant all his weight on my neck. He was kneeling on top of me with one knee on my chest and one on my neck and the more I struggled the tighter he held me. I was terrified and really thought I was going to die. I literally gave up and stopped moving. I think I passed out before he stopped. I came to in real agony and hyperventilating. I don't know why I ever let him get away with it?'

More pertinently, she also revealed that Robbie had a somewhat sinister fixation with knives and wouldn't think twice about holding one to her throat. Indeed she recalled how he would often sit in a restaurant playing games with his knife, stabbing it between his outstretched fingers or moving it between them like a trick. Demonstrating how he used to move the knife from finger to finger, she recalled how it used to unsettle people. 'I'd have to order him to put it down as you could see it was making people uncomfortable,' she explained. 'But he just had this mad fixation with knives and loved demonstrating his skills. He certainly had no qualms about threatening me with them and on quite a few occasions he put a knife to my throat. He'd do it during arguments or to get his way in bed.

'I deliberately only kept a couple of sharp knives in the apartment and would hide them as much as possible, so he couldn't get hold of them in a fit of rage. I even kept them under my pillow a few times. Robbie is crazy and wouldn't think twice about stabbing you, or using something to hurt you. He would often throw knives at me in anger and would pick other things up and smash them in a rage. He was always destroying my stuff. He would pick things up and just throw them, smashing them. He would throw things at me and sometimes I would think, God, how close was that to my head?'

She also knew about his violent reputation with women and in particular about the ex-girlfriend Michelle, who had almost killed him when she turned the knife on him. 'I knew he had this big scar on his leg from this girl Michelle who he lived with in Madeira. I knew she had stabbed him and he had been to hospital and nearly bled to death and was told by friends that she had done it through self-defence. He never told me exactly what happened and the story changed all the time, but I knew this girl Michelle had moved to the Costa del Sol a couple of years ago and a mutual friend told me she was absolutely petrified of Robbie. Why didn't I heed the warning I do not know.'

Pointedly, Louise recounted how Graham would also try and rape her. Usually late at night in a drunken rage, he would pin her down in bed and force her to have sex. 'Sex was never that good, despite Robbie being well endowed. We would often go for ages without sex, usually after we had had a violent argument, and pretty much the only time I could bring myself to have sex with him was when I was drunk. He used to like watching porno movies and would make me get them for him at the video shop and when we did have sex it was at best so-so and the only way he could come was doggy style.'

She is convinced that it was his reacquaintance with his old timeshare colleagues, including Tony King, when they moved back to the Costa del Sol in 2001 that heightened his sexual deviance. 'I believe Robbie would have violent, orgy-style sex with Tony when they had been drinking. Drink flips him out and makes him aggressive. He told me that when the two of them had lived together after Celia had dumped Tony they were out all the time getting up to mischief. He talked about going on these missions – mish-mashes, he called them – and being completely wrecked, it sounded very sordid.'

Sensationally, she also believes he is guilty of raping other women. 'Yes I think Robbie has raped people before,' she stated matter-of-factly. 'Put it this way, he would disappear quite often late at night, like Tony did. One minute he would be in the pub with me and next he would be gone. I used to think he was simply off taking cocaine but now I think he might have been out doing other things. The way he behaved, I can just feel it. He was always making crude remarks about young girls he saw in the street. He would say things like they deserved it if anything happened to them, and how could their parents "let them out dressed like that?" There was also the way he tried to justify Tony's behaviour after he was arrested. Saying things like it wasn't his fault and: "What the fuck were those girls doing walking around late at night dressed like that anyway?"'

But there were other clues like the times he had frequently mentioned how he had been accused of trying to rape a girl at a wedding in England. 'I've no idea whose wedding but he said it had happened after he tried to kiss this girl in a doorway at the reception and she suddenly went running back into the wedding saying he was trying to rape her. I don't remember any other details, but it certainly wouldn't surprise me if it was true.'

She also caught the timeshare salesman cheating on her on various occasions. 'I actually left him for two months in early 2003 after catching him out with this Australian girl Christina, who had recently joined the team. I found out when I saw a text message she had sent him saying "I enjoyed it last night – love from C". Robbie, of course, completely denied it, but the next night I had it out with Christina when I went over and asked her straight: "Did you shag my boyfriend?" And the stupid girl actually admitted she had.'

It should have spelt the end for their relationship, Louise admits, and for a time she went to stay at her boss's house in a huge villa in Fuengirola. With everyone's encouragement she should finally have left her violent boyfriend, but somehow he wormed his way back into her affections and by the middle of March 2003 they were again living together.

'I was really, really stupid,' she admits today. 'I had spent the best part of a year desperately unhappy and wanting to leave him but had been too scared to try. Next thing I was living with him again and things were as bad as ever. The beatings got worse and I stopped being able to think straight. I was on sleeping tablets to help me blank it all out and I would often pour my heart out to my family in England, crying down the phone, promising I would leave him, but somehow I never could. I know I should have left him, but I was beginning to lose face. He had some sort of control over me and I was lacking courage and felt isolated. I was in a rut and lacked energy to pull myself out. At times I felt I was literally about to crack up. All my friends were back in Benidorm and I had no one to turn to.'

Strong words. I had first got a definite hint that Louise wanted to come clean about Graham in November 2003, on the day of King's second testimony in Fuengirola court. I had heard a series of nasty stories about the way he had mistreated her, but every time I suggested it to her, she evaded the subject and went on to something else. This time she finally admitted it was true. Calling her to find out if she had heard from Robbie she suddenly blurted out that she was 'sure' that Graham was much more involved in the death of Rocío than he had let on.

Once Graham had left to take a timeshare job in Egypt, Deravairere found herself free from his grip. Perhaps accidentally, perhaps not, she blurted out on the phone: 'I know I've only got half of the story from him. Robbie had something to hide and I've got a feeling that he is involved . . . and a lot more than he has let on. I can just tell from the way he speaks; the way he is; the way he has tried to condone Tony's behaviour.

'He was trying to make out that Tony was pushed to do it. That it was some sort of accident, nothing more. I can tell he was involved.' It was intriguing stuff and only added to my hunch that Graham was perhaps a lot more involved than anyone was giving credit.

Watching her words carefully (and never, it should be noted, asking for a penny for her story) she told me that Robbie had landed a new job with a Russian company in Aswan (I later discovered this was through his old friend Peter Moore). She said that she was still in contact with him despite having broken up when he left and said he had told her he had no intention of going back to 'fucking Spain', because of the way he had been treated. 'First he lied by telling me he did not have to make any declaration and when I found out he said he was too scared to go back because he thought he was going to be rearrested. He had started acting really weirdly when he heard that Tony was about to make a statement. He kept saying he was going to try and go to Egypt as soon as possible. He said something about Interpol and said that Egypt would be one of the best places to go because it didn't have an extradition agreement with Spain.

'I told him I did not believe a word he was saying and told him he needed to go back to Spain to sort everything out. I tried to provoke him into telling us what had really happened but we ended up having a big argument, which, luckily, was in front of my family. It ended with me telling him to leave and he finally left. The next day he took the flight to Cairo.'

It seemed clear to me that she had a good deal more to tell me about the timeshare salesman and I told her I would be coming back to England at Christmas and would like to come down to Brighton to interview her for my book in the new year.

Having moved back to her parents' and gone on a course of

antidepressants in a bid to get over her ordeal, she was starting to get her life back together with a steady job as a call-centre manager. But, before I could get down to see her in early January 2004, it emerged that Graham had already paid her another surprise visit. The shock visit had come after he had lost his job in Egypt by going to Spain to testify for a week without telling his bosses. Despite having neither family, nor friends in the Sussex town, he hoped to be able to persuade Louise to have him back and turned up unannounced on her parents' doorstep just before Christmas, begging to stay. Charming and meek, with no money and nowhere else to live, the family agreed to let him stay for a few days while he went flat hunting in the area.

But inevitably things quickly turned sour and he found himself thrown out after an extremely disturbing incident on New Year's Eve. Details are sketchy as Louise still finds it hard to recall anything of the night, but it appears that at some point during the early hours of New Year's Day Graham attempted to strangle her in her sleep.

Her parents confirmed that an incident had happened after a heated row – in which it is alleged Robbie once again confessed his involvement in the murder of Rocío. Louise revealed how her teenage sister Laura had heard a stifled scream coming from her room and signs of a struggle at around 3a.m. Worried about her older sister, she had burst into the room to find Robbie on top of Louise with his hands around her neck. She was clearly struggling to be freed and Laura ran out to get her dad, who rushed in to order Robbie back downstairs. 'I can hardly remember anything as by 8p.m. I was completely out of it. I don't know why and fear that maybe my drink was spiked. But the next day I awoke in pain with a really sore wrist. I ended up having to go to hospital where they told me I had a fracture and put it in a splint. It seems Robbie had been trying to strangle me and luckily my sister had walked in

240

at just the right time. I might be lucky to be alive and had I not been so drunk would definitely have gone to the police.'

Her mother Mary confirmed: 'I think he lost his rag and launched himself at her and although I didn't see it, nothing would surprise me about him. There was certainly a lot of commotion and my younger daughter says she saw him with his hands on Louise's neck and thought he was strangling her. Louise always told me about the beatings he would give her and I begged her to leave him. I hate the fact that he's still here in Brighton, hanging around.'

He didn't stop pestering Louise, and from January to March 2004 he put her through a terrifying stalking campaign in which he would regularly turn up at her house, as well as her local pub the Damner Park.

He was certainly there one night in mid-January when I phoned up to see how she was faring. Amazingly she was able to joke about it as Robbie stood talking to a couple of regulars at the bar just ten yards away. 'He keeps bloody turning up,' she explained. 'He has been getting pally with all the regulars and even the landlord, buying various people drinks. They have no idea what he is really like, but he has continued to be a nightmare for me and the other night started giving me loads of abuse, telling me I was a scumbag and a bitch.'

A week later, on 22 January 2004, she told me he was following her 'everywhere' and was growing increasingly worried that he might try and attack her. By now living in a rented flat on the outskirts of Brighton – and pregnant from a new boyfriend, a local builder – she was adamant there was no turning back with Robbie. 'Things are completely over with him now. He's made my last three years sheer hell and there is no way I am going back to him. I am very happy with my new boyfriend Russell and we are having a baby together. I feel I had the blinkers on with Robbie. I had lived happily in Spain for three years until I met him and he is without a doubt one of the most manipulative, aggressive and nasty men around.

'I am pleased to have finally escaped him and at the end of the day they have let a guilty man walk free. The fact that he is able to walk the streets unhindered, while Tony is in prison is an outrage. They have put more women at risk and some day another girl is going to turn up dead. Robbie's ex-girlfriend Michelle is lucky not to be dead. I'm lucky not to be dead. Every day there is a small part at the back of my mind that says: "Watch out! He is going to get me", but I just try and brush it aside and hope he will move on. I'm scared and pray he moves on and leaves me alone one day.'

However, her words proved to be sadly prophetic when, a few weeks later, she found herself in hospital following a vicious attack from Graham. The dramatic development had certainly been a long time in coming, and building up from the first death threat she received from Graham on 7 February 2004. It was just as the relationship between them was becoming a bit more amicable. She had been due to meet him the following day to return some belongings he'd left at her house, but on the phone that night he suddenly launched into a diatribe against her. 'He said he was going to kill me. He said he knew where I lived and that he was going to sort me out. My whole family heard the phone conversation and it was at that point that I decided I wanted to testify against him.'

And that is when things started to get really nasty. Perhaps sensing that Louise was making plans to return to Spain to give evidence (and by now certainly hearing that I had been to Brighton to interview her), Graham increased his stalking campaign against Louise. With increasing numbers of aggressive phone calls and a couple of rows in the pub, by the end of the month she had had enough and through the encouragement of her family reported his behaviour to Sussex Police.

By 10 March 2004 she told me she had been for a series of

interviews with detectives detailing his behaviour in England as well as his alleged involvement in Rocío's murder. 'I told them about the attack on New Year's Eve and how he had been stalking and threatening me by phone ever since,' she said. 'I gave them his address and they told me to be careful and said they would keep an eye on him.'

A few days later, it is understood, Graham was actually brought in for questioning. While the circumstances of the arrest are vague – and it is unclear exactly what they asked him – Louise claimed that the minute he was released he was on the phone to berate her. She told me (on 15 March 2004): 'He said he had been brought in for questioning over "a couple of sex offences" and another crime in Spain that Tony might have been involved in. He said the two detectives, who said they were from Scotland Yard, did not know much about the case and once again threatened me to keep quiet. He was really quite scary.'

And naturally, of course, the overstretched and under-staffed force did remarkably little and Graham continued plaguing her with threatening calls, usually withholding his number, until she stopped answering. The final straw came when she told him about her planned trip to Spain and that she was pregnant to her new boyfriend and had no intentions of going back to him. 'He was furious and said he was going to pin me down and force a load of tablets down my throat to make it look like suicide,' she said.

The next big attack had come on the evening of 28 March 2004, when Louise had been walking across Preston Park to meet some friends in a local pub. It was just getting dark on that Sunday evening when she saw Graham – who had shaved his head – walking towards her 'at a brisk pace' with a new girlfriend Beverly Chopin in tow.

As Louise recalled a few days later: 'As soon as he saw me he started screaming at me that I was a traitor, a liar, and a scumbag and then he pushed me to the floor and started punching and kicking me in the stomach and head. His girlfriend was hitting me too and he must have punched me three times in the head and had me pinned down while he hit my stomach before my screams managed to attract attention and some local woman called the police.'

According to Louise, they ran off the minute they heard police sirens, but were arrested at his new girlfriend's home a few hours later, only to be somewhat inexplicably released without charge, having completely denied the attack.

Louise, meanwhile, had been rushed to the Royal Sussex Hospital where she claimed to have had a broken nose, two black eyes and bruises right across her body, with particular pains in her kidneys and stomach. Incredibly, a scan showed that her two-month-old unborn baby appeared unharmed.

A few days later on 1 April 2004, however, there was to be more trouble, when Graham's new girlfriend and teenage daughter turned up at Louise's parents' house making threats. 'They started banging on the window, shouting and screaming that I was a liar and threatening me to drop the charges. It was really terrifying and I admit I lost it and stupidly ran out with a knife in my hand to tell them to get lost. One of our neighbours had obviously seen the whole thing and a few minutes later the police turned up and arrested me for possessing an offensive weapon. It was ridiculous but luckily my lawyer managed to get me off saying it was self-defence.'

Incredibly, Graham – who the police had still not charged with any offence – was to continue mocking Louise's family by phone and on Saturday, 3 April, made a particularly nasty verbal threat to her mother in Brighton town centre. 'He came storming over to her, his face all twisted and aggressive and spat out that I should watch out and that he was going to drive me out of Brighton,' claims Louise. 'It really scared my mum, who again called the police.'

But while the police continued to try and calm the family down, insisting that they would be given Grade 1 status for rapid response and panic alarms, nothing actually materialized.

Indeed, it wasn't until 14 April 2004 that the police are understood to have finally arrested Graham and his girlfriend Beverly Chopin again. Hauling them in for questioning about the 28 March attack, they had their passports taken and were ordered to be available for further inquiries. Graham was told not to contact Louise under any circumstances.

Meanwhile, Louise was asked to make an in-depth video testimony for Interpol and on Thursday, 20 April 2004 she spent the day detailing Robbie's claims. Interviewed for five hours at a safe house more commonly used for rape victims, she gave a full and frank account similar to the one she had given to me in January. In the eight-page statement – which was later sent to the police in Spain – she talked, among many other things, about Graham's close friendship with Tony King and the violence he subjected her to.

The main difference was that in her new statement she claimed that Robbie only told her about his involvement once he was safely back in England. Telling me she had done this 'to prevent being charged later for covering up for Robbie', she claimed that he had first told her in October 2003 after a night out at a local pub. She added that he had gone on to admit it two more times over the next three months. The second time she said was after a night out at the Walkabout bar, in Brighton town centre, a few days before his trip to Egypt. She said, by then, his attitude had changed and he didn't seem at all worried that Tony was going to take the rap for the crime. She said: 'He had a much more every man for himself attitude and he seemed to be saying to me: "I don't give a shit. Tony can take the rap." It seemed to me that he was thinking that Tony was going down for a load of crimes, he may as well go down for this one too.'

The only other main difference was that she claimed that

Robbie had actually stabbed the girl 'two or three times' to finish the job, rather than hit or smother her. Otherwise, her claims in the witness statement, of which I got a copy, were remarkably similar.

Convinced she would quickly be summoned to give evidence to the judge in Fuengirola, it came as something of a surprise when she had heard nothing by the beginning of May. And that was when things took another sudden unexpected turn for the worse.

Having told me by phone that she would come over to give her evidence regardless the following week – and having booked her flights for 12 May 2004 – the text message I received on Wednesday, 5 May came as something of a bombshell to say the least.

It was short and to the point. 'Jon I stabbed Robbie yesterday – could not take his threats anymore – just been released.' Received as I was having dinner with my wife in Seville, I could hardly believe my eyes. In terms of confessing to a crime it was pithy and to the point; in terms of Louise's case against Graham it was a disaster. Straightaway I got on the phone to find out what had happened and got a tearful Louise begging me to understand how she had come to leave Graham in hospital with a four-inch laceration in his abdomen and a deep wound to his hand.

The attack had happened the previous day after she had received yet another text message from Graham – one·of many over the previous week – which meant he was breaking his bail conditions. While it hadn't said anything specific, she admitted she lost her temper and decided to go and confront her ex-boyfriend. 'I'll admit I was tense and lost my rag,' she told me. 'He has been calling me three or four times a week and making my life hell. I know I shouldn't be talking to him, but I talk to him in a bid to keep him close. It feels safer that way. I am terrified of him and think he is going to try and kill me, and it seems more sensible to know your enemy and what he is doing. Anyway, he was staying just around the corner from my mum's and I was worried for her. I wanted to go and face him once and for all. Tell him it was over and to please leave me alone. I jumped on a bus, and started banging on his door the minute I got there. The next thing I know he is at the front door with this bloody great knife, about 20cm long and he lunged at me.

'But luckily because he is right-handed and it was in his left hand he lost control of the knife and it fell on the floor, leaving me with a small cut on my hand. Realizing he had lost it he slammed the door and I picked it up. It had made me even more furious and I started throwing stones at the window, when I heard him running back to the front door and he came charging at me again. I didn't know what happened exactly but I just reached the knife up in self-defence and it stabbed him in the stomach. The next thing I know he is lying on the floor and the police are arresting me and rushing him to hospital.'

A nasty incident, the long and short of it was Graham spending a couple of days in hospital being stitched up, while Louise found herself charged with actual bodily harm. Ordered to appear in court on 11 May 2004, it was looking extremely unlikely she would make it to Spain the following day. But due to a last-minute appeal to the judge (on the basis of self-defence), and after much deliberation and demands from Graham's lawyers that she be remanded in custody, she was awarded bail. Her solicitor Richard Frank told me: 'She was eventually given bail, but it was touch-and-go and looked like she might have had to spend a few months in prison awaiting trial. His side were certainly hoping that, and argued aggressively. It is a very odd case and I have a lot of reading up to do.'

He certainly did. Meanwhile, Louise against whom the case has since been dropped, bravely made her way to Malaga airport on 12 May 2004, where I was waiting, first to take her to make a deposition to King's lawyers, Javier Saavedra and

Ignacio Prieto, and then the following day to the judge in Fuengirola.

It led to yet another major shock. All squeezing into Prieto's small Mazda sports car, we knew we were in line for a somewhat frosty reception from the judge, who was said to be wrapping up her investigations into the case and keen to send it to trial. But what we got was, in my opinion, one of the most scandalous, reckless examples of judicial work ever imaginable. Having arrived at the court, the two lawyers had gone in to ask if Louise could make a deposition in the King case, only to be told by Judge María del Rio that she was not in the slightest bit interested.

Perhaps she had an important lunch appointment (or maybe the paperwork was stacking up) but she insisted Louise was not an important witness and moreover claimed she was lying. She told them that she had received her testimony from England via Interpol some days earlier and, without informing the relevant parties, had already brushed it aside. Prieto was furious. 'She said Louise was making the whole thing up for financial gain and that she just wants to go on television to make money,' he spat out disgustedly. 'She said she knew all about her testimony and it was bullshit. It was quite amazing.'

And this was in spite of the judge actually meeting her – and the crucial fact that she was meant to be compiling the evidence for the case, which would actually be tried by a separate judge and jury in Malaga at a later date.

But that was the end of that, as far as she was concerned, and she told them to take Louise to the local police, if she really insisted on making a report. And that is exactly what they did.

Taking the stiff 15-minute walk uphill to the Guardia Civil's Mijas barracks, which is actually based just inside Fuengirola, she and the two lawyers duly went in to ask if she could give evidence in the case. And while, unlike the judge, the police could not refuse, they insisted she came back in a couple of hours, by which time, who should be outside and taking photographs, but none other than Juan Gey Vicente (who was unwittingly snapped himself by Prieto's mobile phone).

It was a case that got stranger and stranger by the day. Particularly so, when a few days later I would once again find myself making front-page news, after being accused of perverting the course of justice by trying to bribe a witness to change his testimony in the case.

The bizarre accusation had come about via an extremely strange turn of events, which began on the night of 12 May 2004 when Louise and I were having dinner at a restaurant in Marbella. Trying to rack our brains as to how to find former colleagues of Tony and Robbie who might remember the sort of work they were getting up to in 1999 and, more pertinently, any connections to Dolores Vázquez, Louise decided to ring her old friends Peter and Jenny Moore to see if they could help. The conversation with Jenny – whose husband had worked at Lubina Sol for years and later organized Robbie's trip to Egypt – was warm and friendly in spite of the fact that it was after 10p.m. Catching up about this and that, Louise finally explained that she was about to testify the following day in court and was hoping to find some other witnesses who might be able to back up her claims about Robbie and Dolores' involvement. Up till then there had been no solid evidence to link them to the case and she hoped to find some.

Her husband Peter had already told me a few months earlier that he was sure that Dolores had been to Lubina Sol a few times and that there was some connection between the trio. He said: 'I remember Dolores from Lubina Sol, one hundred per cent. But it was not until I saw the picture of her in the paper that I recognized her. She was not staff, but I certainly saw her at Lubina Sol half a dozen times. She had connections there.'

When asked what her involvement might have been with the business, he said he was pretty sure she was finding clients for the timeshare side of the hotel she ran, Club Sultan in Marbella. 'There was certainly something going on between them (Robbie and Tony) and she was there quite a few times,' he said. 'I expect she was trying to sell timeshare packs in her place.'

These claims were backed up by another former boss of King's (known as Chalkie), who had actually worked in the Club Sultan. 'I'm sure they knew each other and Tony and Dolores are liars if they say otherwise. A lot of people say Tony worked there, and if he did then they knew each other: fact. She has been director there for years and I worked for her when it was a timeshare resort. I don't know how many other timeshare decks sold for it, or if it is still a timeshare resort, but she was definitely in charge and had a lot of connections with the timeshare world.'

What Jenny was saying now to Louise and I completely backed these claims. 'Robbie, Dolores and Tony were friends and everyone at Lubina Sol knows Dolores used to go there,' she stated clearly. 'I know Dolores and it is a known fact that there was a connection and she used to come [to the deck] regularly.'

It was at this point that Louise asked her if she would consider making a witness statement to the police or court to this effect. She said she would 'think about it' and talk to her husband, who would be back around 12p.m. She gave Louise her mobile number and told her to give her a call 'any time' the following day.

But when Louise called at around 10a.m., before her aborted trip to testify in front of the judge, Jenny had already made up her mind to decline the plea. She reiterated to Louise that while she herself had seen Robbie, Tony and Dolores at Peter's house her husband had told her not to get involved. 'He does not want to get involved with that lot. He does not want his name used,' she said.

And that was that until, perhaps foolishly, I went back to

Peter the following day on 14 May 2004. With Louise growing disheartened and desperate to find people to back up her claims in court – and with the Spanish media increasingly sensing that Dolores and Graham would be imminently discharged – I agreed to go back to Peter to see if he could help.

As a journalist it came as more of an irritation, than a surprise, to hear him desperately trying to back-pedal. But while it was annoying, he unwittingly backed up much of what he had earlier told me and even gave more information in the process. He told me: 'I never said I saw Tony and Dolores talking together. Yes she had been at Lubina Sol and I believe that it is more than very likely that they knew each other. We knew Dolores through the cleaner and yes, we have seen her there, but whether she talked to Tony or Robbie I really can't say.' I soon discovered one of the reasons why not, when he added, almost as an explanation, that a certain person – one Juan Gey Vicente – had been 'pestering' him over recent days. He wouldn't tell me what exactly he wanted, but after giving me a few names of people who might be able to help, he closed by saying: 'There is certainly a lot more than meets the eye.'

I would discover this to my horror when, a few days later on 19 May 2004, I heard my name mentioned on the afternoon news. According to the reports – that were soon on the television news as well – Louise and I had been accused of offering money to Peter and Jenny Moore to give false information implicating Dolores Vázquez. It was a horrific accusation and well wide of the mark. It had stemmed from a report (or a *denuncia*, as it is known in Spain) being filed by the couple at Fuengirola police station on 14 May. In the *denuncia*, Peter Alan Moore and Jennifer Margaret Francom (who I had previously intended to use as off-the-record sources in the book) claimed that Louise and I had put them under 'considerable pressure' to step forward publicly to say the trio knew each other. They even claimed that Louise said she would make sure they got the money back that Robbie apparently owed them from an earlier job if they helped.

And at the bottom of the page, in thick black ink, were the words: 'Interpreted into Spanish by Juan Gey Vicente.'

It was serious stuff and having seen the four-page report, Dolores Vázquez's lawyer held an immediate press conference, insisting he was personally going to take out a private prosecution against both Louise and me on Dolores' behalf. The words he used were both inflammatory and outrageous. Describing it as a plot bordering on 'mafia levels' he said, somewhat poetically, that he was concerned about the 'lack of scruples and ethics on the part of whoever is conducting this orchestra'. More alarmingly, I read that the maximum sentence was four years in prison.

While complete and utter claptrap – I had listened to every single word of the two conversations Louise had had with Jenny, as well as taking copious notes of my call to Peter – that night, every time I heard a noise outside, I was convinced the police were coming to arrest me. They were anxious moments, particularly when every daily newspaper in Spain carried the story the following day, and I was being hounded and receiving calls from dawn to dusk. While angry and desperately wanting to put my side forward I was beginning to get the message: someone wanted me off this case!

It became even more apparent when the next day Louise and I took a ride up to speak to the manager of a rent-a-car business, who had earlier told Louise to be particularly wary of Graham. The company Royal Cars in the El Zoco centre in Calahonda, had rented numerous cars to Graham and his colleagues at Lubina Sol over the years. But it was after Louise had returned one of these cars a few days overdue the previous year, that the Scandinavian manager Nel had told her to watch out, saying he was 'a nasty piece of work'. While she refused to elaborate any more, she did agree to retract the police report she had filed into the missing car, which was only three or four days late.

A year on and Nel still refused to tell us anything specific about Graham (saying only: 'He was a real troublemaker and bad news'), and she was completely stunned by the coincidence of our visit, as that morning the police had been on the phone about the very car that Louise had allegedly stolen. The car in question was a white Clio, which Robbie had hired in Louise's name in the summer of 2003. Driven around by both Louise and Robbie – despite the fact that he had been banned from driving in the UK – they had not returned the car on the agreed date. It was at this point that Nel recalled how she phoned Louise, who agreed to come up with the car and the remaining payment the following day. But with all the drama of Robbie's arrest she had got waylaid and wasn't able to come, leading to Nel filing a report with the Guardia Civil in Fuengirola. Early the following week, however, Louise returned the car and Nel agreed to waive the outstanding fee and went to the police station to retract the *denuncia*.

Said Nel: 'That was the end of that, as far as I was concerned, until I got this very odd phone call this morning from the Guardia Civil in Fuengirola asking about a certain *denuncia* against a Louise Deravairere. They said they wanted to pursue it and could I give them some more details. I looked in the files and told them I had retracted it a year ago and there was no problem. Why were they calling? They sounded a touch crestfallen . . . and next thing I know you suddenly walk into my office. That is one strange coincidence isn't it? And why now? If I wanted a bet I'd say the police were making a bid to try and discredit Louise.' It was all a little creepy.

Chapter Seventeen

So, Was He Helped?

Louise Deravairere is certainly not alone in believing that Robbie Graham is guilty of far more than just covering up for Tony King. And there is a fair amount of evidence to suggest that she might be right. First and foremost, her concerns that her ex-boyfriend could have been a sex offender are reinforced by the chilling claims of one of his former colleagues Jeremy Stokes.

Confirmed in a statement given to police the day before Graham's arrest, Stokes revealed that Graham had 'boasted' to him about raping girls on the Costa del Sol. Alarmingly, the sickening boasts – in which Graham claimed of gang-raping one particular girl with King and another friend – were made less than a month before the death of Sonia Carabantes.

Graham had made the alleged claims while hiding out in King's home town of Alhaurín for a few days, in a bid to escape a police investigation into the stolen hire car (in which his girlfriend Louise had been arrested). Teaming up with his old friend King, he had soon managed to persuade Stokes to put him up temporarily in his four-bedroom apartment in the

254

centre of the mountain town. Stokes could hardly refuse. He had not long arrived in Spain and was desperate to protect his job to support his wife and three children, who were planning to join him from England. Living on his own, Graham knew his employee at Lubrina Sol would agree and he was soon borrowing his car and generally lording it around the town.

Stokes's friend Simon Bowers (who also employed King in his bar) recalled the concerns he felt about having to put Graham up. 'He came into the bar telling us how upset he was with the situation. How Graham had simply forced himself on him and wouldn't tell him when he was going to leave,' recalls Bowers, who also met Graham in his bar on various occasions.

But these concerns were more than compounded by what Graham is alleged to have told his colleague over a series of raucous late-night drinking sessions. According to Bowers, Graham bragged to his colleague about raping women and, in particular, one attack, in which he had gang-raped a girl with two or three friends. Bowers said: 'Jeremy told me how Robbie openly talked about various rapes he had been involved in. He said he, and unnamed friends, would sidle up to some tipsy young girl in a club somewhere, get her completely drunk – possibly with a pill in her drink – put her in a car and drive inland, where they would gang-rape her together. In particular there was this one teenager, a few weeks earlier, who they had left crying and bleeding beside the road with no clothes.

'Jeremy said the stories had done his head in and he hadn't been able to sleep afterwards. He hadn't wanted Graham staying in his house in the first place, and just didn't know what to do. I think he just hoped Robbie would move out and leave him alone.'

The momentary relief he felt when Graham returned to the coast didn't last long when King was arrested a few weeks later. Knowing that police were putting together a profile on every last detail of King and his friend Graham's movements over the previous few years, Stokes knew that they would almost certainly want to interview him. 'Jeremy didn't know what to do,' said Bowers. 'He knew it would be much better if he went to the police first, but was terrified that if Robbie found out he would certainly lose his job and probably a lot worse. He was tortured about what to do for a couple of days and poured his heart out to us.'

Finally, after a series of long conversations with his friends and his wife Jackie back in England, Stokes took the brave decision to give a declaration to the Guardia Civil, on 21 September 2003, three days after Tony's arrest. I eventually got a copy of that report, which made for shocking reading.

Taken at the Guardia Civil barracks, in Fuengirola, at 4.15p.m., it explained how Jeremy Graham Stokes, born in Windsor in 1961, had met Graham after landing a job at Lubina Sol in February that year. It continued that they had soon become friendly, working with each other every day and then read: 'Some days ago Robbie Graham told him that he, with Tony King and a third person, had anally raped a girl, who "would have needed stitches in her arse". He said the attack had taken place in Miraflores urbanization, in Riviera del Sol, using a vehicle that had its number plates covered with black plastic, so no one, and in particular the girl, would be able to take down the registration. He did not give an exact date for when it had happened and he didn't mention who the third person was.'

In the two-page report – which was later submitted, but somehow ignored by the judge – Stokes described Graham as an 'aggressive' man, who regularly attacked his girlfriend, and recalled tellingly, how Graham had recently told him that he had some 'unfinished business' to sort out with Tony King, without saying what it was.

Intriguingly, Stokes (who also knew King socially) continued that after the murder of Sonia Carabantes, Tony seemed to be behaving normally, 'whereas Robert seemed to be behaving very nervously'.

Stokes – who had arrived in Spain in October 2002, working initially at Jon Daniels's company Dreamworks – said he had broken the news of King's arrest to Graham via a phone call on the morning of 18 September 2003. The report read: 'Graham called him from a phone box in Nerja and reacted with surprise when he told him that Tony had been arrested. He hung up quickly and then phoned back later to tell him he knew every-thing about 'the first murder', and referring to Tony, said: "I know that he committed the first one".'

That same day Stokes flew back to England to spend a week with his wife Jackie and three children. Dramatically, less than three months later, the timeshare salesman, who was only 42 years old, had died in unusual circumstances. His untimely death, which happened on 12 December 2003 at a private clinic in Malaga, was put down to liver or kidney failure, according to Simon Bowers. But, according to a source close to the family, it was more than exacerbated by the case and in particular Graham, who they believe was behind a series of threatening phone calls to his mobile.

In an extremely tense conversation, Jackie Stokes told me how her husband had had a nervous breakdown on his return to England, from the stress of the affair. 'The stress of it all drove him into a downward spiral and he never recovered,' revealed the mother of three, who had stayed in England, while her husband, a former IT consultant, tried to get his career off the ground in Spain. 'He had a breakdown in the week he was here and spent his whole time in tears recalling the horrific details he had heard from Graham. He was unfortunate to have had to hear all that crap and he could simply not take it. It frightened the hell out of him. That was his downfall and that is what bloody killed him.'

But while she blamed his death on Graham and King, it is

one particularly nasty phone call that really makes her angry. While she is too scared to reveal exactly what was said, according to a good friend of her family, it referred directly to Jeremy's statement. 'Jeremy was dying and she received this nasty phone call,' said the source. 'It frightened the hell out of her. I don't know if it was from Graham, but we strongly suspected him. It was on Jeremy's phone and she answered it. It was a man's voice and she listened to what the caller had to say and then hung up. It was not at all nice and the long and short of it was that Jeremy was a grass – and under no circumstances should he say anything else.

'I can tell you she is scared and does not want to get involved. She is worried about her children and is very concerned about where Robbie might be living now and whether he could find her.'

Jackie admitted: 'I really can't say any more about it as I have my children to protect, but it was very unpleasant and came as I was on the way to the hospital to see my dying husband and decide whether to turn off the machines that were keeping him alive.'

She explained how her husband had first met King and Graham after they had made the decision to start a new life in Spain the previous year and had taken the initial step of renting a house in Alhaurín.

'Before all this stuff, Robbie had been a friend. We had no idea what he was really like. He and King had seemed quite normal and we saw them socially. But Jeremy didn't want him staying at our house. Our house had been invaded by him and King, and he wasn't happy. To think that I have stood there and folded Robbie's underpants and he has played with our children. It makes me sick.'

Jackie, who had been hoping to join her husband in a new life in Spain, was scared to say much more. 'All I want to say is that as I see it, all Jeremy had done was what any decent person would have done in a murder inquiry. He was just unlucky to have got into the wrong crowd and heard something he shouldn't have. How was he to know what Graham and King were really like. All I know is that he was not involved. And, of course, I wish he had just kept his mouth shut now. I see no point in getting involved. Nothing is going to bring my husband back. It is all in the past now and all that matters to me is to somehow provide for his three young children.'

Further evidence of Graham's strange behaviour came when police contacted the owner of the last flat he rented in Calahonda before doing a 'midnight flit' to Nerja, owing 3,000 euros in rent. Getting hold of the lettings agent Alex Anderson through a business card which Graham had in his wallet on his arrest, they discovered that among other items cleaners found at the vacated flat in the El Alarife development, was a crude white hood, with eye-slits cut in it. Found wedged down the side of the sofa, the cleaners – not seeing any significance in it – had thrown it away with all the other rubbish.

While there is no suggestion that Graham ever used the mask (or indeed that it was even his), police were made aware of the discovery, which must be seen as suspicious at best. As Anderson explained: 'It was a case of really bad luck for the police and good luck for Graham that the police got in touch with me two days after the cleaners had gone through the place and thrown out the rubbish. They had left it in a real state and there was lots of rubbish, but typically the dustman had been the day before the police called.'

Anderson, whose company Royal Executive manages 150 properties on the Costa del Sol, explained that Graham and his girlfriend Louise had taken over the lease of the flat three months earlier, after being recommended by a mutual friend. But straightaway he knew there would be problems. 'They paid their deposit, but when it came to paying their second month's rent, nothing arrived. They kept saying it was coming but, of course, it never did and I was preparing to have them evicted. Then one night a week or so before his arrest he did a runner.

'When the police came to us I straightaway asked the cleaners if they had found anything and they said, in particular, was this hood, made out of a pillow case with eye-holes cut into it. It looked like a typical Ku Klux Klan-type mask, but, of course, the cleaners had no idea and threw it out. You find all sorts of kinky gear left in flats and they assumed it was just that. One thing is for sure, it must have come from Graham as the cleaners are very thorough and would have found it before they moved in. The police were obviously investigating as to whether he might have been using it outside, and I guess we'll never know.'

He added that the police did, however, take a number of items away, including a series of sheets, as well as mattresses and blankets, which haven't been returned. Most interesting of all was a stack of around half a dozen VHS videos. 'I don't know what was on them, but the police have still got them. I assume they are of interest.'

Intriguingly, Graham's ex-girlfriend Louise Deravairere also claimed that Graham had once cut eye-holes in a pillowcase. 'He did the same thing in Benidorm once,' she told me. 'He came in with this thing over his head in a bid to scare me, saying the Ku Klux Klan were going to get me because I was black. It made me jump, but once I knew it was him I laughed and quickly forgot about it. I have no idea what happened to it or if he ever used it, but it is odd that there was another one in Calahonda.'

While there is no suggestion that these masks were ever used outside the house, Graham was, however, linked with three more serious crimes on the Costa del Sol. The first, which has already been mentioned, was the disappearance of María Teresa Fernández, in Motril, in August 2000 (when he was apparently seen in the small town on various occasions but with no known friends or business reasons to be there) and the second was said to have taken place in the same week as Rocío's death in 1999. The incident, which was reported in the Spanish press, involved a young Dutch girl going to the police after a man had pestered her relentlessly on her way home late at night in Mijas, where Graham was living at the time. The girl, who had been coming back from her job as a waitress in a restaurant in Torremolinos, recognized Graham after he was seen on television following his arrest, but a positive identification could not be carried out because Graham had already left the country to return to England.

The third incident involved a student, who had disappeared in 1995, in Cabopino, near Marbella. The link to Graham came out after a letter was sent by Tony King to his wife Celia. In the letter, written from prison, he came out with a series of tantalizing clues about his former friend and colleague. After berating his wife for selling her story to the newspapers and swearing on his daughter's life that he did not murder Rocío, he asked her to pass on a message to Robbie from him. He wrote cryptically: 'I want you to give Robbie a message. Say "Walk like a chicken?" Say "London Underground". Tell him I know every single dirty thing he has done and that I swear on my daughter's soul that if it takes my last breath on this planet I will make him pay for what he did to Rocío, to the girl from Motril and for the man in Cabopino.'

The man in question was one José Manuel Lopez Martin and he had disappeared in strange circumstances on 16 October 1995, with remarkably little headway made by the police into the matter. Indeed, his family claims that because he was a 23-year-old student – and therefore an adult – and there was no evidence of any attack, the police did practically nothing.

The facts, however, pointed at something far more sinister. José Manuel had been dropped off by his sister Juani at Marbella bus station that morning to catch an early bus to Malaga, where he was in his second year at university studying information technology. He had told her he would be back for lunch, but never turned up, and only finally got in touch with his family in a bizarre phone call home at around 9p.m. that night. Clearly panicking and in tears, he promised he would call back, but never did.

In a heart-rending description of the events that took place, his sister Juani told me: 'It was very strange when he didn't come home, but as we didn't have mobiles in those days, we could only wait for him to come home. At 9p.m., however, the phone rang and it was him. He was clearly in tears and said he couldn't talk. He said he only had a few minutes. I asked him, where are you? Tell me where you are and I'll come and find you. But all he said was: "I'm very far away". I said what's wrong? Are you OK? And he said: "Don't worry I'll phone you back" and that is all I remember as, by then, I was also in floods of tears.'

Suffice to say he never called back and after calling all his friends and the local hospitals they reported him missing at Estepona police station.

According to the family, the police did not seem very interested in José's disappearance and simply told them that he had probably left home voluntarily. The family were, however, not prepared to lie down and accept it, and spurred on by the sinister late-night phone call, decided to put up hundreds of posters all around the area. After a month, their action bore fruit when they received a phone call from a woman who said she had seen Martin on the bus that evening going from Malaga to Marbella. She told them that she had noticed him because he seemed very nervous, before getting off the bus at a stop in the pine woods just before arriving in Marbella. That stop could have been only one of two: Las Chapas or Cabopino.

'But the police were still completely uninterested in the information we gave them and didn't actually go to interview that woman for a whole year,' continued Juani. 'It is incredible that a decade has passed since my brother disappeared and the police have been incapable of finding any clues as to his disappearance. It is as if, just because he was 23 years old and an adult he disappeared voluntarily. But that is no way the case. He had no reason to disappear as he was not depressed, nor had had any big rows with any of us. He was a successful student, he had a girlfriend and would have at least called us to let us know he was safe. This is the first good clue that we have had for years and we demand to know whether King's accusation could be true.'

They believe King might be telling the truth for a variety of reasons. First and foremost because whenever anyone, and in particular, the media refers to José Manuel's disappearance it is in relation to the man 'missing from Marbella or Las Chapas' and never Cabopino. 'So how does Tony King come to mention Cabopino?' said the sister. 'How does he know it was actually Cabopino where he got off the bus? We are sure that he was referring to our brother because there are no other unresolved disappearances or murders in either Las Chapas or Cabopino.

'Another reason they should investigate is that if King arrived in Spain in 1997, how would he know about someone missing two years earlier? I am convinced he was murdered that night and if the police can establish whether Robbie Graham was in Spain in 1995 then he needs to be interrogated. I don't understand why they haven't done that yet.'

While it is almost certain that Robbie Graham was on the Costa del Sol in 1995 (all the evidence suggests that he was either living in Spain or southern Portugal at the time – and he was certainly in Tenerife that year, as he was charged with theft there) there is one other very intriguing link. According to the family there used to be a brothel close to the Cabopino bus stop, which was once investigated by police for drug dealing. And intriguingly José Manuel had told his brother-in-law Juan

that he and a friend from university had visited the brothel
Sauna Eva – which was owned by a trio of foreign owners, at
least one being English.

According to the Spanish magazine *Así son las Cosas*, Guardia
Civil sources confirmed that, among other things, the brothel
was investigated for its links to the selling of cocaine, a drug that
Graham, by his own admittance, was heavily involved with.

It is these drug connections that are worth looking at. Louise
Deravairere claimed that Graham got a regular supply of
cocaine and Viagra from both Peewee Bachour and former
colleagues at Lubina Sol. 'Everyone knew that a number of the
salesmen there used to deal in cocaine and Viagra, which was
imported from Gibraltar,' she told me. 'Robbie often bought
both drugs from them and there was always plenty of drug
money floating around.'

Others such as Jon Daniels's right hand man Peter Moore and
Ingrid Pantoja confirmed that a fair amount of drug dealing went
on at Lubina Sol. Talking at the small apartment where she lives
with Daniels's two sons, Pantoja (Celia King's younger sister)
revealed: 'I knew a couple of the main dealers and at one point
stupidly even got talked into storing 2,000 ecstasy tablets in one of
my cupboards for a while. I didn't have much choice. One of the
guys later told me that he had a kilo of cocaine buried in his
garden and I have no reason to doubt it.'

Moore, who worked at the Lubina Sol office for a couple of
years, added: 'There were a lot of things I was privy to, one
being the issue of drugs. Put it this way when you are in a car
coming back from Estepona and you are told that there was a
load of drugs in the boot, you are not going to be very happy. I
was against drugs and far from happy when I found out that I
was unwittingly transporting them.'

While Moore confirmed that a number of the staff were
involved in one way or another with drugs, his words are also
extremely useful in shedding light on the connections between

King and Graham. Few people knew the pair as well and it was more than a decade since the Gibraltar-based businessman had first met Graham while working in Tenerife in the early 1990s. While careful with his words, the construction boss revealed: 'Robbie had an extremely bad reputation even back then. He was always getting into scrapes and climbing off balconies to get away from the police. He always seemed to be on the run from something. Small things, he would say, stuff like getting drunk and causing trouble, but with Robbie you always thought it would be something more serious. The thing was he was such a good liar, you never knew what to believe. And another thing for sure: he was the master of scamming people.'

Once back on the Costa del Sol, Graham's behaviour hardly modified and he was soon back to his old tricks, in particular through a special hold he had over timeshare boss Jon Daniels. Said Moore: 'Robbie always had some special hold over Jon and I never understood what it was about. But there was some special power that made Jon always do what he wanted, and always pay him on time and by the day, while everyone else had to wait. I was always against Robbie coming to work with us in Fuengirola, as he always managed to make things more complicated and tense, but somehow he ended up working there. Those two were as thick as thieves and always forged something of a deadly partnership.'

Intriguingly, Moore also went on to back up the so-called 'Russian mafia' connections with Lubina Sol, which Tony King had brought up in court during his second testimony, something that was much ridiculed by the Spanish press. 'Tony was completely right that Lubina Sol was dealing with Russians at the time. There was a woman who ran that side of things for Roscoe, until she got the boot and stole £20,000 in the process. There were always Russian fly-bys about and later, after he moved back to England, I helped Robbie get a job with a Russian company called Holiday World in Egypt.'

The former British soldier explained how he had managed to land the job for Graham through an old contact, who specifically deals with the Russian timeshare market. 'Robbie was desperate and really down after being hauled in with Tony, and begged me to help him. Against my better judgement I stupidly agreed to try and get him a job in Egypt. Nobody else would help him after what had happened and somehow we found him a management post, sorting him out with flights and $1,000 on his arrival to tide him over.

'But, of course, being Robbie, he dumped on us badly and still owes us money,' continued Moore. 'It was classic Robbie doing the normal thing; trying to invent a new system to suit him. He was meant to be managing the deck, but without telling anyone where he was going, disappeared back to Spain to give evidence . . . and then he was surprised when there was no job when he got back after a week. Is it any surprise that he was nicknamed Robbie Nightmare?'

Moore was unequivocal that Tony was being wrongly blamed for the Wanninkhof murder. 'I feel sorry for Tony,' he continued. 'I think more has been heaped on him than should have been and I have said to Robbie's face that he's more involved than he lets on. There is certainly a lot more to this crime than meets the eye and there are a lot of things that could be true in King's statements. Robbie was certainly into drugs and Tony steroids and there were a lot of drugs swilling around.'

Is it possible then that Rocío Wanninkhof or her mother might have discovered something that led to the killing? Alicia was the cleaner at Lubina Sol and had been for three years. She knew the place and its staff very well. What was going on in the office that she was privy to?

It is a theory that Jon Daniels's long-term partner Ingrid Pantoja has given serious consideration to. 'Did Alicia stumble across something dodgy or did Jon try to talk Alicia or Rocío into doing a drug deal for him?' she said. 'He could talk anyone into doing something for him. He was very persuasive and managed to talk me into doing all sorts of dodgy things for him. I just have a suspicion that maybe they were somehow involved in a drugs deal that went wrong. I don't know, it is just a hunch.'

She also believes that on the night of Rocío's death, it is highly likely that Daniels was out with Graham and King. She said: 'Jon was out that night and quite likely with Robbie and Tony. He was also acting particularly weirdly at the time and I don't know if it was a coincidence that he dumped me a few weeks after the murder and Tony King moved in for a few weeks with him. He said Tony was staying for a few weeks as a favour and he was lending him money. I could never understand why he was being so kind to someone he had previously called a waster and said he couldn't stand him,' she recalled.

There is no doubt that King and Daniels were much closer than Daniels has let on. Indeed, intriguingly, Daniels told me that he and King had discussed an idea for making porno movies for an Internet site based somewhere inland. 'It would involve Tony shagging women live on camera and he wanted me to help him finance it. We would hire a house somewhere out in the hills and drag all these women up there. He reckoned we could make a killing from it and he was the perfect man for the job.' It is also interesting to note that a week or two after the murder, Daniels also inexplicably paid for Robbie Graham to have a holiday in Majorca. While exact details of the holiday are difficult to get, Graham did at least confirm to the police that Daniels paid for him to have a holiday around that time.

In further evidence that Graham may have been more involved than he has let on, two timeshare salesmen, who worked at Lubina Sol at the time, said that Graham didn't come into work the day after the murder. Indeed, according to the salesmen, who worked for the company for a couple of years, Graham had given the excuse that he had been in a car crash the previous day.

Over a beer at Johnny's bar in Benalmadena, one of them, the former OPC manager, told me: 'The night of Rocío's murder they were both out together and the next day neither of them came to work. They both said they had been in a car crash and simply didn't appear. It was all very suspect at the time and nobody believed it. But we had no suspicions that they were involved in the death. We knew Robbie was a wanker to women. We knew a few of his girlfriends, including Michelle, who he used to treat very badly . . . but we didn't know if it was worse than that. Another thing for sure, Jon Daniels knew everything Robbie and Tony were up to. He was giving Tony a lot of jobs with A Man Who Can! and Tony was always hanging around.'

Either way, it is Graham's own evidence that perhaps best indicates his involvement in the crime. Over the course of the year he consistently changed his tune to police, the courts and the media about what happened. Sometimes saying he didn't remember what happened that night, sometimes putting King there and not Dolores, sometimes admitting he might have been in the car, sometimes admitting he had helped dispose of the clothes. Everything points to the fact that Graham knew a lot more than he has let on.

Perhaps the best indication of this is his first statement given to police on his arrest in September 2003. Riddled with contradictions and possibly lies, the interview (which I managed to get a copy of) demonstrates that he was, at the very least, giving Tony King guidance on how to cover up the crime. Translated back from the official court transcript in Spanish, it was taken over a period of six hours by three detectives at the Guardia Civil barracks in Malaga on 22 September 2003. At the top, it clearly states that Graham is charged with the crime of 'covering up the murder of Rocío Wanninkhof'.

So, Was He Helped?

The ten-page transcript begins with Graham first telling detectives that he had only been living in Spain for 'five to six years', on both the mainland and Lanzarote. Neglecting to mention his long stay in Tenerife, he claimed that he had lived on the Costa del Sol for 18 months from 1999 to 2000 before contradicting himself just four paragraphs later, by saying that he had actually met Tony King at Lubina Sol in 1998.

In terms of girlfriends, he said he had lived with a French girl called Nora, 'who later moved back to Marseille', as well as a Spanish girl in her mid-twenties called Rocío Martin, whom he'd broken up with two weeks after the death of Rocío Wanninkhof and who mysteriously, it should be noted, nobody seems to know or have met. He continued that on his return from a holiday in Majorca, paid for by Jon Daniels, he started dating Jon's sister Justine, a receptionist at the timeshare company where they all worked in Fuengirola. He said she was pregnant and they had soon moved in together.

Continually denying that he knew Tony King well, he first of all said he had met him through his wife Celia, at Charly's Bar, in Riviera del Sol, in 1999, before admitting that he had actually met him a year earlier at Lubina Sol in 1998. He said that he had given King a job at Lubina Sol in 1999, describing him as 'simple and strange', but perhaps more crucially 'friendly and obedient'.

While stressing that they were not close friends, he admitted that they DID go to the pub after work to talk, when Tony would open up about the problems he was having with his wife. But he claimed he drank much more with Jon Daniels and the others and, somewhat comically, described the timeshare industry as a complicated world revolving around 'a lot of drink and a lot of football'.

When asked specifically what his relationship was like with Tony in October 1999, he said that at the time King was working for 'some Liverpudlians' and doing 'odd jobs and sometimes cleaning the windows of Lubina Sol'. He claimed that he had stopped being friendly with King after he left Lubina Sol in 1998, but then admitted they had got reacquainted the following summer when Tony was working as a window cleaner.

While he still tried to make out they were not good friends, he finally accepted that King visited him at his house in Balcon del Mar and that he himself had visited the mobile home he shared with Celia on the Calazul camp site.

When asked specifically where he was on the night of Rocío's disappearance on 9 October 1999, he couldn't remember whether he was at his apartment in Balcon del Mar, or the one in Fuengirola, 'he can't remember exactly, although he thinks it was Balcon del Mar'.

But, to be fair, his whole recollection of the night when he claimed that Tony King had killed Rocío Wanninkhof, was vague in the extreme. The transcript read:

He remembers that one night around that date, he thinks it might have been 9 October, Tony came round in a very strange state. It was the only time he had seen Tony in such a state. Tony arrived at after nine or ten at night, while Robbie was alone and waiting for his girlfriend Rocío Martin, who worked at Miraflores. He thinks Tony had been drinking and he brought beer with him because usually Robbie didn't have drink in the house. Tony had a dark look. He spoke rubbish, he seemed to be drunk and Robbie thought about chucking him out. He started talking about problems with girls and his wife. He doesn't know if that was the night that the girl disappeared but when he went to work on the Sunday, Rocío's mother, who worked in Lubina Sol, started to put posters up with her photo. But he admits it could have been the following Sunday.

At that point, he clammed up, before saying that he had gone to Majorca a week or two later for a holiday and didn't see

King until about a month after that. By then, late November 1999, he was living with Justine in Fuengirola and Jon Daniels had just offered Tony another work opportunity to make some money in the run-up to Christmas.

When asked what vehicles Tony drove he said he had a white Ford Fiesta, but that he sometimes used to borrow the car of his neighbour Jane Maynard, who was a friend of Justine's. He stated clearly however that 'Jane would not have lent Tony the car on that night because he was drunk'.

He was then asked when he had discovered that Tony had been arrested and he said he had seen it in the English newspaper *Sur*. It was at this point that he claimed to have had a flashback to the night in question, when he 'realized' that Tony had wanted to confess. In yet another major contradiction he then said that Tony 'DIDN'T look like he had been drinking or consuming drugs' and that he remembered the car he was driving was a light Ford Fiesta 'because he said goodbye to him from the terrace of his flat, which was on the third floor'.

Clamming up again, the police changed tack and asked him if he knew Jeremy Stokes and he confirmed that he worked with him, before admitting that it was Jeremy who had called him with the news of King's arrest (and not newspaper *Diario Sur*). He admitted that he had spent a couple of nights at Jeremy's house a few weeks earlier but claimed that Jeremy was a much closer friend of King's than he was.

And that is when he suddenly started to open up. There is no indication of what the police said or put to him to encourage it, but when he was asked if he wanted to say anything else, he replied spontaneously that on the night of 9 October (he now remembers the date!), Tony told him that he had been driving between Torrenueva and La Cala, when 'he thinks he might have killed a girl'. Robbie claimed, however, that he didn't want to know any more, as 'it would make him culpable', and he told him he wasn't going to listen and asked him to leave.

271

So, Was He Helped?

A few minutes later though he continued that Tony had not 'asked him to help move the body'. That night he told him that he thought he had killed somebody, that she was unconscious or dead. Tony told him that he was going to have another look or cover the body. He didn't say any name and he arrived without warning at his house. He arrived in a Ford Fiesta but he didn't know whose it was, because in those days he didn't have a car. (He had said earlier that Tony owned a white Ford Fiesta!)

He thinks that Tony said to him that he had seen a girl while driving. He had picked her up, given her a 'good shagging' and had left her unconscious or dead. Robbie told him to leave his house, he didn't want to hear anything else. Tony answered OK, but said I am going to cover or hide her, I don't know where. Robbie is sure that he hid the body immediately, and that he didn't give him any ideas about how or where to put it.

He insisted he didn't directly help Tony, despite talking to him for two hours between 9p.m. and 11p.m., but he agreed that he had 'collaborated in some way because he didn't report him'. And then in a hint of confession, the report continued:

Robbie insists that he didn't go out to see the murder site. But he added that if he had helped Tony to move Rocío's body, if he drove the car or helped in any other way, it could only have been if he was very, very, very drunk and if he had done it if he was very, very, very drunk he wouldn't have remembered anyway.
  When Tony told him what he had done he told him to 'go away and cover it up [the body]' and Tony went to cover it up, as if he had given him an order, but it wasn't his intention to give orders. He adds that whenever he told Tony to do something Tony would jump because he was simple and obedient.

272

In further contradictory evidence, he was asked if he had met Tony in the Irish Times bar a few days after the murder, to which he first of all gave a definitive 'no' and then admitted that he might have done, but didn't remember as he was drunk. Some minutes later, he suddenly came out with yet more recollections, when he said that he remembered seeing 'black plastic bags full of clothes in the car', which meant that Tony must have returned a second time, as 'the first time he is sure he didn't go down'.

He said that he remembered that there were two bags of clothes, 'but no blood' and said that he had felt 'terrorized' by the situation. 'He felt he had committed a crime and because he was so frightened he does not remember if he went with Tony anywhere. He remembers that when he saw the bags in the back of the car, he made a point of not touching anything. Tony told him that they were the girl's clothes and he didn't know what to do. Robbie told him to leave. Tony insisted and pleaded with him to accompany him but he didn't go.' In terms of leaving fingerprints in the car Graham said it would be highly likely as he had been in the car before, on various 'drinking sessions'. Now remembering suddenly that the car was Jane Maynard's despite saying earlier than Jane would not have lent the car to Tony if he was drunk, he added: 'He doesn't think that he shut the boot because he didn't want to touch anything, although he may have touched the car previously.'

He then started talking for the first time about weapons and, in particular, a hammer, as well as well as various other tools. 'But he didn't see blood or a body.' He continued that he believed Tony had 'gone to hide the body' when he had told him to, and that he might have come back because he didn't know what to do with the clothes. He told Tony that he should 'burn the clothes' and that 'because of the state of terror he was in he may have accompanied Tony to destroy the clothes'.

Then, giving considerably more detail, he added that the bags were only 'squeezed closed' and not tied and added that:

If he had accompanied Tony to get rid of the bags, it would have been because he had threatened him with a knife, although he only remembers having seen a hammer. Tony had the hammer in his hands when he opened the bags. From then on his mind is blank. He doesn't remember going back up to his house, or going anywhere in the car.

But after a pause of about 35 minutes of not remembering anything, the report noted how he finally remembered – for the first time – that he had been taking cocaine all day and he had gone back upstairs to take some more.

He again denied having been in the car but said that:

If he had got in, it would have been under threat. He doesn't know the place that they might have gone to, nor what they might have done because he was so frightened. And in any case had he got in the car it would have been on the second visit to his house. And apart from anything, many years have gone past and he has been trying to forget what had happened.

Strangely, even though you would have thought this should have been one of the first questions, he is then finally asked about the alleged rape that Jeremy Stokes had reported him for and he denies all knowledge.

The report concluded:

Finally he wants to declare that whatever was happening that night he was completely terrorized and it is perhaps for this reason that he doesn't remember if he got in the car or not. He also wants to say that he is not a person who is easily scared, but the tension and panic that he went through at that time was caused by the seriousness of the situation. He had never been in such a situation before. The reason he didn't report it was that he was really scared for his life. Tony told him that he was in prison for murder, and he is a very dangerous person and is in the right place. And that since he has been with Louise he has stopped drinking alcohol and cocaine and is trying to lead an ordinary life and work every day.

That same day Robbie Graham also appeared for the first time in front of the judge in Fuengirola. In the session – with both Rocío Wanninkhof's mother and her lawyer also present – he found himself cross-examined with some extremely enlightening results.

Giving his address as Room 207, Hotel La Ermita, Nerja, the judge first tried to establish when Graham and King had met and exactly how close they were. It was put to him that if, as he claimed, they were not close, why then had Tony been sleeping in a car outside his house in April 2000 and the pair had then shared a tent together after he split up from Justine? In a weak response he said that Tony had joined him because he had problems and that he was 'afraid to say no'.

Eventually they got to the night in question, in which, while Graham did not remember the exact date, he did now remember for sure that it was at his apartment in Balcon del Mar. He said that Tony had arrived in 'a terrible state' and that he had started talking very critically about his wife. He said that Tony was drinking and had 'a bottle in his hand' and they sat there between an hour and an hour and a half, while Tony confessed to him what had happened. Tony told him he had picked up a girl on the other side of the campsite, behind the BP station . . . he told him he had had sex with her and had been 'very hard' with the girl. He then told Robbie he had to help him. He said he had abandoned the badly injured girl on the other side of the campsite near La Cala and needed help to deal with the situation.

He was then asked why he had gone down to see the car,

rather than simply tell King to leave, to which he replied: 'I don't know why I did it.' He then said he didn't remember what was in the boot of the Ford Fiesta, but quickly admitted that he saw two plastic bags in it, which Tony touched with a hammer. He remembers something about a knife, but he did not see it and that there was no blood on either the bags or on Tony. He also thinks that Tony had asked him for shoes and clothes that night.

Asked if he knew that Rocío's body was in the car he replied, in an apparent contradiction, that yes he knew, but he was too scared to go near the vehicle. Asked if he was scared because he suspected the body was there he said yes, that is why he didn't look.

Despite not looking, however, he claimed to have been able to see some female clothes in the car, but didn't want to touch them because he was 'scared'. He said he advised Tony 'to get rid of the clothes.' And that Tony told him that they were the clothes of the girl.

When he was pressed to remember where he might have gone with Tony in the car, he said that he didn't believe he got in the car and that if he did he doesn't know if he went to Fuengirola or Marbella. He added that he 'really did not remember' if he was in the car or not, although he felt that he must have been in the car because lots of police have told him he was. He said he would need psychiatric help to remember what happened.

Despite his earlier denial, he now admitted that he had met Tony in the Irish Times a week later and got angry with him about the night in question, after Tony refused to be drawn on what happened. All he would say was that 'she was not a girl; she was older, maybe 25 and it was not Rocío'. He said he didn't really remember the conversation because he had been drinking all day and that he left Tony there after the row.

He again confirmed that he knew Jeremy Stokes, but denied

the allegations in his declaration. While he admitted that they had had various conversations, none was about that apparent crime. And he then launched an attack on Stokes's credibility claiming he was 'a strange person. Depressive, alcoholic and taking medicine'.

There was little more said apart from confirming that he had been in prison in England for two spells: one of six months when he was under 18; and another when he was aged 29 (1993), when he was sentenced to 20 months for drink-driving, but served only nine months. He also made the point (quite incorrectly, as I have already established) that this time did not correspond to the time that King was in prison and that they were in different prisons at different times. He added that he had not taken drugs for six months and lived a normal and organized life with his girlfriend Louise, a claim she has more than dispelled.

From the two sessions we can not only clearly see how he was changing his story by the hour, but that he showed a remarkably (perhaps unnaturally) poor memory for a night only four years earlier when one of his closest friends had allegedly killed a girl and then confessed it to him. But over the course of the next few months his memory would improve dramatically, particularly after he had been hypnotized by police a few weeks later in Madrid. Indeed, after the voluntary session, in an interview I organized for the *Sunday Express*, he claimed that while King had been involved – and was paid some £800 – the main attacker had been Dolores Vázquez.

As mentioned at length in earlier chapters, he said:

> *The main thing I can tell you is that while Tony King was heavily involved with Rocío's murder he did not do the stabbing. He said he had been hired to do something for this woman, who was the lover of the mother of the victim. He told me the name of the woman was Loli or Dolly, which I never connected to Dolores Vázquez at the time, as*

So, Was He Helped?

I didn't know her. He told me he had been paid to hurt somebody. He told me he got 150,000 pesetas, which was about £800 at that time just to assist and drive a car.

Graham added:

Anyway, there is no way that Tony could have got that body to the place she was found without that woman taking him to that site. Whether she paid him first and then he did it, or she went with him, I don't know. But I believe she went with him. I believe she stabbed the girl, maybe after Tony had given her a bump. But Tony said she had got out of the car to let the girl get in and then when they dragged her out of the car he couldn't stop the woman stabbing her. He said she stabbed her about 20 times.

It was certainly a marked change from his earlier statement, in which he seemed decidedly vague, but his claims of remembering all the new information from hypnosis must be seen as highly suspect going on the claims of his ex-girlfriend. As Louise said: 'All this bullshit about being hypnotized is nonsense. Robbie was not under hypnosis and told me so. Only 20 per cent are susceptible to hypnosis and there is a small per cent that can pretend they are. Robbie is one of those. He knows how to do hypnotherapy and he told me that years ago he used to be a hypnotist, like Paul McKenna, only not on the telly. He said he was taught by some guy in the north and that was the end of the conversation really. I don't think he ever tried to hypnotize me. But I just know he was not hypnotized, he was not fucking hypnotized. He even admitted that he hadn't gone under. He is just blagging his way out to put the blame on anybody but himself.'

On his return to Spain in December 2003 he would end up contradicting himself again. In a testimony labelled 'useless' by some of the Spanish media he changed his story in quite a few ways.

At the session at the Guardia Civil barracks, in Fuengirola, on 4 December 2003, he first of all said, for example, that 'Loli' had stabbed Rocío 'twenty times with a knife'. However some time later he completely contradicted himself by blaming the murder on Tony saying that he had 'hit her with a stone'. 'Tony was the one who killed her, he did 99 per cent of the killing,' he claimed.

With regard to the car that Tony was driving that night, in this session he said that it was Tony's own car, whereas before he had said it belonged to Tony's neighbour Jane Maynard. In terms of the number of times that King had visited him at the house, Graham changed his tune saying he had come once, when previously he'd said King must have come around twice. Regarding what he saw in the car, in the new testimony he said that he saw bags in the car but he 'didn't look inside them', whereas before he said specifically that he had seen two black bags with women's clothes inside.

He also denied that Tony King had ever changed his clothes or shoes in his house, when before he had said that he thought he had.

With reference to the money Tony was allegedly paid for the crime, on this occasion he specified neither how much, nor, indeed, that Dolores had contracted him. He did, however, say that Tony suddenly had money in the days after the murder. He claimed this after admitting that he had met King at the Irish Times pub, in Fuengirola, the following week.

All in all, the session was considered useless. Experts believed that it carried no legal weight as he had used 'a job' in Egypt as an excuse to hear what King would testify first before he gave evidence. Ultimately, perhaps only one or two people – apart from King and Graham – knew the real truth. One of those might have been Nora, who had mysteriously 'gone back to Marseille' in 1999, while another would surely have been his Spanish girlfriend Rocío Martin, whom nobody has been able to trace.

There is one final theory that needs to be explored and that is the idea that King and Graham might have been closet homosexuals, with a deep, misogynous hatred of women. It is a suggestion that has certainly been brought up by a number of people during the course of my inquiries, including Celia Pantoja and her sister Ingrid, as well as Robbie Graham's dad, among others.

Indeed, it had been Graham's father, who had first put the idea in my head that Tony might have been gay. It had been towards the end of our interview at his house in Yorkshire that he had made the off-the-cuff remark that I didn't really pick up on at the time. After telling me that he had met Tony a number of times on his visits to Spain he said: 'I must say I thought he was queer.' He didn't wish to elaborate, and it was up to Louise to fill me in, when she told me that Graham's father had told her that Tony was 'a real keep-fit queen' when he was first introduced as Robbie's minder. 'He told me that he thought their relationship was quite odd. Tony was always with Robbie and he felt there was some infatuation with Robbie on Tony's part.'

Louise herself has always had doubts about the exact relationship they had between them. 'I often had a suspicion that something sexual was going on between them. Robbie was clearly fixated with anal sex and preferred it to normal sex. He also had these fantasies about having sex with other men quite a lot and told me on a number of occasions about a night he had had in Malta when this gay bloke made him feel his dick and they played with each other.

'There is no doubt they were unnaturally close and were always very tactile with each other, always hugging and even cuddling each other. At the same time he found it almost impossible to give me a hug and I had to practically order him to do it.

'I have always thought that Tony was gay. He is not very

masculine despite his muscles and he has a high-pitched squeaky voice. I certainly got the impression that Tony would do anything for Robbie, including sexual favours if he asked. He mentally brainwashed Tony – and got him to do all these errands. Tony was infatuated with Robbie and seemed to be prepared to do anything for him. I used to say to Tony, why do you let someone like him mentally brainwash you? But Robbie had the brains and money and Tony seemed to like getting looked after by him.

'I am certainly not the only one to have come up with this theory. Both the police and other friends have said that they think Robbie and Tony had a bizarre father-son type relationship, with Robbie being the papa and Tony the son. Certainly Robbie is a manipulative bully and it wouldn't surprise me if he was directing Tony and using him for his pleasure.'

King's wife Celia also had her suspicions about Tony's relationship with Robbie. 'I always thought that Robbie and Tony might be having some sort of sexual relationship. They were so close and had some weird bond, maybe something that comes out of being in prison, I don't know, but I just felt that there was something more. I got this feeling that Tony was queer while in prison, that he had had a few relationships. It is impossible to say for certain, but I just felt he might be storing up his sexual appetite and drive for Robbie rather than me.'

Perhaps unwittingly giving something away in the interview he had given to the *Sunday Express*, Graham himself claimed King was gay, and that he might be responsible for the deaths of men as well as women.

He said: 'I think you can almost guarantee there are probably a couple of blokes as well. You know, young lads, because it's not a sexual thing that Tony was into, but throttling somebody. I can actually see that in Tony. It wouldn't have been a rape thing it would be just doing that to them and having a little fiddle or interfering with them. I can't see Tony being bothered whether it was a man or woman and I think they [the police] have concentrated too much on women. There could be loads of young lads missing – no one looks for them do they?'

Conclusion

While some feel strongly that both Dolores Vázquez and Robbie Graham might have been involved in the murder of Rocío Wanninkhof, there are many people who believe they are innocent. Could it be possible that Vázquez was singled out after an acrimonious split with her former lover? Or feasible that Graham – while undoubtedly something of a rough diamond – was little more than an unfortunate confidant of Tony King, and was stupid – or scared – enough not to report to the police what his friend had told him?

Vázquez has an undeniably good defence, with neither a clear motive for wanting to kill the daughter of her ex-lover, nor any physical evidence linking her to the crime. There has certainly been a groundswell of support among many of her neighbours. English businessman Cliff Stanford, who personally put up a reward of 150,000 euros to help capture Rocío's killer, was in complete agreement with the decision that no further action was to be taken against her. The millionaire said, 'I believe she has been wrongfully convicted and treated badly from the start. I am pleased there is finally light at the end of the tunnel for her.' Even the staff at the nearby Oasis restaurant – where she was said to have arrived late on the night of the murder, sweating profusely and agitated – are now quick to back her up. After offering his restaurant as the venue for her supporters to hold a celebratory party and a press conference after her discharge, the owner said: 'There is no doubt she is innocent. She has been through hell and back.'

To her credit, the hotel manager has certainly managed to maintain a dignified silence throughout the five years leading up to the trial of Tony King – even after the case against her was thrown out of court. Indeed, while her supporters crowed loudly to the media on that day in August 2004, she decided to return quietly to the house she has long lived in, in La Cala, to try to get on with her life. Having driven to the court alone, she looked relieved, but neither cheered nor smiled, when the verdict was given. Indeed it wasn't until after she had left the courtroom that she showed any emotion, when she broke down and cried at the wheel of her car outside.

For the record – while the family of Rocío Wanninkhof remain convinced that she was involved and up until press date of this book continue with their private prosecution against Vázquez – Judge María Jesús del Rio threw out the case against both Vázquez and Graham on 2 August 2004. Citing as a reason the lack of evidence linking either of them to the murder, state prosecutor Antonio Gonzalez told a packed Court Number 6 in Fuengirola, that the Crown's case was that King alone killed the teenager.

Whether the right or wrong decision, it is certainly true that there was no phone record linking Vázquez with either King or Graham, nor was there evidence of any payment to them. And with neither fingerprints nor positive identifications putting her at the crime scene, the lack of evidence does indeed point to her innocence. While sources in this book are adamant that

Vázquez knew both King and Graham, no one, it should be pointed out, has been able to provide material proof.

On top of that, despite sending a policewoman to work undercover in an effort to get close to Vázquez, the Guardia Civil were still unable to find any strong signs of involvement. Most crucially of all, the prosecution was never able to come up with a concrete motive for why Vázquez would want to kill the daughter of her former lover. The likelihood of Tony King – a man with a history of attacking women – having committed the crime, remains statistically much higher.

Could it turn out to be one of Spain's worst miscarriages of justice? This, we won't know for sure for at least another five years, as the authorities – in a distinctly cautious move – only conditionally discharged Vázquez until 2009, when she will be completely absolved if no new evidence has come up. Something of a bitter-sweet victory, she will have the shadow of a possible retrial hanging over her until then . . . not to mention a five-year wait to seek redress from the authorities for effectively losing four years of her life, nearly two of them in prison.

With Graham, the situation is in some respects the same, in that the police were unable to find any evidence linking him to the crime scene. While he more or less confessed to covering up for King (and admitted he should have reported him to the police), his behaviour could easily be seen as someone panicking in a far from ordinary situation. It could also be argued that Graham, a timeshare salesman with a long criminal record, might well be loath to have any more dealings with the police than were absolutely essential. And the truth is that while he worked in an extremely unscrupulous and unregulated industry for over ten years, it doesn't make him a murderer. Moreover, while there are many claims that he has a violent temper and occasionally strikes out at his partners, there is no evidence to suggest that he has a pathological enjoyment of hurting women, or that he might have been paid to do it.

Most crucial, however, is the absence of fingerprints or any positive identification at either crime scene. Could it also be possible that the claims of Louise Deravairere, who paints a very dark picture of Graham, are tainted by the fact that her ex-boyfriend apparently dumped her to go to Egypt? Having paid for his flights home and put him up for his first few weeks in England, could she have had some desire to get even? Unlikely as it is, it cannot be discounted.

Questions do, however, remain about the apparent lack of investigation into Graham's behaviour, both past and present, by either the police in Spain or the UK. Given his obvious proximity to the case it seems odd that, according to a high-level source in the UK, Scotland Yard was asked to do little more than dig out his previous convictions, which were sent to Spain via Interpol. This was despite the numerous claims of his mistreatment of women, and the apparent need to clear up whether or not he crossed paths with Tony King in prison. 'Once they had King inside and apparently confessing to the crimes, they felt they were home and dry and quite frankly lost interest in anyone else,' said the source who was involved in the case. 'Quite honestly we have done very little on Graham. No one has asked us to and that's the end of that.'

The possibility also remains that had the timeshare salesman stepped forward when, as he claimed, his best friend Tony King admitted to killing teenager Rocío Wanninkhof in October 1999, at least one girl might still be alive today, and others may not have been raped or sexually assaulted. And, but for a bizarre technicality under Spanish law, Graham would currently be awaiting trial with his friend in Alhaurín prison, on the charge of 'covering up' for Rocío's murder, a charge that by his own admittance he was guilty of.

There are further questions about why Graham was not prosecuted for the theft of hire cars, and why no action was taken over the money he owed to landlord Alex Anderson in

Calahonda. And why was he allowed to live and travel around Spain with an expired passport, which ran out on 10 April 2003. Also, why was he not handed to the Portuguese authorities, who still had a warrant out for his arrest until the end of 2004?

These need to be answered by the Spanish Criminal Prosecution Service and the police, whose apparent cock-ups in the case were numerous. Aside from the flimsy case against Dolores Vázquez, it emerged, for example, that they had failed to interview King over the Wanninkhof murder in 1999, despite reportedly having him on their list of potential suspects. It turned out they had actually made inquiries in the road in which he lived and even went to his local pub, the infamous timeshare haunt, David's Bar, in Riviera del Sol. On top of this, according to his flatmate Simon Bowers, they had also picked him up at least twice in Alhaurín and once in Miraflores for other offences.

It certainly wouldn't have been hard to find him had they really wanted to. Unlike a large percentage of Britons who move to Spain, he had actually officially registered at Fuengirola police station in November 1997 and was a well-known figure on the coast. Could it be that the police simply did not – and perhaps still do not – have King down as the sort of gruesome murderer who could commit the sort of crimes that he has been convicted of?

The affair has also had some important international ramifications, aside from the Spanish minister of the interior being forced to explain how King had moved so easily to Spain from England unchecked. The most important of these has been the tightening up of intelligence information shared among European countries. In a new accord that from 2005 will allow Spain, France and Germany to share crime databases, the case of Tony Alexander King was used to highlight the reason why information sharing is vital. The United Kingdom is due to join in 2006 with the rest of Europe following soon after that. The new accord will allow a daily interchange of data regarding convicted criminals, meaning law enforcement agents will have full and up-to-date information on people living in their country who have a criminal record in one of the other countries. As Spanish justice minister Juan Fernando Lopez Aguilar explained, in the case of Tony King such information sharing might have 'potentially prevented one or even both of the murders of which he was accused'. This may well be the case, in light of the fact that information provided to the Spanish police from Scotland Yard was not held on Spanish databases due to privacy laws. Under the new law, this has changed.

In addition it was announced in October 2004 that Great Britain and Spain were studying the creation of an organization to combat organized crime on the Costa del Sol. The body will concentrate, in particular, on drug trafficking and kidnapping, but will also look into fraud, including timeshare.

But despite these new measures, the problems associated with foreign criminals profiting on the sunny shores of the Costa del Sol are unlikely to stop overnight. Indeed, one recent report by Spanish police claimed that there were 18,000 criminals living on the Costa del Sol alone. While the majority were 'probably' Eastern European and North African, it stated that a large proportion is made up of English, French and Italians involved in drug dealing, prostitution and fraud.

Another thing for sure, the scams, most commonly associated with timeshare, are not going to go away. With an estimated five million British holidaymakers alone coming to Spain every year, not to mention around 350,000 already living in Andalusia all year (with another 700,000 coming for periods of the year), there is a big ready-made market. Constantly evolving with new names and ideas – whether it be holiday clubs, or whatever – there will always be a large number of bad eggs feeding off the timeshare idea. The latest scam is in the resale bracket, where timeshare salesmen first find out who owns a property, then send a letter or call the owner to say that if they are thinking of selling their property the company has a series of guaranteed buyers at, say, four or five times the market value. With numerous timeshare owners already keen to get rid of their properties and many others tempted, it doesn't at first seem like a big outlay to give the company £500 from their credit card in order to start the process of picking up the names of the mystery buyers. However, when the mysterious list fails to turn up, it suddenly seems like a lot of money. But by then there is normally no comeback and often the company has changed its name and moved. When inquiries are made, either through solicitors or the police, you often find that the company is not properly listed, the letterheads of the company's lawyers are fictitious and the company has mysteriously disappeared up the coast.

As Bruce McIntyre, British consul in Malaga, says: 'Timeshare is still very much alive and full of fraudsters and while we shouldn't paint the whole concept of timeshare black there are undeniably an awful lot of dubious companies. And the sad thing is people are getting taken in every day, and I have heard of some people being conned three or four times. The scams they pull seem to be cyclical and move from one nationality to another, hence once they have flooded the British owners with calls, and got a bad name in the process, they move on to the French.

'The problem quite simply will not go away while there is so much money to be made and people are so gullible. The system feeds on inherent greed and we estimate that the timeshare scams are netting tens of millions of pounds every year. It is a very lucrative business.'

Even the timeshare industry itself revels somewhat in its unsavoury reputation. Scanning the industry's unofficial bible, the website www.crimeshare.com, which details the timeshare business's scurrilous activities, it quickly becomes apparent how important violence – both real and perceived – is to the industry. Used by disgruntled punters, investigators and often the industry as a whole as a sort of mouthpiece to set the record straight – it is a fascinating barometer of the latest comings and goings, movements and takeovers. Taking one small snapshot of the site's message board, between October and December 2003, for example, the following messages stood out:

15 Oct 2003 I heard today that David Stronach was found dead with multiple stab wounds in the Marbella area, now there is a thing. Who has he upset, apart from hundreds of clients he and his partners have ripped off? Having Roy Buck as one of his partners did not do him any good here. Paying Big Dennis for Protection did not work too well here either . . . or did he forget to pay last month? I am sure we will get to know in due course – the Costa Eye

27 Oct 2003 I read the message about the Harris Twins having to be aware of the timeshare crowd. The writer obviously does not know the Harris Twins. He would do better to tell the timeshare people to beware of the Harris Twins. The timeshare guy's underworld connections are not going to do him much good when they find him in a back alley beaten to death or with his throat cut. Think I'm kidding? I know these lads. They are very nice lads as long as you don't upset them or their families. And someone has upset their Mum. A good idea: send the money back now. You do not want these lads calling on you – Geezer

24 Nov 2003 Tommy be quiet we know its u – watching wot u do

In colourful language, these everyday threats of violence are sadly quite often backed up by action, as King's brother-in-law

Garry Leigh discovered to his misfortune in November 2002. According to sources, the attack happened not long after he had been pulled in and grilled over his close connections to a variety of fraud and protection rackets in Spain. After a four-day spell in prison, and under threat of a lengthy sentence, he cracked and agreed to help detectives reel in the crime bosses.

Refusing to pay any more protection money for his business, he was, apparently, trying to go legal and sort out his affairs. Having set up a new office in a plush block behind the popular waterpark in Fuengirola – and with a snazzy new website for Timelinx – it was a nasty surprise (although surely not that much of one?) when three men in balaclavas burst through the door with the intention of teaching him a lesson he would never forget. A vicious attack that even made it into the *Guardian* newspaper, the trio (two black, one white) had let off CS gas canisters before slashing Garry so badly in the face that 'he almost lost an eye'. They cut tendons in his arms, and he lost pints of blood. As his step-sister Ingrid Pantoja says, he was 'lucky to be alive'. 'There were two cuts so deep on both sides of one eye that his eyelid practically came off,' she told me. 'I had to hold it tightly together to try and stop the bleeding and doctors said if I hadn't done that he might well have bled to death.'

Scary stuff, the attack – which took place in broad daylight – was thought by one source to be for 'grassing' to police in connection with the ongoing and high-profile fraud prosecution of Brits Richard Cashman, Dennis New and Lebanese kingpin Mohamed Derbah, who are all closely connected to John Palmer. A 'supertrial' is to take place in Madrid some time in 2005 and Garry is expected to be a key witness. He has since been forced to completely change his work routine – and, according to rumours in the timeshare world, is guarded around the clock by up to six private security guards, each ex-Guardia Civil. As Celia Pantoja's new partner David Cooze explains: 'The place was bedlam and the poor guy got a terrible hiding. He had cuts all over his arms and face. There was no stopping them even when Garry's step-sister Ingrid jumped on one of their backs and hit another with a fire extinguisher. They wanted to teach him a lesson. They knew he was grassing and wanted to talk him out of testifying. Despite the new security arrangements, I understand it might have done the trick.'

Another person apparently 'taught a lesson' after a violent attack was Jon Daniels, who took a beating from Ingrid Pantoja outside a pub in September 2004. He was found lying on the floor outside the Irish pub in Calahonda after his ex-partner hit him on the back of the head with a glass. Ingrid claimed that he was withholding maintenance payments for their two children. Coming after a lengthy argument over his behaviour to her, witnesses confirmed, he was rushed to a nearby clinic to have eight stitches put in the deep gash. 'He had been refusing to pay for the boys' school-books and then started chiding me that they were only two one-night stands to him,' Ingrid admitted to me. 'I lost it and slashed him round the back of the head.' In a classic example of timeshare law, the incident was never reported to the police, and Daniels – after apologizing to Ingrid – has since had regular maintenance payments docked from his salary by boss Garry Leigh at Timelinx.

For Tony King then, the aptly named Costa del Crime was never going to be the best place for him to make a fresh start and get away from his violent past. His family contacts aside, the 350km stretch of coastline is anything but the crime-free idyll that so many British and other foreign buyers at first envisage. Indeed, rarely a week goes past when there is not a shooting or stabbing involving a foreigner.

In this complicated and murky episode that will go down in the annals of British crime in Spain, the last word should perhaps be given to one of the main protagonists, Robbie Graham. He knows better than anyone what really happened from the time the former Holloway Strangler Tony King relocated to Spain from the UK in 1997. Coming from an unused interview I had set up for an English newspaper soon after his return to the UK, they not only illuminate well the sort of people he and King were . . . but the relationship they had.

'Tony King was like a very loyal lapdog who was always extremely useful to have around. He was a game lad and would be right up for anything. In fact he did and would have done anything I told him . . . literally!

'The problems came when he was left on his own. He was all right if he was with people like me or Jon [Daniels] that knew how to handle him. But as soon as he was left on his own he was different. We weren't babysitters, you know. But I'll admit I did look after him . . . and I still think about him every day. I just can't think where he went wrong. I know people find it hard to understand, but to know someone like I knew him, to understand all that has happened is impossible.'

Then finally after a very pregnant pause, he added somewhat poignantly: 'There are undoubtedly more nutcases per square mile on the Costa del Sol than anywhere else in the world. So many people somehow filter through to Spain from the UK and elsewhere . . . there are probably a lot of victims who have not come forward, or never been found . . . even tourists maybe.'

How many more might there be? And could Robbie Graham be able to help?

Postscript

A sensational new twist came in September 2005, when a bag of bloodied clothes, some allegedly belonging to Rocío Wanninkhof, were dumped on the doorstep of her mother's house.

Almost six years to her death in 1999, the sinister discovery also included a tangle of matted hairs, 11 cigarette butts, 12 coins and a money-belt. Inside it, in two pockets, were a photograph of Rocío at the age of ten and a pair of blood-splattered knickers.

A chilling discovery indeed – could the knickers have been the ones apparently missing from the night of her death and, if so, why had they surfaced now? The Spanish press were unsure how to treat the discovery. Might it have been a sick practical joke? Could this be the missing link to solve the crime once and for all? And, if so, who had been hiding them for all that time?

The ring on the door had come at around 10a.m. on the morning of 23 August. But when Rocío's mother Alicia Hornos had opened the door of her house on the La Cortijera estate, in Mijas, there was nobody to be seen. The items had been stuffed in a bag from her local supermarket Supersol and left at the foot of her front door. She had at first been scared to touch it. 'I was frightened. Could it contain some animal, or worse a bomb,' she recalled.

Unlikely as it might seem to the passive observer, Hornos had every reason to be cautious. A little over a week earlier she had received a series of threatening letters insulting her and warning her to watch out for bombs. With postmarks from Murcia, Málaga and Seville, the letters had been decorated with swastikas and warned her that 'the countdown had begun.'

She said it was not the first time she had received such frightening letters and revealed that every time there was a new court hearing they started arriving. For that reason she did not touch the bag until her boyfriend Julian had come home from buying some bread. Meanwhile she phoned her two other children Rosa Blanca and Guillermo. 'I was worried that someone might have left something underneath their cars. Mothers are like that,' she said.

Later that day with much trepidation she and Julian opened the bag. 'I noticed a strong smell like camphor and the first thing I saw was a white T-shirt that had a money-belt tied around it. It was tied up very tightly. In one of its zips I found a bunch of brown hair. It looked like it had come off a comb or from a plughole.' Opening up the money-belt she found 'the pair of white cotton knickers with blood stains in them' and the photo of Rocío, which sent 'a chill up her spine'. In another pocket were the cigarette butts which came from the brand Nobel, as well as three broken cigarettes. At the bottom of the plastic bag were a series of old fashioned peseta coins, 12 in total.

'I recognized the knickers straight away,' said Hornos. 'Rocío had bought them a couple of weeks earlier for a friend's wedding. She had her period at the time which might explain the blood. I am one hundred per cent sure they were Rocío's.'

But perhaps more importantly, it wasn't the only item of clothing that she recognized. In particular was a skirt, which had been worn to her house by 'someone else' some years before. 'It was a long time ago that someone came here dressed in these clothes and I cannot give you the name of the person for legal reasons.'

Speaking carefully, she went on to state that she thought the discovery was probably a sick joke and that, above all, she did not want to incriminate anyone, in particular Dolores Vázquez. She merely added that she hoped that the police would confirm that the DNA matched the clothes 'as soon as possible', and continued to believe that Tony King was not the only person present at the death of her daughter.

King's lawyer meanwhile simply went on to reiterate that Dolores Vazquez had, as yet, only been discharged provisionally.

At time of going to press, there was still no word from the Guardia Civil as to the result of the DNA tests.